To:
PAM,
So nice to meet you!
May you enjoy your journey
in Revelation! Thanks for your support.
God Bless,

Revelation, Simply Put.

A Visual Commentary on the Book of Revelation

Blessed is he that readeth... (Rev. 1:3)

Jodi A. Matthews

innovo PUBLISHING

Published by
Innovo Publishing, LLC
www.innovopublishing.com
1-888-546-2111

Providing Full-Service Publishing Services for
Christian Authors, Artists & Organizations: Hardbacks, Paperbacks,
eBooks, Audiobooks, Music & Film

REVELATION, SIMPLY PUT.

Unless otherwise noted, Scripture quotations are taken from The King James Version of the Holy Bible. Some material has been excerpted by permission: **Copyright Notice:** Taken from "A Survey of the Old Testament." 2009 by Andrew Hill & John Walton. Used by permission of Zondervan. www.zondervan.com. **Copyright Notice:** Taken from "The Four Views on the Book of Revelation." 2010 by Stanley N. Gundry and Marvin C. Pate. Used by permission of Zondervan. www.zondervan.com. **Reprinted by permission:** "The Book of Revelation: The Smart Guide to the Bible Series." Daymond R. Duck, 2006, Thomas Nelson, Inc. Nashville, Tennessee. All rights reserved. **Reprinted by permission.** Kirsch, Jonathan "A History of the End of the World: How the Most Controversial Book in the Bible Changed the Course of Western Civilization." New York, NY: Harper Collins, 2007.

Some material has been substantially excerpted by permission from the following sources, taken from:

CHARTING THE END TIMES
Copyright ©2004 by Tim LaHaye and Thomas Ice'
Published by Harvest House Publishers
Eugene, Oregon 97402
Used by Permission

THE POPULAR ENCYCLOPEDIA OF BIBLE PROPHECY
Copyright ©2004 by Tim LaHaye and Ed Hinson
Published by Harvest House Publishers
Eugene, Oregon 97402
Used by Permission

The following article was excerpted substantially from: Zukeran, Patrick, "Four Views on Revelation." Probe Ministries. 2009. http://www.probe.org/site/c.fdKEIMNsEoG/b.5110361/k.5D09/Four_Views_of_Revelation.htm. **Digital Animations:** Unless otherwise designated, all graphics are retrieved from JUNIPERIMAGES "A© 2012 Juniper Corporation," animationfactory.com. **PLBL: Pictorial Library of Bible Lands Photos**, Volumes. 6, 10, 12 & 16, CD-ROM, copyright © 2001 by Todd Bolen/BiblePlaces.com with the exception of Didyma Temple of Apollo, credited to Enery Hsu/BiblePlaces.com. **Revelation Digital Artwork:** Revelation Chapter Four, Chapter Five, Chapter Six, The Beast, The Great Harlot, Tree of Life, Copyright: David Miles: www.davidmiles.net. Permission to use these images does not necessarily suggest David Miles' endorsement of the views contained within this publication. **Can Stock Photo, Inc.** (Royalty Free Images): Europe Shaded Relief Map © Can Stock Photo Inc./MSchmeling; European Union Shaded Relief Map © Can Stock Photo Inc./MSchmeling; Turkey Shaded Relief Map © Can Stock Photo Inc./MSchmeling; Locust © Can Stock Photo Inc./yio; Myrrh © Can Stock Photo Inc./marilyna; Israel Shaded Relief Map © Can Stock Photo Inc./MSchmeling; White, Red, Pale Horse © Can Stock Photo Inc./krisdog; Black Horse © Can Stock Photo Inc./mariait; The Bible © Can Stock Photo Inc./CJP; 3D Star of David Shalom © Can Stock Photo Inc./Irisangel; Light Angel Wings © Can Stock Photo Inc./zven0; Tripple Sixes 666 © Can Stock Photo Inc./karimala; 3D Star of David © Can Stock Photo Inc./GeorgiosArt; Thunder Storm © Can Stock Photo Inc./Palych; Golden Star © Can Stock Photo Inc./Ancello; Silver Number 8 © Can Stock Photo Inc./Eraxion; Silver Number 6 © Can Stock Photo Inc./Eraxion; Scroll © Can Stock Photo Inc./Digitalstudio; Golden Royal Crown © Can Stock Photo Inc./scanrail; Blank Paper with Wax Seal © Can Stock Photo Inc./SSilver; Ancient Bowl © Can Stock Photo Inc./elenaray; Svitok_pechat(126).jpeg © Can Stock Photo Inc./aleksangel; Silver Number 7 © Can Stock Photo Inc./Eraxion; Old Books © Can Stock Photo Inc./piai; Blue Jigsaw Puzzle 3D Solution Box © Can Stock Photo Inc./michaeldb; Man with Magnifying Glass © Can Stock Photo Inc./texelart; Computer Laptop © Can Stock Photo Inc./ifong; Mountain Lake © Can Stock Photo Inc./karlnaundorf; Spotlight © Can Stock Photo Inc./cobalt88; Israel Travel Photos, Jerusalem © Can Stock Photo Inc./lucidwaters; Israel the New Temple © Can Stock Photo Inc./compuinfoto; Cube © Can Stock Photo Inc./jc_cards; Fire Tire © Can Stock Photo Inc./derocz; Wild Bear © Can Stock Photo Inc./openlens; Very Old Paper with Wax Seal © Can Stock Photo Inc./inxti; Megiddo © Can Stock Photo Inc./vblinov; Roaring Lion © Can Stock Photo Inc./jmhite. **Fotolia** (Royalty Free Stock Photos): Dome of the Rock © *Renewer - Fotolia.com;* Man Jumping in Sun Rays © *B-C-designs - Fotolia.com; Leopard in Bushland © klauspivi - Fotolia.com; Turkey Euphrates River at Artaturk Dam © tella0303 - Fotolia.com.* **CopyArtWork:** Vectorized Daniel Chapter Two Statue created digitally by CopyArtWork.com.

ISBN 978-1-61314-079-6
Library of Congress Control Number: 2012955114

Cover Design & Interior Layout: Innovo Publishing, LLC
Printed in the United States of America
U.S. Printing History

First Edition: December 2012

In loving memory of my mother
Nedra Hunter
(1950–2007)
who introduced me to Jesus.

Your resilience, thoughts, and spirit
live on through me.
Thank you for your "Legacy."

"Blessed is the man that feareth the LORD,
that delighteth greatly in his commandments
His seed shall be mighty upon the earth."
(Psalm 112:1–2)

Acknowledgments

The completion of this spiritual project deserves special thanks to some extraordinary people, beginning with those under my roof:

- To Vincent, my husband. Thank you for your midnight prayers, support, and most of all, trust. This project took the devotion of long hours at the library and travel across the country researching this important subject in the Bible. You are the invisible second author of this book. What a blessing you are to me in the home.

- To my two daughters, Destiny and Jazmine. God could not have given your father and me more wonderful children. Destiny, the oldest, who cooked dinner for the family while Mom wrote in the office; and Jazmine, the youngest, who listened to her older sister without incident. Thank you for allowing Mom to have undisturbed time in the home office. You two are the reason I labor tirelessly.

- To my immediate family—father, Henry, and sister, Toni. Thank you for your prayers and support, especially my younger sister, Erika, who prayed for my strength and for this project's success. The prayers of the righteous do make tremendous power available! You are my twin in the Spirit.

- To Bruce Beecher, my second pair of eyes. Thank you for meeting deadlines. It has been a laborious undertaking, and a pleasure, for both of us.

- To Todd Bolen, David Miles, and other professional photographers. It is because of you that this visual commentary was made possible. What an awesome testimony to the Body of Christ of the different gifts He has placed within the church.

- To my Innovo Publishing family. You have helped to bring this manuscript alive and into the hands of people. Terry, our paths have crossed for a reason. You have been wonderful throughout this process, motivating me to produce fantastic visuals that create a stunning book. Deserving special mention is Darya Crockett, whom I gratefully acknowledge the assistance and contribution to the final editing of this manuscript, ensuring each page reads simply wonderful.

- And finally, to The Father, The Son, and The Holy Spirit (These Three are One). Your Word is Truth! It is true that "A man's heart may be full of designs, but the purpose of the Lord is unchanging" (Proverbs 19:21, Bible in Basic English). It is You who gives me purpose and directs my steps. May You smile upon this project and may it glorify Jesus in the highest. Holy Spirit, what can I say? You are the Great Adviser! Thank You for sticking with me, inspiring me to write and finish this manuscript. It is in You that I live, move, and have my being. Glory to God in the highest!

Table of Contents

III. LET US BEGIN
REVELATION, SIMPLY PUT.

<u>A PANORAMIC VIEW OF REVELATION: CHAPTER LABELS</u>
Chapter days and divisions designed for a four-day study at one-and-a-half-hour increments
or a full-day workshop of eight hours

I. PREFACE

INTRODUCTION

WELCOME!

Your arrival to the study of this last book of the Bible, Revelation, is greeted with great delight. With few visitors stopping by to read Revelation, in honor of your arrival, many have gathered in anticipation of meeting the one who has chosen to read the words of this prophecy. John, the revelator, is your personal escort through the reception gathering. The VIP room is filled with such guests as Wisdom, Knowledge, Foresight, and Understanding. Applause is given as the guest of honor enters the VIP area. The Great Guest, Jesus Christ, is also rendering laudation to this guest of honor: **you!** For **"Blessed is he that readeth, and they that hear the words of this prophecy, and keep those things which are written therein: for the time is at hand" (Revelation 1:3)**. Welcome to Revelation, Simply Put.

THE K-I-S-S PRINCIPLE

The adage, "a picture is worth a thousand words," refers to the idea that a complex idea can be conveyed with just a single still image. "Visualization makes it possible to absorb large amounts of data quickly."[1] This visual publication serves that purpose.

This optic, page-by-page commentary to the book of Revelation is motivated by the K-I-S-S Principle. **"K-I-S-S"** is an acronym for the design principle, **"keep it simple and short."**[2]

The K-I-S-S Principle states that most systems work best if they are kept simple rather than made complex; therefore, simplicity should be a key goal in design, and unnecessary complexity should be avoided.

The book of Revelation, as one twentieth-century Bible scholar suggests, ". . . has been abandoned by the readers of the Bible as being almost completely unintelligible."[3] Sadly, this feeling of despondency is shared by many twenty-first century Christians today. To some scholars, due to its complexity, it is dangerous to teach; to the Bible student, with symbols too difficult to comprehend, it is left forsaken.

THE MOTIVATION

The motivation for writing this visual guide to Revelation is to aid Bible students to succeed at reading Revelation and to help one's study of Revelation in a most productive and fruitful manner that leads to clarity, understanding, and solid answers. An unequivocal blessing is declared to the one who reads, hears, and keeps this written prophecy **(Revelation 1:3)**. The reading of Revelation is not exclusive to the scholar, the savant, or the wise man; it is readily accessible to the pupil. Poignantly revealed in **Revelation 1:1, "This is a revelation of Jesus Christ, which God gave John to show unto <u>his servants</u>"** (New Living Translation). Expressly stated, the word *servants* is all-inclusive! Thus, **Revelation is not to be abandoned but pursued.**

If one is to pursue this blessed book, simplicity should be a key goal in design, and unnecessary complexity should be avoided. Typically, in studying commentaries, publications, or writings on Revelation, it usually requires large amounts of reading covering many months, which can cause one to lose focus, place, and direction to **connect** all the pieces. This type of study may be well-suited for the scholar, the astute, or the Bible pupil, but for many laymen, the task is, as one spectator states, "Revelation has as many mysteries as it does words."[4] It is no wonder one would abandon this blessed book as unintelligible, complex, and difficult to understand.

THE BOOK'S SCOPE AND PURPOSE

The design of this book is purposely illustrated in two specific ways: **"portraiture"** and **"simplification."**

- **Portraiture** (picture form; a single still image)
- **Simplification** (easy to understand, not elaborate but plain)

"Success comes with many different learning styles."[5] With pictures, one can take a mental picture of information. In this publication, alongside each chapter are colorful charts, timelines, or maps for a **visual view** as one reads Revelation. Adopting this method of seeing the single still image will lessen the confusion of words, assisting the student to a productive study of Revelation. Applying the K-I-S-S Principle will garner comprehension of the designated Scripture, simplifying difficult words and passages that have been transformed into pictures, symbols, charts, and diagrams.

TO WHOM THIS BOOK IS WRITTEN

To the Bible layman, "servants" (Revelation 1:3), may this book be a light for your soul and an exceptional study reference for guiding you through the book of Revelation in anticipation of the blessed coming of our Lord and Savior, Jesus Christ!

To the Bible scholar, may this publication continue to build upon the bountiful years of ruminated study and writings of faithful men and women of God who ardently exhort the teaching of the book of Revelation.

And to the men and women in the modern world, may this writing open your understanding to the **"Revelation of Jesus Christ"** that you may know the height, depth, and width of His love for you.

Revelation is a sacred, yet glorious book. May this message be conveyed in such a way that people of all intellectual levels can comprehend its communication, in hopes that this comprehension will harvest further teaching of the book of Revelation to others. For the reason that, "Whether one approaches the Book of Revelation as drivel or divine, the fact remains that Revelation is still embraced with seriousness by a great many men and women in the modern world." [6]

ABOUT THE AUTHOR

Jodi A. Matthews, a twenty-first century teacher of the Word of God with a twist: bringing the Bible alive with technology. Her passion is marked by a great intensity to empower and propel Christians to a deeper relationship in Christ and to an excellent spirit within. Teaching the Word of God, line by line and precept upon precept, she equips God's people in the Word of God, whereby they grow and are nurtured in the things of God.

Professionally, she is a court reporter for the United States District Court of Michigan; **spiritually**, she is answering the call of God on her life as teacher of His Word. **Educationally**, a student at The King's University in Van Nuys, California, Jodi is pursuing her Bachelor of Theology degree with a concentration in Jewish Messianic Studies. She has a profound appreciation for the Hebraic roots of the Christian faith. Jodi passionately upholds the school's motto: "Servant Leadership. Kingdom Building."

Jodi holds the **futurist** interpretation of the book of Revelation and is a **pretribulational believer** (one who believes the Rapture will occur before the Tribulation). She teaches from this view, while graciously examining the other major views. She undertakes the age-old Golden Rule of Interpretation, which states, "when the plain sense of Scripture makes common sense, seek no other sense . . . the Bible explains itself."[7]

As an earnest prophecy student and an addendum to her educational matriculation, Jodi attained her Certificate of Completion in Eschatology Study Courses: The Book of Revelation, The Prophecies of Daniel, and Basic Bible Prophecy from World Prophetic Ministry with Dr. Ed Hindson, respected Bible prophecy scholar in Colton, California. She has designed and taught "Revelation, Simply Put" (a four-day study), which includes colorful charts, interactive PowerPoint technology, a world history timeline, and an original master design Revelation timeline, allowing students to finish the study of Revelation in less than a week.

Jodi is a member of the Peoples Community Church-Westland, where she actively serves in the ministry faithfully teaching Sunday school, and serving in the music ministry. She is married to Pastor Vincent Matthews, Pastor of Peoples Community Church of Westland. They have two beautiful daughters, Destiny Rachael and Jazmine Eve Matthews.

A PERSONAL WORD FROM THE AUTHOR

Revelation & My Personal Journey

The inspiration for the writing of this book did not surface at the beckoning of an overnight inspiration, but came at the behest of reading God's Word for the "pure joy of it." It has been a laborious exploration. My first personal reading of the entire book of Revelation took place as I traveled on an airplane in 2006. It was upon takeoff that I chose to open and read the entire book, since I would be confined in the air for more than four hours. This reading would exclude the aid of commentaries, dictionaries, or periodicals—again, it was simply for pure joy. The initial reading evolved into a yearly reading, where I would purposely schedule a personal reading of Revelation at least once during the course of the year in addition to church Bible study lessons, Sunday school curricula, and sermon series preached by my pastor.

    This yearly reading progressed into a most arduous, painstaking study. Each year I began to gain additional insight and understanding of its relevancy to the generation at hand (this generation). Reading Revelation brought the pieces together in answer to questions that plagued me for years as a Bible student. Serving as Sunday school teacher, the personal study and research of Revelation in the class curriculum aided me in drawing timelines and pictures to help with understanding difficult passages, making its comprehension simple. When the opportunity arose for me to be a guest Bible class teacher, VBS instructor (Vacation Bible School), and/or Sunday school instructor, I was able to use many years of studies, drawings, and personal notes to teach this blessed book in a most **simplistic** way. Witnessing students leave class with a sense of "I've got it!" confirmed that the many years of my personal reading and study of this book was not happenstance, but Divine.

Revelation & Prophecy

The ancient prophecy of Revelation is not a folklore story of Scripture pondering past history. The ancient texts of prophecies speak today in the local news. "Revelation starts in antiquity but continues into our day."[8] In baseball, the adage is used, "keep your eye on the ball." There is a ball to follow in prophecy. Prophecy is progressive. This simply means, the closer you get to the end of the **last days**, the clearer and more vivid the prophecies will become because prophecy advances day by day. "It is important to note that prophecy can be compared to looking into the distance at a mountain.[9] From the present state you see **one** mountain, but as you get closer you find it is not only one but **two**, and even closer, it is not two but **three**."[10] Such is prophecy.

    The great commentator, Matthew Henry (1662), whom I respect, and others were only privy to see one mountain; so their view and comments validated only so far. But the generation to see Israel become a nation again, (May 14, 1948)[11], forthwith saw another mountain appear clearly, indicating God's prophecy program extends into our day. Matthew Henry did not see this mountain, for it was not revealed until the year 1948.

Revelation & Technology

John the revelator, author of Revelation, whose words were recorded some 1,900 years ago in AD 95–96, testified about today's technology. Revelation 13 depends heavily upon technology. Technology distributes data globally, delivering information to man **instantaneously**, linking the world together **simultaneously**. This information age will aid the Antichrist greatly in his pursuit to rule all nations concurrently as relates to the economy and worship (Revelation 13:7, 15–17).

"Notice, in the days of David and Abraham, man communicated with handwritten messages and traveled at the speed of horseback. Tracing history to George Washington (1789), man still communicated with handwritten messages and traveled at the speed of horseback."[12] Not until the end of the nineteenth century (1876) did technology come on the horizon. Now man travels at the speed of sound **(trains, planes, automobiles)** and sends messages at the speed of light **(emailing, texting, facebooking, tweeting)**.

Numerous mountains are appearing simultaneously, which is indicative of how close we are to the arrival of Christ and the establishing of His earthly kingdom. If these signs poignantly reveal Christ's Second Advent, most assuredly the Rapture ("the catching away of believers <u>before</u> the Tribulation") is on the horizon.

If your eye is on the ball, the stage is set for pivotal prophetic moments to be fulfilled. You can readily acknowledge the genesis of an increase in technology beginning near the end of the nineteenth century: **Alexander Graham Bell** (1876) inventor of the first telephone; **Thomas A. Edison** (1879) inventor of the first widely marketed incandescent lamp; **Charles E. Duryea** (1892) first automobile produced; **The Wright Brothers** (1904) credited with building the world's first successful airplane; **The Internet**, International Computer Network (1969); **cellular telephones** (1979);[13] and **Israel** declared a nation again on May 14, 1948.

Then technology was openly enhanced by the hands of **Steve Jobs** (1976), Apple Computer Industry Pioneer; **Google** (1998), a search engine and organizer of world information; **Mark Zuckerberg** (2004), CEO of Facebook, a social networking service; **YouTube** (2005), a video sharing Web site; **Twitter** (2008), a micro-blogging service, to name a few.[14] These present-day moments are being used to synthesize the coming fulfillment of the book of Revelation in our day. This advancement in technology represents what we have been labeling as "paving the road" to the Tribulation and the arrival of the man of lawlessness (the Antichrist). The role of technology will answer the questions: How will the Gospel be preached in all the earth? **(Matthew 24:14)**; How will one man (the Antichrist) govern the world? **(Revelation 13:7–8)**; How will the entire world behold the two witnesses' dead bodies lying in the streets of Jerusalem simultaneously? **(Revelation 11:9)**. These questions will instinctively be fulfilled through the powerful infrastructure of **technology**.

Revelation & You

A respected African-American historian, Dr. Carter G. Woodson stated, "Real education means to inspire people to live more abundantly, to learn to begin with life as you find it and make it better."[15] May *Revelation, Simply Put* aid you to become better at understanding its message. It is my hope you are not "tossed to and fro . . . with every wind of doctrine" **(Ephesians 4:14)** as it relates to Bible prophecy. That you are always ready to answer every man of "the hope that is within you" **(1 Peter 3:15)**.

Leonard Ravenhill (1907–1994) states, "The **opportunity** of a lifetime **must be seized** within the lifetime of the **opportunity**." Questions are being asked by the modern world, and now is the time for believers to seize the opportunity to educate others on the blessed return of Christ!

May you enjoy your study in the book of Revelation!

II. BEFORE YOU BEGIN: THE BLUEPRINT

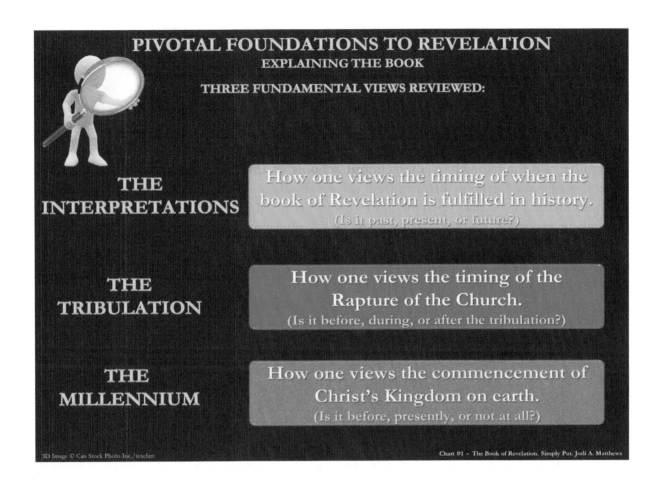

PIVOTAL FOUNDATIONS TO REVELATION
EXPLAINING THE BOOK

THREE FUNDAMENTAL VIEWS REVIEWED:

THE INTERPRETATIONS	How one views the timing of when the book of Revelation is fulfilled in history. (Is it past, present, or future?)
THE TRIBULATION	How one views the timing of the Rapture of the Church. (Is it before, during, or after the tribulation?)
THE MILLENNIUM	How one views the commencement of Christ's Kingdom on earth. (Is it before, presently, or not at all?)

Chart #1 - The Book of Revelation, Simply Put. Jodi A. Matthews

PIVOTAL FOUNDATIONS TO REVELATION: EXPLAINING THE BOOK

The Foundational Pieces

Every structure must have a foundation. Foundations are crucial to the solidity of a structure. A house has a foundation, human families have foundations, and even one's spiritual life of salvation is built upon the foundation, Jesus Christ (1 Corinthians 3:11). A foundation, according to Merriam-Webster's Dictionary is ". . . an underlying base or support upon which something is built or overlaid." Most are familiar with the term *foundation* as it relates to building a dream home. Whether it's your dream home or not, building a house can be a rewarding experience, and like all things it starts with the foundation. The success to understanding Revelation comes at the behest of the setting up of one's foundation in interpreting its precious words. **"The foundation is of utmost importance."**[16]

Establish Your Foundation...
Where do you stand?

It is sobering to note, although every home has a foundation, not all foundations are solid enough to bolster the weight of materials overlaid upon it. If the foundation is of utmost importance, it is vital that one remember "the foundation shoulders the weight of the house and even disperses the weight so the house does not cave in where support is not offered."[17] What despondency a builder must feel when his house has collapsed, not from the result of strong winds, earthquake, or a major storm, but from a poor foundation.

The above house illustration may answer why many encounter this collapse and despondency when reading Revelation; what's missing is a strong **foundation**. When one approaches the book of Revelation, he first must put on his glasses, so to speak, as to how the book's meaning will be understood. **Chart #1** proffers fundamental views one should adopt as he reads passages in Revelation. Each view will be expounded on independently, which will wholly structure one's foundation as he reads the verses written in Revelation.

    "There are at least four schools of interpretation of Revelation"[18] (known as how one explains or tells the meaning of a verse); **four schools of interpretation on the Tribulation** (a time of great suffering upon the earth); and **three schools of interpretation on the Millennium** (the personal reign of Christ upon the earth for 1,000 years). To simplify this, when one chooses his view of interpretation, this will usually choose one's Tribulation and Millennium views.

    Let's examine a further example of this using the four schools of interpretation: **preterists, historicists, idealists**, and **futurists**. If one chooses the futurist interpretive view, he will most likely undergird a pretribulational and premillennial outlook on Revelation. These three views combined will shape one's foundation in studying Revelation. Personally speaking, my foundation status is: **futurist, pretrib**, and **premillennial**. I do not hold this view because it is a popular view and the most widely adopted outlook in Christendom, but I am convinced that the Bible teaches and supports the futurist foundation after study of this view and graciously examining the other major views.

The Prophetic Pieces

Bible prophecy can be best understood as a **"prophetic puzzle."** The pieces are all there, but must be arranged with diligent study of each individual piece for placement together as a whole. The Bible deserves as much diligent study and thorough examination of each piece as possible to view the

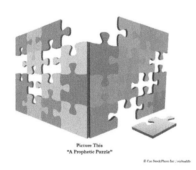

Picture This
"A Prophetic Puzzle"

© Can Stock Photo Inc. / michaeldb

panoramic view of the Scriptures, especially concerning subjects of prophecy. As with puzzles, many pieces derive the whole picture. For example, if there are two **blue** pieces, although both are blue, the pieces may not fit together perfectly. The reason being, one blue piece snaps into place in the sky, the other piece in the ocean. Most often, it isn't until the puzzle is almost finished that one sees where the **blue sky** piece fits and where the **blue ocean** piece fits, and how these pieces finally "snap" into place perfectly.

    I believe the futurist pretrib view **fits** the pieces of the prophetic puzzle together perfectly; wherein the other views force pieces in where they do not belong or there are missing pieces in the puzzle. Each person who reads Revelation will fall under one of the four schools of interpretation. Whether he chooses to adopt one or not, he will find himself peering through the glasses of one of the **major views**. It is best to educate oneself as to these views, which makes for easier understanding of Revelation. This guide represents the futurist view, while graciously examining the other interpretations. "In spite of one's adoption of interpretation, may its readers be aided by the Holy Spirit to form the whole"[19] **(See Chart #2 for Schools of Interpretations.)**

Conclusion

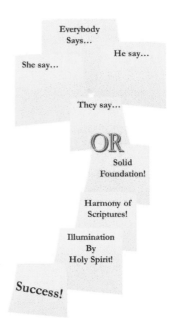

Humbly submitting, no one view ultimately has all the answers. "What is called for is the realization that we as humans, with finite understanding, need each other's insights enlightened by the Holy Spirit, in order to grasp the intent of God's Word."[20] May it be applauded that each view speaks great truths; although some have advanced more than others. In that light, this manual does not sarcastically condescend upon the other respective views, but simply states the facts researched, its strengths, and its weaknesses.

However, when a Bible pupil follows the breadcrumbs of Scripture, undergirded with the futurist outlook, he will be able to gather enough crumbs to mix and bake a cake. "Many important biblical doctrines are not derived from a single verse, but come from a harmonization of several passages into systematic conclusions. Some truths are directly stated in the Bible. Other doctrines, like the Trinity and the incarnate nature of Christ, are the product of harmonizing the many passages that relate to these matters."[21] Such is Bible prophecy.

God has not left the Christian destitute with no answers as it relates to the hearing, reading, and studying of Revelation. He has not thrown this book in the air, leaving its pages to fall scattered where they may for one to guesstimate or decode. But with one's **proper foundation**, harmonization of Scripture, and the illumination by the Holy Spirit, the person who hears, reads, and keeps Revelation can accomplish this task most successfully.

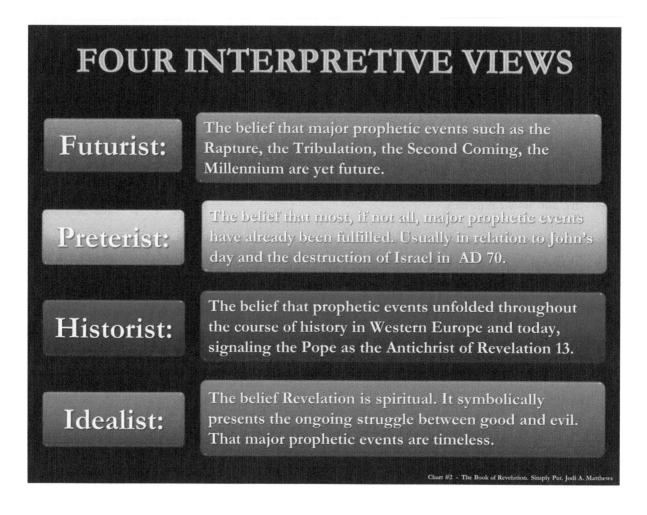

FOUR INTERPRETIVE VIEWS

Futurist: The belief that major prophetic events such as the Rapture, the Tribulation, the Second Coming, the Millennium are yet future.

Preterist: The belief that most, if not all, major prophetic events have already been fulfilled. Usually in relation to John's day and the destruction of Israel in AD 70.

Historist: The belief that prophetic events unfolded throughout the course of history in Western Europe and today, signaling the Pope as the Antichrist of Revelation 13.

Idealist: The belief Revelation is spiritual. It symbolically presents the ongoing struggle between good and evil. That major prophetic events are timeless.

Chart #2 - The Book of Revelation. Simply Put. Jodi A. Matthews

THE FOUR INTERPRETIVE VIEWS

Over the centuries, there have been four main approaches regarding the proper interpretation to "the unveiling" or "book of Revelation." Each view argues for the integrity of its outlook. **Chart #2** is a simple explanation of each school of thought. As relates to each respective view, much of what follows is drawn from an article by Patrick Zukeran of Probe Ministries called, "Four Views of Revelation." All quotations that follow come from this article. Zukeran states, "Each view attempts to interpret Revelation according to the law of hermeneutics—simply the art and science of interpretation. This will be a brief overview and presentation of the strengths and weakness of each view:"[22]

Futurist (Future): "This view teaches that the events of the Olivet Discourse and Revelation Chapters 4–22 will occur in the **future** (emphasis added). Futurists apply a literal approach to interpreting Revelation. Literal interpretation of the Bible means to explain the original sense, or meaning, of the Bible according to the normal customary usage of its language. Futurists acknowledge the use of figures and symbols in the light of its biblical context to find the meaning; however, noting figurative language does not justify allegorical interpretation."

© Can Stock Photo Inc./zentaut

Noted Scholars of this Position: "Charles Ryrie, John Walvoord, Dwight Pentecost, Ed Hinson, David Jeremiah. Tim LaHaye and Jerry Jenkins made this theology popular with their end-times series of novels."[23]

Major Weakness: "Some futurists have been involved in setting dates of Christ's return, which does not represent the biblical futurist's view."[24]

Preterist (Preter, Latin for "Past"): "There are two major views among preterists: 'full preterism' and 'partial preterism.' Both views believe that the prophecies of the Olivet Discourse of Matthew 24 and Revelation were **fulfilled** (emphasis added) in the first century (AD 1–100) with the fall of Jerusalem in AD 70. Partial preterists believe identically, with the exception that Chapters 20–22 point to future events such as a future resurrection of believers and the return of Christ to the earth. Partial preterists view full preterism as heretical since it denies the Second Coming of Christ."

Noted Scholars of this Position: (particularly the partial preterists): "Hank Hanegraaff, R. C. Sproul, Kenneth Gentry, and the late David Chilton (who later converted to full preterism after the publishing of his books)."

Major Weakness: "Preterists stretch the metaphors and symbols in order to find fulfillment of the prophecies in the fall of Jerusalem," states Zukeran. "An example is found in Matthew 24:15 regarding the destruction of the Temple. General Titus did not set up an 'abomination of desolation' object as prophesied by Daniel and Jesus in Matthew 24:15, rather, he destroyed the Temple and burned it to the ground. This creates a **missing piece** in the prophetic puzzle, as earlier stated, that requires preterists to allegorize in order to find fulfillment of the prophecies in the fall of Jerusalem in AD 70."[25]

Historicist (Procession): "The third view is called the historicist approach. This view teaches that Revelation is a symbolic representation that presents the course of history from the Apostle John's life through to our present day and on into the end of the age," informs Zukeran. "Revelation is fulfilled through **history**. That the symbols in the apocalypse correspond to events in the history of Western Europe. This view rose to popularity during the Protestant Reformation because of its identification of the Pope and the Papacy with the beasts of Revelation 13. They often hold that the Antichrist is the Pope and Roman Catholicism."

Noted Scholars of this Position: "John Wycliffe, William Tyndale, John Calvin, Matthew Henry."[26]

Major Weakness: "This view focuses entirely on the events of the church in Western Europe, and the overthrow of Catholicism; thus, its narrow scope fails to account for God's activity throughout Asia and the rest of the world. John Walvoord points out the lack of agreement among historicists. Since the beginning of the twentieth century, this view has declined in popularity and influence."[27]

Idealist (Timeless): "The idealist view or spiritual view uses the allegorical method to interpret the Book of Revelation. According to this view, the events of Revelation are not tied to specific historical events, they are **timeless** (emphasis added). The imagery of the book symbolically presents the ongoing struggle throughout the ages of God against Satan and good against evil," comments Zukeran. "That Revelation should be used as a 'guide to life' for Christians enduring and/or undergoing persecution presently, not any prediction of future or past events."

Noted Scholars of this Position: "William Milligan, Robert Mounce, Paul S. Minear, Elisabeth S. Fiorenza."

Major Weakness: "There are several weaknesses of this view. First, this view denies that the Book of Revelation has any specific historical fulfillment. Second, the symbols portray the ever-present conflict, but no necessary consummation of the historical process. Finally, reading spiritual meanings into the text could lead to arbitrary interpretations which fail to seek the author's intended meaning."[28]

Conclusion

One should not allow "the views" to discourage the study of this blessed book! The reader of Revelation must understand Satan's par excellence in the discouraging of the reading, hearing, and keeping of this book written specifically to his servants **(Revelation 1:1)**. One does not need to become hostile, but educated in light of these outlooks. "Each believer should advance the dialogue in a cordial, respectful manner which will challenge every believer to accurately study and interpret the Word," replies Zukeran.[29]

No one view ultimately has all the answers. Granted, the nearing of the end of the age has advanced some views more than others. In a comparative study like this, it is necessary to consider similarities and differences to gain a balanced picture. Being ever mindful when the Bible pupil follows the breadcrumbs of Scripture, he should be able to gather enough crumbs to mix and bake a cake or henceforth see where each **blue** piece fits: "the sky" or "the sea."

Zukeran highlights, "Despite the various schools of interpretations, there are common threads upon which Christians agree. **All views** (emphasis added) believe that God is sovereign and in charge of all that occurs in history and its ultimate conclusion. **All** (emphasis added) agree upon the importance of the study of prophecy and its edification for the body of Christ. **All** (emphasis added) await the return of our Lord and together with the saints of all ages say, 'Amen, come Lord Jesus!'" **(Revelation 22:20)**.[30]

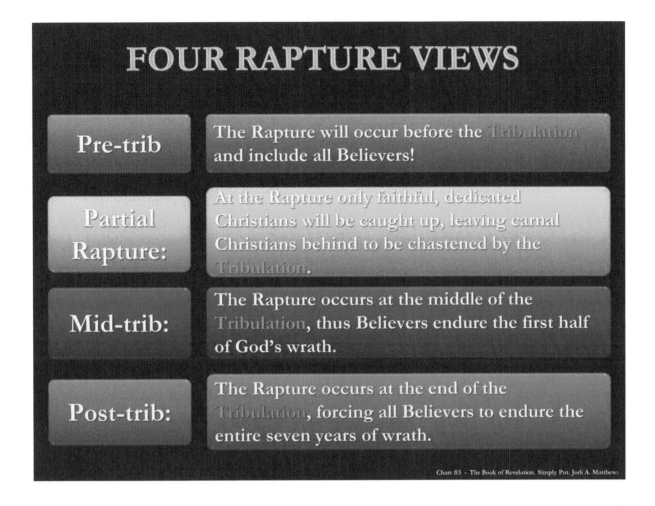

FOUR RAPTURE VIEWS

Pre-trib	The Rapture will occur before the Tribulation and include all Believers!
Partial Rapture:	At the Rapture only faithful, dedicated Christians will be caught up, leaving carnal Christians behind to be chastened by the Tribulation.
Mid-trib:	The Rapture occurs at the middle of the Tribulation, thus Believers endure the first half of God's wrath.
Post-trib:	The Rapture occurs at the end of the Tribulation, forcing all Believers to endure the entire seven years of wrath.

Chart #3 - The Book of Revelation. Simply Put. Jodi A. Matthews

THE FOUR RAPTURE VIEWS

"Many believers believe in a 'rapture' of the church to the Father's house according to Jesus' promise in John 14:1–3; there is, however, a divergence as to the exact timing of the Rapture and the question is asked, **'Will the Lord come back for His church before, in the middle, or at the end of the Tribulation?'** The timing of the Rapture is a matter of deduction based on a careful study of all Bible passages on the Lord's return. And when properly understood, the Scriptures are quite clear on this subject."[31] A more thorough understanding concerning the "Two Phases of His One Coming" will be examined later.

What Does Rapture Mean?

"The English word *rapture* comes from the Latin word *raptus*, which in Latin Bibles translates the Greek word *harpazo*, used fourteen times in the New Testament. The idea of the word means, 'to suddenly remove or snatch away' . . . 'to steal or plunder.'"[32] "The Rapture is often referred to as 'the blessed hope' (Titus 2:13), because it provides assurance to believers who are concerned about the coming Tribulation, and it offers comfort to those who long to be reunited with their departed loved ones who share a faith in Christ."[33] **Chart #3** outlines the four rapture views. Below are fast facts why the Bible supports a pretrib rapture view:

Pretribulationism most clearly fits the flow of the book of Revelation. Both Jesus and the apostle Paul promised believers they would be saved from the "wrath to come" **(Matthew 3:7; Luke 3:7; 1 Thessalonians 1:10)** and kept from "the hour of trial which shall come upon the whole world to test those who dwell on the earth" **(Revelation 3:10)**.

"For God hath not appointed us to wrath, but to obtain salvation
by our Lord Jesus Christ . . ." **(1 Thessalonians 5:9)**.

"And to wait for his Son from heaven, whom he raised from the dead,
even Jesus, which delivered us from the wrath to come" **(1 Thessalonians 1:10)**.

"Much more then, being now justified by his blood, we shall be saved from
wrath through him" **(Romans 5:9)**.

Conclusion

"The persecution of the church in this age is not the wrath of God. The future Tribulation will be a time of God's wrath upon a Christ-rejecting world. Our Lord has promised to exempt the church from it (Revelation 3:10)."[34] Prophecy scholar Ed Hindson expresses, "The church may be subject to: **1)** the discipline of Christ; **2)** the chastisement of the Father; **3)** the judgement of Christ; **4)** tribulation in the world; **5)** persecution of the world; **6)** even martyrdom and rejection; but never the **wrath of God**."

All other viewpoints contradict these Scriptures by stating that at least a portion of the church will experience all or some of the Tribulation, failing to fit in the **missing piece** of the blessed hope and coming of Christ who will "deliver" the church from the wrath to come **(1 Thessalonians 1:10)**. The other viewpoints direct Christians to the expectation of the Antichrist and not the blessed coming of the Christ, which Scripture announces repeatedly **(Titus 2:13)**.

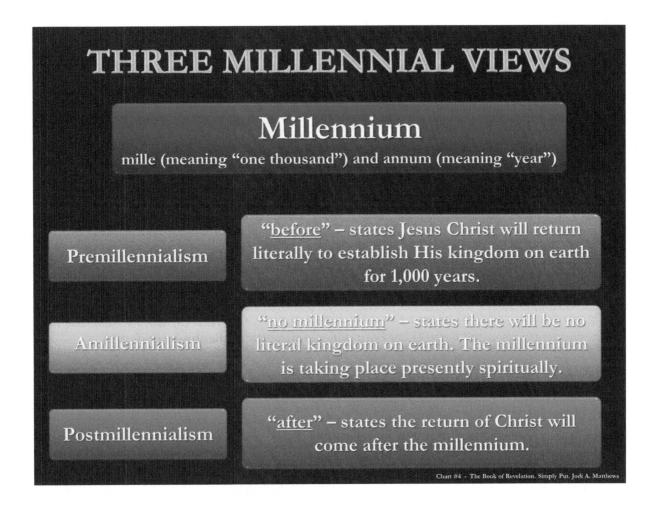

THREE MILLENNIAL VIEWS

"The word *millennium* comes from the Latin word *mille*, meaning 'one thousand,' and *annum*, meaning 'year.' The Greek word *chilias*, also meaning 'one thousand,' appears six times in Revelation 20, defining the duration of Christ's kingdom. The Millennium, therefore, refers to one thousand years of Christ's future reign on earth. During the Millennium, Christ will reign in time, space,"[35] and human form.

Positions on the Millennium

Chart #4 briefly outlines each position. Below is a more thorough examination of each belief:

Premillennialism: The premillennial interpretation teaches that "the kingdom will follow the Second Coming of Christ and will be a literal thousand-year reign of Christ on earth."[36] Simply put, when Christ returns to earth, after the battle of Armageddon, Christ will not return to heaven; **Christ will commence the millennial dispensation!** Christ will fulfill the covenant promised to David by God **(2 Samuel 7:16)** by sitting upon His father David's throne **(Luke 1:32)** ruling in human form as His father King David did from Jerusalem with the rod of iron **(Revelation 12:5)**.

Then there shall be one LORD in all the earth **(Zechariah 14:9)** with the government upon His shoulders **(Isaiah. 9:6)**, thus fulfilling the kingdom of God upon the earth **(Matthew 6:10)**. At that point, the words of Isaiah the prophet will be fulfilled: ". . . the earth shall be full of the knowledge of the Lord . . ." **(Isaiah. 11:9)**.

"The idea of the kingdom of God on earth is central to all biblical teachings. The Old Testament prophets predicted it, Jesus announced it, and the New Testament apostles foretold it again. The Greek term *a thousand* is used six times in the original text of Revelation 20 to define the duration of Christ's kingdom on earth."[37]

The Numeral Six

The numeral six often refers to "man" in the Scriptures. Using deduction, with the reference of a one thousand-year reign mentioned "six" times in Revelation 20 as it relates to Christ's reign on earth, one can positively conjecture and harmonize from numerous Scriptures that Christ will be in "man form" during this duration of the thousand years. The kingdom of God on earth will reach its apex during the thousand-year reign of Christ. **(Day Four will examine the Millennium in depth)**

Amillennialism: "With the Greek negative *a* in front of the word *millennium*, this view says that there will **not** be a literal, earthly kingdom established."[38] They tend to spiritualize and allegorize the prophecies concerning the Millennium and attribute yet-unfulfilled prophecies relating to Israel to the church instead. Those who hold to amillennialism also believe that Satan was bound at Christ's first appearance on earth two thousand years ago; hence, Christ's kingdom is reigning presently through believers. This view is partially correct in light of the spiritual, but not physical reality. Those who hold to this view do not adhere to a simple and plain literal interpretation of Scripture. The integrity of this argument fails wherein the New Testament shows Satan is a very active person. He continues to oppose all that God purposes to do in this present age. "The epistles offer numerous examples of Satan's current activity:[39]

> 1) He walks about like a roaring lion **(1 Peter 5:8)**.
> 2) He blinds the minds of the lost **(2 Corinthians 4:3–4)**.
> 3) He appears as an angel of light **(2 Corinthians 11:14)**."

Postmillennialism: "Those who hold to this perspective believe that the world will continue to get better and better until the entire world is Christianized; at which time, Christ will return to a kingdom already flourishing in peace. Although this view was popular at the beginning of the twentieth century, it was all but eliminated as a result of world wars, the Great Depression, and the overwhelming escalation of moral evil in society. Many who previously held postmillennial views adopted the amillennial position."[40]

Conclusion

In summary to the amillennial and postmillennial positions, there are many passages that show Satan is anything but bound during the present age—therefore, the binding of Satan must be a future event that has not yet occurred. It can be affirmed that Christ's kingdom reigns **spiritually** within believers presently; except for the fact His kingdom shall also reign **physically** (without), instituting a world of utopia (perfect peace). This interval of time did not take place in the past, neither is it currently realized; thus, this event must be in the **future**, affirming the writings of the prophets Isaiah, Ezekiel, Zechariah, and John **(Isaiah 2:1–5, 11:6–9, 35; Ezekiel Chapters 40–48; Zechariah 14; Revelation 20:1–6)**.

In addition, the world is not presently at a stage of utopia, neither is the world's circumstances getting better and better. Harold Hoehner wrote, "Attempts to 'spiritualize' the 1,000 years as symbolic often go hand in hand with attempts to 'spiritualize' the biblical promises of a glorious future to the nation of Israel."[41]

T. F. Torrance of the University of Edinburgh, Scotland, said, "God has not cast off His ancient people (Romans 11); for the covenant with Israel as God's people remains in force, and cannot be 'spiritualized' . . . without calling into question the whole historical foundation of God's revelation."[42]

These are ultimate answers to the amillennial and postmillennial views.

HOW TO "READ" THE BOOK OF REVELATION
"Blessed is he that read the words of this prophecy . . ." (Revelation 1:3)

Now that the **"Pivotal Foundation"** is built, the next few preliminaries should be much easier. Finding one's foundation might have been an arduous task, but it was necessary. Remember, *the foundation shoulders the weight of the house and even disperses the weight so the house does not cave in where support is not offered.* The foundation you choose is the same foundation you will use while reading the book of Revelation. The charts will offer sufficient recollection of one's pivotal foundation.

Three Tools That Will Greatly Aid Your Study:

Chart #5 lays out "Tips for Study." You may embark upon a more laborious study, but the goal of this manual is keeping it simple so there is no collapse in study. Here are three tools that will greatly aid you when reading Revelation:

> **1. Bible**—A parallel Bible of KJV or NJKV and translation of choice is recommended. This will help you understand Revelation in the most widely read version, KJV, and when misunderstanding arises, a simpler translation is immediately available.

2. Commentary—One has an efficient study Bible if a commentary is combined with it. Study Bibles contain notes or footnotes located at the bottom of each page. This will prevent you from having to carry multiple books. Some recommended study Bibles—complete with notes, book introductions, study articles, charts, and diagrams—are:

- *The Tim LaHaye Prophecy Study Bible* (NKJV) AMG Publishers
- *The Life Application Study Bible* (NLT) Tyndale House Publishers
- or any study Bible version of choice (a great study Bible should include the above-mentioned applications)

3. Timeline—Timelines help outline the Bible's historical setting and aid greatly in understanding the timing of when events occur. A book of Revelation timeline has been included in the back of this publication.

Conclusion

These tools are simple, but add considerable understanding to the study of Revelation. It is recommended that you read the book of Revelation once a year in its entirety.

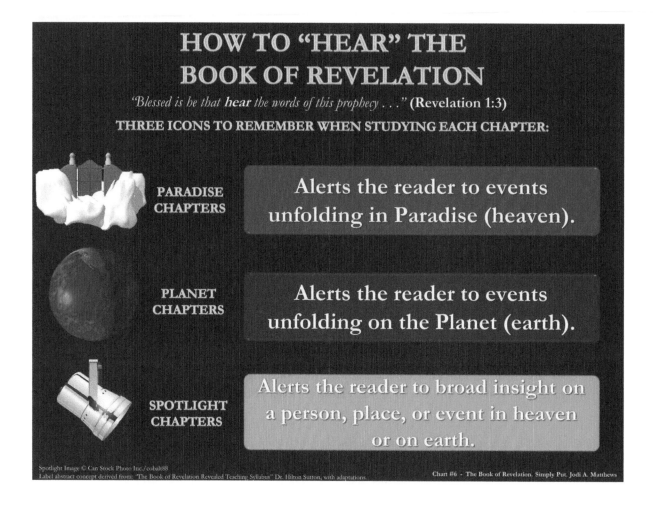

HOW TO "HEAR" THE BOOK OF REVELATION
"Blessed is he that hear the words of this prophecy . . ." (Revelation 1:3).

In ancient times, Christians, in their public worship, followed the Jewish custom of **public reading** of the Scriptures (2 Corinthians 3:14). "Today, the public reading of the Bible is an important part of worship that is often poorly done."[43] Revelation was meant to be read aloud in the churches.

Three Icons to Remember When Studying Each Chapter:

As one "hears" each chapter read, much comprehension is gained in labeling each chapter. This manual adopted this concept from Dr. Hilton Sutton's, "The Book of Revelation Revealed Teaching Syllabus," which marks each chapter, giving you insight into the chapter at large. A vast amount of understanding is attained by tagging each chapter before its reading. Tailoring the label concept to this manual, **Chart #6** alerts you to the content of each chapter. Icons are indicators to each chapter, identifying its main focus and intent. This will keep you alert to things going on in heaven, earth, or whether chapters give broad insight on a person, place, or thing..

- **Paradise Chapters**—Gives great details of events happening in heaven

- **Planet Chapters**—Gives great details of events happening on earth

- **Spotlight Chapters**—Gives you information on a person, place, event, or thing. These chapters provide information about the broader events taking place in Paradise and/or Planet chapters.

Conclusion

Feel free to use these icons or identifiers in your Bible to familiarize yourself with each chapter.

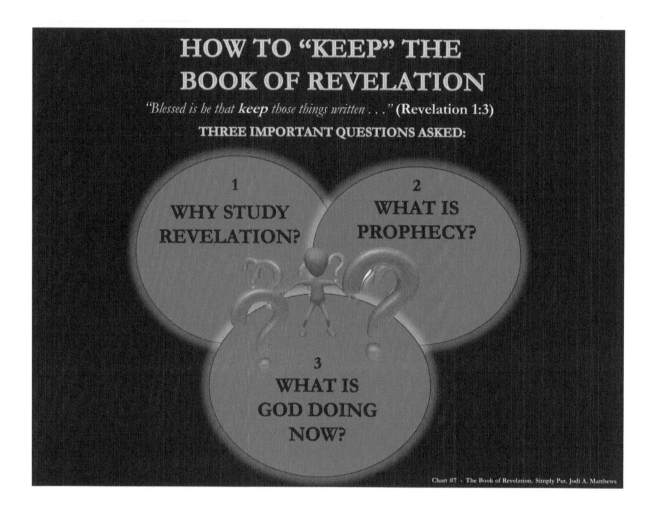

HOW TO "KEEP" THE BOOK OF REVELATION
"Blessed is he that keep the words of this prophecy . . ." (Revelation 1:3).

"The content of the Apocalypse is not merely prediction; moral counsel and religious instructions are the primary burdens of its pages."[44] "Observe here the great encouragement which the Spirit of God gives to all Christians to read and regard, to consider and meditate upon the things contained in this Divine book, that is, the necessary parts of Christianity."[45]

Three Important Questions Asked:

A great motivation in knowing "why" helps a person to keep a promise, covenant, or discipline. In order to "keep" Revelation, **Chart #7** outlines three important questions that will be examined independently and answered.

WHY STUDY REVELATION?

The ultimate answer is, Jesus encourages us to study Revelation. **"I Jesus have sent mine angel to testify unto you these things in the churches" (Revelation 22:16).** Weymouth's New Testament says, "I Jesus have sent My angel for him solemnly to declare these things to you <u>among the churches</u>" (underline added). This speech is from Christ, illustrating the beauty of the "reading," "hearing," and "teaching" of Revelation in the churches.

As outlined in **Chart #8**, the study of prophecy provides three things:

1. **Provides an outline of God's program.** "We are not isolated creatures living in a vacuum without cause or purpose. We were created body, soul, and spirit by a loving God who has a detailed plan for our future, which is revealed only in the Bible."[46]

2. **Provides us God's calendar in our day.** "God, in His marvelous grace, began revealing His will to man right from the beginning, in Genesis 3:15, which is the first prophecy related to God's redemptive plan for the salvation of mankind. From there

onward, through the pens of many writers, God continues to reveal more of His plan, which we find in the Bible."[47]

3. **Provides answers in uncertain times**. "Despite easy access to modern technologies and conveniences, bits of information at the blink of an eye, many people still believe that the Bible, a book written thousands of years ago, holds the answers to life and the life hereafter."[48]

Conclusion

God has a plan to proclaim in history. In reference to the study of end-time events, Hill & Walton states, "It was only the Israelite concept of a totally sovereign God that allowed for the development of eschatology. Eschatology should be understood as dealing with the final stage of the plan of God in history. No other deity had such a plan to execute in history. The possibility of a final stage of history was nowhere considered by any ancient deity."[49] It is God who unveils **when all heaven breaks loose** to the seven churches in Revelation and throughout history.

WHAT IS PROPHECY?

Prophecy is history written in advance; a prediction of something to come that relates to our own day.

Source: "Charting The End Times" by Tim LaHaye & Thomas Ice   Chart #9 - The Book of Revelation, Simply Put, Jodi A. Matthews

WHAT IS PROPHECY?

Briefly displayed in **Chart #9**, "prophecy is history written in advance."[50] American Tract Society Bible Dictionary states, "Prophecy is the foretelling of future events, by inspiration **from God**. It is very different from a sagacious and happy conjecture as to futurity, and from a vague and equivocal oracle, without any certain meaning. A true prophecy can come only from God."

It is vital that Christians understand the word play of the meanings concerning prophecy. Distinctions must be understood between a Bible dictionary versus a secular dictionary. Merriam-Webster's Dictionary defines the word *foretell*: "applies to the telling of the coming of a future event by any procedure or any source of information" (underline added). American Tract Society Bible Dictionary undergirds its meaning with: "foretelling of future events, **by inspiration from God**."

The Marks of True Prophecy

A true prophecy may be known by these marks: "**1)** being announced at a suitable time before the event it foretells; **2)** having a particular and exact agreement with that event; **3)** being such as no human sagacity or foresight could produce; and **4)** being delivered by one under the inspiration of the Almighty."[51]

"Many of the prophecies of Scripture foretold events ages before they occurred—events that, at the time, had no apparent probability, and the occurrence of which depended on innumerable contingencies, involving the history of things and the volitions of persons not then in existence; and yet these predictions were fulfilled at the time and place and in the manner prophesied. Such were the predictions expecting the coming and crucifixion of the Messiah, the dispersion and preservation of the Jews."[52]

Conclusion

Psalm 25:14 says, "The secret of the LORD is with them that fear him; and he will shew them his covenant." God has revealed His will through His Word. Through His Word it is revealed: the Abrahamic Covenant, the Davidic Covenant, the New Covenant, and His long-range plan for humanity. Prophecy can make one uneasy, but that is not its purpose. Ed Hindson remarks: "The purpose of prophecy is not to scare us, but to prepare us." As Jeremiah the prophet prophesied to Israel before their seventy-year captivity, he revealed God's thoughts toward them: **"For I know the thoughts that I think toward you, saith the LORD, thoughts of peace, and not of evil, to give you an expected end" (Jeremiah 29:11)**.

May these thoughts of the Lord follow you as you read Revelation.

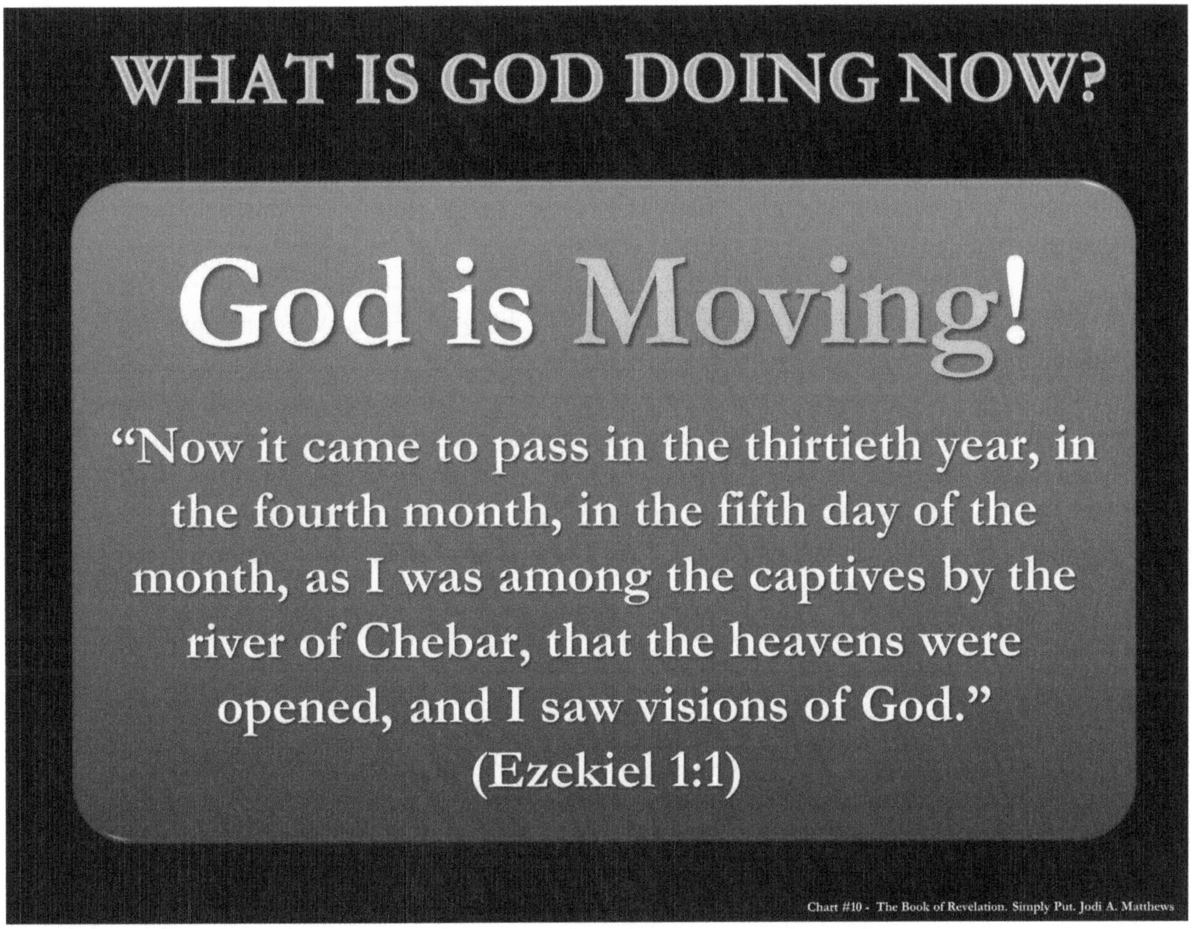

WHAT IS GOD DOING NOW?

God is Moving!

"Now it came to pass in the thirtieth year, in the fourth month, in the fifth day of the month, as I was among the captives by the river of Chebar, that the heavens were opened, and I saw visions of God."
(Ezekiel 1:1)

Chart #10 - The Book of Revelation. Simply Put. Jodi A. Matthews

WHAT IS GOD DOING NOW?

Chart #10 introduces an extraordinary vision of the Divine witnessed by Ezekiel, the prophet. Most are familiar with its words, ". . . wheel in the middle of a wheel," rather than its location (Ezekiel 1:16). "Although the account of this ecstatic vision was at the behest of being a captive who survived the trek to Mesopotamia,"[53] Ezekiel's vision gives insight into what God is doing **now**.

Significance of Ezekiel Chapter One

Familiarize yourself with Ezekiel Chapter 1. Therein lies not only a vision and message to the Jews held captive, but the answer to a question continuously inquired of by Christians: **"What is God doing now?"** Under the examination of Ezekiel Chapter 1, **God is moving**. There in the land of the Chaldeans, where the Jews were bound for seventy years, Ezekiel sees a vision that God is not bound. What a display, seeing the glory of God upon wheels.

Simply put, Ezekiel witnessed the "Throne of God" and the Throne of God was supported by wheels. When something has wheels, it moves from one place to another. The word *wheel* is a function word, which means, "to convey or move on or as if on wheels; to cause to change direction."

The account of this passage of Scripture was composed sometime between 571–562 BC. When we see what God was doing then, we can deduce what He is doing now: **MOVING!**

Conclusion

God is moving, progressing, and advancing. He is watching over His Word; bringing to pass His plans; advancing prophecies, and preparing to perform and conclude His everlasting covenant to the apple of His eye—the Jewish nation **(Zechariah 2:8)**. Let the theologian, the pupil, the prophet, the preacher, and the layman be ever mindful that the timing of God's prophecies are not contingent upon when an author writes a best seller, when a pastor reaches a thousand-member congregation, when the pupil obtains a PhD, when an individual gets married, or when the layman procures million-dollar status. God will bring to pass all of His promises at the appointed time, fulfilling His Word and keeping His covenant.

III. LET US BEGIN: REVELATION, SIMPLY PUT.

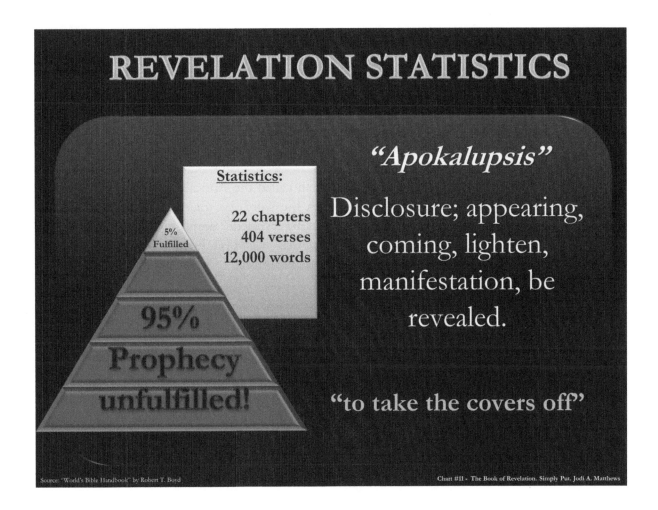

REVELATION

Let Us Begin!

Preliminaries. Since we will be studying Revelation in a very simplistic manner, keep in mind the simple way this manual will guide. Not every verse will be dissected in its entirety. Some verses should be taken at face value, meaning the verse explains itself. Others will have their core meaning explained, while some will be studied with a fine-tooth comb. Remember, charts, diagrams, and maps will provide vital information to help with your study. "To explain this book perfectly," says Bishop Newton, "is not the work of one man, or of one age; probably it never will be clearly understood till it is all fulfilled."

Fit the Missing Pieces

This **piece** will guide you to further explanation of a Scripture or subject at hand, filling in the "missing piece" of the puzzle for Scripture harmonization. To maintain continuity when studying Revelation, these pieces can be found **at the end** of each chapter when referenced.

Judge the Book by Its Title

Revelation. There is more to the title of this book than its meaning. Foremost, the pronunciation of this blessed book has suffered immensely by the addition of an "s" at the end. The mispronunciation of an individual's name can be sensitive. Thankfully, God is not sensitive; nevertheless, let us begin this study by making sure the pronunciation is correct. **Chart #11** exhibits the spelling, R-E-V-E-L-A-T-I-O-N, minus the "S." Although the "s" might flow easily off the tongue, the book is called Revelation, not Revelation**s**.

The last book of the New Testament is often called the Apocalypse. The word *revelation* comes from the Greek word *apokalupis* from which the word *apocalypse* is derived. This means, "disclosure; appearing, coming, lighten, manifestation, be revealed." Simply put, "to take the covers off." This book, by some, is considered "full of mysteries." However, judging the book by its title, God wants to make **Revelation** known. The title speaks for itself.

Vital Statistics

Author: John the apostle
When and Where it Was Written: AD 95, from the Isle of Patmos
Special Features: "Revelation is written in 'apocalyptic' form—a type of Jewish literature that uses symbolic imagery to communicate hope (in the ultimate triumph of God) to those in the midst of persecution."[54]
Statistics: "Revelation has 22 chapters, 404 verses, and 12,000 words."[55]

REVELATION CHAPTER 1

Press Rewind

Planet Chapter

> **Revelation 1:1–2** *¹The Revelation of Jesus Christ, which God gave unto him, to shew unto his servants things which must shortly come to pass; and he sent and signified it by his angel unto his servant John: ² Who bare record of the word of God, and of the testimony of Jesus Christ, and of all things that he saw.*

Don't jump ahead! Let's look at the most important subject of the Revelation—**Jesus Christ.** If you skip ahead to the hot-potato topics like the mark of the Beast, the seven seals, the Antichrist, and false prophet, you are skipping parts of the Bible that contain many great truths.[56]

v. 1 "The Revelation of Jesus Christ" indicates the **subject** of the entire book (not the Antichrist, 666, the seven seals—but Jesus). There are fifty-four references to Jesus Christ in the book. The primary author of this revelation is God the Father, the first Person in the Trinity. "The order in which God gave forth this revelation; first, it is given to Christ, next unto the angel, then unto St. John, to reveal it to the church."[57]

"to shew unto his servants" Revelation is not revealed to the world, and it is not unveiled to the unbeliever; it is revealed to **"His Servants."** Many, who do not have the Spirit of God, will lack understanding the book of Revelation for ". . . the natural man does not receive the things of the Spirit of God, for they are foolishness to him; nor can he know them, because they are spiritually discerned" (1 Corinthians 2:14, NKJV).

FIT THE MISSING PIECES!

See **Chart #12** for further explanation of Verse 1 and Meaning of Numbers

"things which must shortly come to pass" The word *shortly* in the original Greek is *en tachos*. The Greek preposition "en" denotes a fixed position; "tachkos" signifies speed, quickness, swift. This bespeaks the action will be a **fixed** position of time occurring swiftly. Announcing the actions will occur in rapid succession (one after another) being swift, not necessarily that it will occur immediately.

Presently, "these last days are rapidly paving the road for end-time events such as: one world currency, the Revived Roman Empire (the European Union Confederacy), the Jewish people's preparation for a Third Temple."[58] With these important prophetic events presently being inaugurated, once they begin, they will allow the end-time events to occur in rapid succession.

v. 2 "Who bare record of the word of God" The apostle John, whom Jesus loved (John 13:23), bore record of Jesus in the flesh. John, the disciple, walked with Jesus on earth. He bare witness with his own eyes to the Word of God enflesh (Jesus), recording all things that he saw.

Blessings, Blessings, Blessings

> **Revelation 1:3** *Blessed is he that readeth, and they that hear the words of this prophecy, and keep those things which are written therein: for the time is at hand.*

v. 3 "Blessed" The word *blessed* implies "to set a high value upon; held in honor or respect." An unequivocal blessing is bestowed upon the ones who read, hear, and keep the words of **this prophecy**. This promise of a particular blessing is not attached to any of the other sixty-five books. Albeit, there is always a blessing when one reads the Word of God; however, there is a peculiar blessing fastened to Revelation.

In illustration, the Bible is comprised of sixty-six books entwined between sturdy, poly canvas material, woven under a single, vinyl cover. When you carry your Bible, you are actually holding in your hand sixty-six detachable books. Hypothetically speaking, in view of sixty-six Divine separate books gracing one's bookshelf, the pupil is encouraged to choose **Revelation**. Why? Because of the high honor and respect (blessed) upon the one who reads, hears, and keeps the words of its prophecy.

"he that readeth" This is a personal account of one's reading. "He" that reads Revelation.

"and they that hear" This refers to a public reading of the book in the churches. The word *and* is a conjunction word, implicating a blessing on those who hear, not merely reading. One is blessed for the hearing of this book.

"and keep those things" Requires obedient action to do what the Bible says. There are admonishments instructed to the seven churches in Revelation. The duties and obligations given by Christ to John and then to the churches are to be kept.

The Salutation

> **Revelation 1:4** *John to the seven churches which are in Asia: Grace be unto you, and peace, from him which is, and which was, and which is to come; and from the seven Spirits which are before his throne;*

v. 4 "to the seven churches which are in Asia" The names of the churches to which John was to write are found in Revelation 1:11. "All seven were in the Roman province of Asia, now Asia Minor. The number seven is fixed on as representing totality."[59] These churches will be examined in detail in chapters 2–3.

"Interesting note on the number seven, it is the covenant number, the sign of God's covenant relation to mankind, and especially to the church; hence, the seventh day."[60] It is on the seventh day the church frequently worships. The number seven appears frequently throughout Revelation.

III. LET US BEGIN: REVELATION, SIMPLY PUT.

"and from the seven Spirits which are before his throne;" This is the Holy Spirit, which proceeds from the Father (John 15:26). The Holy Spirit is strongly presented throughout Revelation.

"This Spirit is one in person according to his subsistence: but in communication of his power, He perfectly manifests Himself as if there were **many spirits**, every one perfectly working in his own church"[61] This is why in Revelation 5:6 they are called the "seven horns" and "seven eyes" of the Lamb, a most absolute power and wisdom. In Revelation 3:1, Christ is said to have these seven spirits of God, and in Revelation 4:5 it is said that "seven lamps" burn before His throne, which also are those **seven spirits of God**. And these three (Father, Son, and Holy Spirit) are **One**.

All Hail to the King!

> **<u>Revelation 1:5–6</u>** *⁵And from Jesus Christ, who is the faithful witness, and the first begotten of the dead, and the prince of the kings of the earth. Unto him that loved us, and washed us from our sins in his own blood, ⁶ And hath made us kings and priests unto God and his Father; to him be glory and dominion for ever and ever. Amen.*

v. 5 "And from Jesus Christ, who is the faithful witness" Acclamation of shouts to the One hailed King of kings! The expressions of praise, exaltation, and hails exuberate through the pages of Revelation. This is the exclusive reason the book is heralded as, **"The Revelation of Jesus Christ."** Christ is unveiled as the One who has: **1)** washed us from sins; **2)** made us kings and priests; and unto whom is ascribed glory and dominion for ever and ever.

> **<u>Revelation 1:7–8</u>** *⁷Behold, he cometh with clouds; and every eye shall see him, and they also which pierced him: and all kindreds of the earth shall wail because of him. Even so, Amen. ⁸I am Alpha and Omega, the beginning and the ending, saith the Lord, which is, and which was, and which is to come, the Almighty.*

v. 7 "Behold, he cometh with clouds" The apostle John gives a *preview* into the Second Coming of Christ. Matthew 24:30 speaks, ". . . and they shall see the Son of man coming in the clouds of heaven with power and great glory." The Second Coming of Christ will not cause everyone joy. To the wicked, they will wail, for Christ will come to execute judgment on an unbelieving world **(Matthew 24:30–41)**. This occasion is not to be confused with the Rapture of the church, which is an event that precedes the Second Coming. Not every eye shall see Christ when He returns for His Church, an event recognized as "the Rapture."

The Rapture and the Second Coming will be examined in detail later. In view of Matthew 24:30, John discloses the conversion of the nation of Israel in which the Spirit of grace will be poured upon the Jewish people or "those also which pierced him" **(the Jewish Nation)**. Zechariah Chapters 12 and 13 set forth great details on the salvation of the Jews. **Zechariah 12:10** forthrightly states, "And I will pour upon the house of David, and upon the inhabitants of Jerusalem, the spirit of grace and of supplications: and they shall look upon me whom they have pierced, and they shall mourn for him, as one mourneth for his only son . . ."

My Brother's Keeper?

> <u>**Revelation 1:9–10**</u> *⁹I John, who also am your brother, and companion in tribulation, and in the kingdom and patience of Jesus Christ, was in the isle that is called Patmos, for the word of God, and for the testimony of Jesus Christ. ¹⁰I was in the Spirit on the Lord's day, and heard behind me a great voice, as of a trumpet,*

v. 9 "your brother, and companion in tribulation" "The climate of the times was great persecution of the church. John was not exempt. He suffered with his brethren. He was such a great companion that it resulted in his exile during the reign of Domitian to the island of Patmos in AD 95."[62] John was exiled **"for the word of God, and for the testimony of Jesus Christ."** May there be enough evidence of one to be found guilty and convicted for the "word of God" and the "testimony of Jesus Christ."

The Isle of Patmos from the East Acropolis
where John received Revelation

v. 10 "I was in the Spirit on the Lord's day" In the midst of tribulation, John worshipped the Savior. The first day of the week, Sunday,— **"on the Lord's day"**—was the day in which the Lord rose **(Matthew 28:1).** This is the customary day that the church (Body of Christ) worships. In contrast to the Sabbath, Saturday, on which day orthodox Jews worship, John, a believer in the Christ, worshipped on Sunday.

"a great voice, as of a trumpet" The beloved John, a believer in the Christ, heard the voice that sounded as a trumpet. It is the church, believers in the Christ, who shall hear the blast of **a trumpet** at the onset of the Rapture. "For the Lord himself will come down from heaven with a commanding shout, with the call of the archangel, and with the **trumpet call of God . . .** Christians who have died will rise from their graves. Then, together with them we who are still alive and remain on the earth will be caught up in the clouds to meet the Lord in the air: . . ." **(1 Thessalonians 4:16–17, NLT).**

The Rapture, a meeting in the air—distinct from the Second Coming, a meeting on earth—is promised to all believers who trust in Christ and to those who sleep in Christ. What a wonderful trumpet sound to be heard on this great day.

The Only Door

> <u>**Revelation 1:11**</u> *Saying, I am Alpha and Omega, the first and the last: and, What thou seest, write in a book, and send it unto the seven churches which are in Asia; unto Ephesus, and unto Smyrna, and unto Pergamos, and unto Thyatira, and unto Sardis, and unto Philadelphia, and unto Laodicea.*

v. 11 "I am Alpha and Omega" Christ gives powerful characteristics of Himself. He ascribes praise to Himself. The reason Christ visited John was for this very purpose: "**What thou

seest, write in a book, and send it unto the seven churches which are in Asia;" Christ has a message for the churches. Although delivered to the seven churches of Asia, each message is to be regarded, esteemed, and kept by the Universal Church of Christ throughout all ages.

Vision of the Son of Man

> **Revelation 1:12–16** *¹²And I turned to see the voice that spake with me. And being turned, I saw seven golden candlesticks; ¹³And in the midst of the seven candlesticks, one like unto the Son of man, clothed with a garment down to the foot, and girt about the paps with a golden girdle. ¹⁴His head and his hairs were white like wool, as white as snow; and his eyes were as a flame of fire; ¹⁵And his feet like unto fine brass, as if they burned in a furnace; and his voice as the sound of many waters. ¹⁶And he had in his right hand seven stars: and out of his mouth went a sharp two-edged sword: and his countenance was as the sun shineth in his strength.*

v. 12 "saw seven golden candlesticks" These candlesticks are defined in Revelation 1:20 as "the seven churches."

v. 13 "in the midst of the seven candlesticks, one like unto the Son of man" May the saints seriously recollect the presence of Christ in church each Sunday. This verse poignantly shares His attendance in every church service. "The Lord is presented in this startling way in order to motivate the readers to pay attention."[63]

v. 14 "His hairs were white like wool" Herein lies a glimpse of His glory, a majestic vision of the risen Christ. An injustice is done to the description of Christ's "glorified person" when cradled into the box of a particular ethnic group. No ethic group can vouch the mark of a "two-edged sword" or a countenance as "brilliant as the sun." This verse elucidates the being of "The Son."

He Reigns Over the Earth

> **Revelation 1:17–18** *¹⁷And when I saw him, I fell at his feet as dead. And he laid his right hand upon me, saying unto me, Fear not; I am the first and the last: ¹⁸I am he that liveth, and was dead; and, behold, I am alive for evermore, Amen; and have the keys of hell and of death.*

v. 17 "I fell at his feet as dead" What creature can come before the face of God and live? In Israel's encounters with God, the Scriptures declare one could not dare to hear God's voice and live, and here, John stands as dead coming face to face with a vision of Christ. "Did ever people hear the voice of God speaking out of the midst of the fire, as thou hast heard, and live?" **(Deuteronomy 4:33).**

"I am the first and the last" "Christ affirms his authority over death and the place of the dead. The Christians' death and resurrection are both in His hands."[64]

A Divine Outline

Revelation 1:19 *Write the things which thou hast seen, and the things which are, and the things which shall be hereafter;*

FIT THE
MISSING
PIECES!

See
Chart #13
for further
explanation of Verse
19 and Meaning of
Dispensations

"There is a divine outline of Revelation. The subject of his record has three tenses: **a) 'Write the things which thou hast seen,'** what he had already experienced; **b) 'the things which are,'** the present experiences; **c) 'the things which shall be hereafter,'** the future."[65]

"What John was told to write was first a record of his experience, his history **(chap. 1)**. Then he was to write the present message of Christ to the seven churches **(chaps. 2–3)**. Finally, he was to introduce the events preceding, culminating in, and following the Second Coming of Christ **(chaps. 4–22)**—the main purpose of this prophetic book."[66]

As earlier stated, this manual adopts the futurist school of interpretation, but herein is a beautiful harmonization of three out of four interpretive views according to the chronological order found in **Revelation 1:19**: "Write, therefore, what you have seen **{preterist}**, what is now **{idealist}**, and what will take place later **{futurist}**."[67]

Revelation 1:20 *The mystery of the seven stars which thou sawest in my right hand, and the seven golden candlesticks. The seven stars are the angels of the seven churches: and the seven candlesticks which thou sawest are the seven churches.*

In Revelation, a symbol of the vision is often presented first, and then its interpretation is given. Thus, the Bible explains itself.

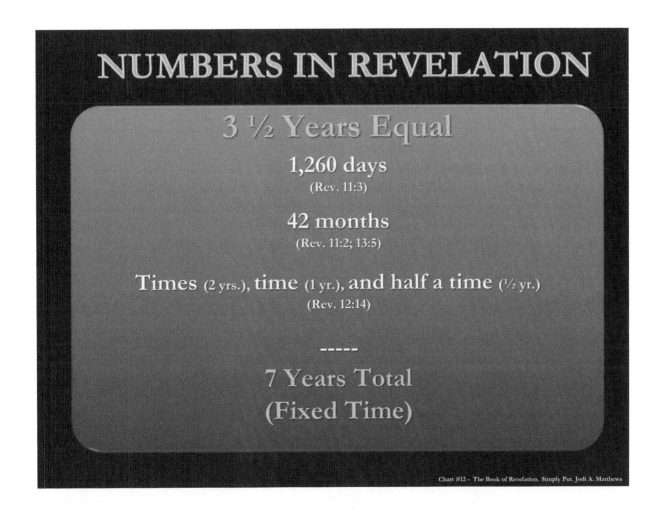

NUMBERS IN REVELATION

3 ½ Years Equal

1,260 days
(Rev. 11:3)

42 months
(Rev. 11:2; 13:5)

Times (2 yrs.), time (1 yr.), and half a time (½ yr.)
(Rev. 12:14)

-----

7 Years Total
(Fixed Time)

Chart #12 - The Book of Revelation. Simply Put. Jodi A. Matthews

NUMBERS IN REVELATION

"In the unveiling of Revelation, God reveals lengths of time regarding events, particularly the one known as a seven-year tribulation. This is often referenced as: the '70th Seven,' the 'One Week,' and the 'Week of Sevens,' denoting **seven years**. The prophetic calendar of Daniel 9:24–27, specifically **verse 27**, shows that the Tribulation will last for seven years."[68] "The 'Week' that Daniel writes of is understood by most prophecy scholars to be a week of years or seven years."[69]

The Significance of Numbers

"The mention of **1,260 days**, **42 months**, and **three-and-a-half years** are all literal and not symbolic. Hence, there is no need to take the 'numbers' found in

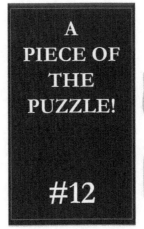

A PIECE OF THE PUZZLE!

#12

Revelation as anything but **literal** years."[70] "The desire to spiritualize the text always places the burden of proof on the interpreter. Without objective proof, it will result in a subjective interpretation."[71]

Numbers in the Bible deserve better than the landscape of "a long period of time" when its literal enumeration is given. The fact is supported that Daniel, through the reading of the book of Jeremiah, was able to understand the **number** of years his people would be in captivity: "In the first year of his rule, I, Daniel, saw clearly from the books the number of years given by the word of the Lord to the prophet Jeremiah, in which the making waste of Jerusalem was to be complete (the captivity), that is, **seventy years**" (Bible in Basic English).

Note, there was no spiritualization to this number of years declared upon the nation of Israel (seventy years); whereas there should be no spiritualization to the number of years revealed to Daniel concerning the "time of Jacob's trouble" **(Jeremiah 30:7)** and/or "the Seventieth week" (final seven years) decreed upon the Jewish nation in the last days **(Daniel 9:24)**.

Are We There Yet?

Chart #12 discloses numbers set forth in Revelation, allowing the pieces of the puzzle to fit together with the Scriptures found in the book of Daniel **(Daniel 7:25, 9:27, 12:7)**. "While Revelation does not contain a single specific quotation of the Old Testament, nevertheless, out of 404 verses in it, 278 contain indirect references to the Old Testament."[72]

Seven years (Dan. 9:27) split
into two halves of 3 1/2 years

1,260 days
(Rev. 11:3, 12:6)

42 months
(Rev. 11:2, 13:5)

Time, times, and half a time
(Dan. 12:7; Rev. 12:14)

The Seventieth Week, most commonly known as "Daniel's Seventieth Week" is vividly described in Revelation Chapters 6–20. Simply put, the "length" of time was disclosed to Daniel (*how long*); the outworking of that "length" of time was revealed to John in Revelation (*what happens*). And this length of time is a "fixed length of time," no more, no less, but en tachos **"shortly"** (Revelation 1:1). Remember, *en tachos* means, a "fixed position encompassing speed and quickness." Revelation 1:1 unveils, **". . . things which must shortly come to pass."**

These "things" are found in Revelation Chapters 6–20 and are known as Daniel's Seventieth Week or the Seven-Year Tribulation, which have <u>yet</u> to begin. Although, when "these things" begin, it will come to pass **shortly** ("swiftly") throughout a "fixed" length of time in rapid succession:

"The book of Revelation gives a number of time indicators. These time indicators, each a different way of indicating three-and-a-half years, reflect the two halves of the seven-year Tribulation period—the Seventieth week of Daniel 9:24–27."[73]

Conclusion

When one reads the Bible in plain view, taking its sayings at "face value," this lessens the confusion of the timing of prophetic events. Set against the background of allowing the Bible to speak for itself (Scripture interpreting Scripture), many thought-provoking questions are clearly answered, such as: **"Is the Tribulation period presently going on in the twenty-first century, dating back from John's day?"** This cannot be in view of a "fixed" period of time of seven years as Scripture indicates. This proffers that the Tribulation period is not currently taking place, but is in the **future**.

As one examines the Scriptures in its proper context, more thought-provoking questions are answered, even in light of the Antichrist and his location today. We will examine this in Chapter 6.

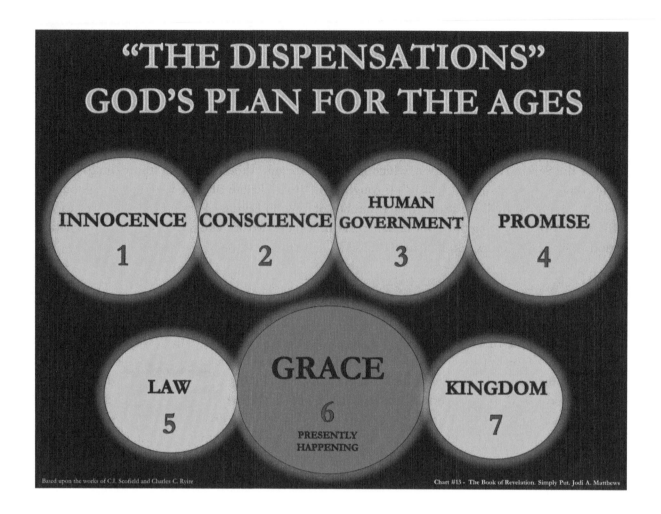

Chart #13 - The Book of Revelation. Simply Put. Jodi A. Matthews

DISPENSATIONS

According to *The Popular Encyclopedia of Bible Prophecy* by Tim LaHaye and Ed Hindson, "God's single plan has multiple aspects to it **(dispensations)**. It has both unity and diversity." The Scriptures speaks of this as, ". . . the manifold wisdom of God" (Ephesians 3:10). Elmer Towns and Thomas Ice were right when they suggested, "Dispensationalism is essential to correctly understand the Bible, especially Bible prophecy. No one will be able to rightly divide God's Word without understanding these great truths. It has been properly developed from the Bible itself."

A PIECE OF THE PUZZLE!

#13

What Is a Dispensation?

Simply put, "a dispensation is **a temporary period of time** based on a conditional test to determine if humanity will be faithful to the conditions of God."[74] "Deepening the discussion, the English word *dispensation* translates the Greek noun *oikonomia*.

Oikonomia is a compound of *oikos* meaning **'house,'** and *nomos* meaning **'law.'"** [75] The Greek word *nomos* further deepens to the primary word *nemo*, meaning "to parcel out." It is in this parceling out that man enters into what is called a new "dispensation." This word encompasses the managing or administering the affairs of a household.

Chart #13 highlights the "temporary time periods" or "dispensations" man has been administered under. Currently, humanity is administrated under the dispensation of "grace." The apostle Paul referenced this dispensation of grace as he explained how salvation has come to the Gentiles. In **Colossians 1:25–27** Paul states, "Whereof I am made a minister, according to the **dispensation** of God which is given to me for you, to fulfill the word of God; Even the mystery which hath been hid from ages and from generations, but now is made manifest to his saints: To whom God would make known . . . this mystery among the Gentiles; which is **Christ** in you, the hope of glory." Also referenced in (Ephesians. 1:10, 3:2).

Paul understood the arrangements of God; wherein those who now believe on the "Lamb of God" were no longer required to bring "a lamb," without blemish, for sacrifice under the dispensation of Law.

The Flow of It All

Putting these dispensational pieces together with the key verse **Revelation 1:19**, the Bible reader can connect and see when the millennial kingdom or dispensation period will take place. Let us examine this verse with a fine-tooth comb, which will bring much clarity in further reading of Revelation. Let us review the final three dispensations (temporary periods of time): **Law**, **Grace**, and **Kingdom**.

FIT THE MISSING PIECES!

See **Chart #14** for further explanation of Key Principles of Bible Prophecy

Most commentators and Bible scholars agree that Revelation verse 19 is a key verse, wherein it outlines the entire book of Revelation. There is no mystery to the order of this Divine book given to John by Jesus. The Christ unveils the outline of its entirety. John was told in verse 19, **"Write the things which thou <u>hast seen</u>, and the things <u>which are</u>, and the things <u>which shall be hereafter</u>;"**

⬤"Write the things which thou hast seen" (Dispensation of Law): John was given revelation or "an unveiling" of three separate dispensations. Remember, John witnessed the Word made flesh. His eyes beheld the Son of glory (John 1:14). Although the Perfect Sacrifice was present (Jesus), the dispensation in operation was **Law** in John's day <u>before</u> the crucifixion. In the days of Jesus and His disciples, the custom of the Jews were the purchasing of animals to bring as sacrifices to the Temple.

An example of this custom in effect is exhibited when Jesus clears the Temple and overturns the money changers' tables (Mark 11:15–17). The sin was not the selling in the Temple, for it was the custom to purchase one's sacrifice to offer unto God. But the inflated, exorbitant prices of the animals is where men were robbed and merchants made wealthy. Therefore, Jesus states, ". . . you turned my house of prayer into a den of thieves" (Mark 11:17).

In view of understanding what John <u>had seen</u>, when given this vision of "the Revelation of Jesus Christ," John did not recollect "animal sacrifices" of what he had seen, but fervently acknowledged the "Perfect Sacrifice" hailing **". . . unto him that loved us, and washed us from our sins in his own blood" (Revelation 1:4).** From this, John began to write the things he had seen concerning Christ in Revelation 1.

◉**"Write the things which are . . ."** (Dispensation of Grace): This refers to John's **present** dispensation, the dispensation of grace and/or the Church Age. The phrase "'things which are . . .' refers namely to the description of the state of the churches given in the second and third chapters of Revelation."[76] The day of Pentecost is the birthday of the Christian Church. The dispensation of grace technically began at the cross when animal sacrifice was no longer required, for Christ, the Lamb, became the Perfect **Sacrifice (Hebrews 10:10).** This dispensation or "the Church Age" was put into effect on the day of Pentecost (AD 30), where Jews began to propagate the Gospel to Israel and Gentile nations. "Before they had been individual followers of Jesus; now they became His mystical body, animated by His Spirit **(Acts 2:41).**"[77]

The church is a body of persons who believes Jesus is the Christ, Son of the living God **(Matthew 16:16–18)**. It consists of both Jews (direct descendants of Jacob) and Gentiles (non-Jewish descent). The Greek translation of this word is *ekklesia*, meaning, "called out ones." During the "Church Age," its members are predominately Gentile. Though a few "elect" (Jews), believe in the Christ today, the rest are blinded during this current dispensation of grace **(Romans 11:7)**. Paul describes the church, of which he comprised, "A great mystery . . ." **(Ephesians 5:32)**. Easton's 1897 Bible Dictionary beautifully comments on this mystery concerning the church:

> The **"Church Invisible"** (emphasis added) consists of the whole number of the elect (Jews and Gentiles) that have been, are, or shall be gathered into one under Christ, the Head thereof. This is a pure society, the church in which Christ dwells. It is the Body of Christ. It is called **"invisible"** (emphasis added) because the greater part of those who constitute it are already in heaven or are yet unborn, and also because its members still on earth (you and I) cannot certainly be distinguished. The qualifications of membership in it are internal and are hidden. It is unseen except by Him who searches the heart. "The Lord knoweth them that are his" **(2 Timothy 2:19)**.

◉**"Write the things which shall be hereafter . . ."** (Dispensation of the Kingdom): "The things hereafter" begins with Revelation 6–22. These are future things to take place within "fixed" periods of time: Seven years for **"The Tribulation"** (chaps. 6–19); one thousand years for **"The Millennium"** (chap. 20); and time infinity for **"The Everlasting Kingdom"** (chaps. 21–22).

Let us focus on the "kingdom dispensation." The age of grace will end, and the millennial kingdom will begin. The **Millennium** is the visible reign of Christ upon the earth for one thousand years. Simply put, the "<u>invisible kingdom</u>" shall become "<u>visible</u>." This is another fixed period or temporary time period that will last one thousand years.

These thousand years will consist of Christ in **human form**, sitting upon the throne of His father David. Christ will reign in the fourth Temple that shall be built by Himself, the BRANCH **(Zechariah 6:12);** and "the earth shall be full of the knowledge of the LORD" during this dispensation **(Isaiah 11:9)**. At last, the world will witness what it desires to accomplish today: one world government. One Ruler will govern the earth and the Scriptures disclose His name—**JESUS (Zechariah 14)**.

However, this dispensation has <u>**yet**</u> to appear "visible" to the eye; currently it is "invisible" within the Body of Christ—the church. Christ reigns today spiritually through the church. The exclusive visible representation of Christ is exemplified in how one conducts himself who <u>professes</u> the Christ. It has been stated, "The world does not read the Bible; they read the ones who profess to read the Bible. The church is the only Bible some people may read in their lifetime."

The burning question of the hour is put forth: **"In one's encounter with the modern world, what do they think after what they've just read (believers)?"**

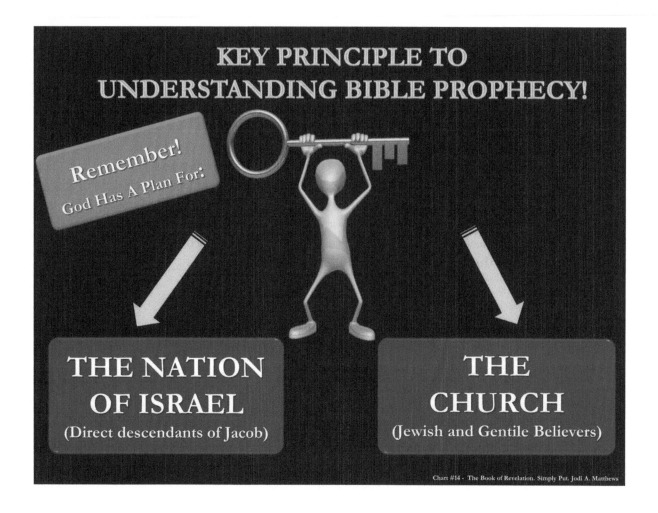

KEY PRINCIPLE TO UNDERSTANDING BIBLE PROPHECY!

Remember! God Has A Plan For:

THE NATION OF ISRAEL
(Direct descendants of Jacob)

THE CHURCH
(Jewish and Gentile Believers)

Chart #14 - The Book of Revelation. Simply Put. Jodi A. Matthews

KEY PRINCIPLE TO UNDERSTANDING
BIBLE PROPHECY

A PIECE OF THE PUZZLE!

#14

There is another essential element to understanding dispensationalism. Charles Ryrie states, "Dispensationalists believe the Bible teaches that God's single program for history includes a **distinct plan for Israel** and a **distinct plan for the church**. God's plan for history has two peoples: Israel and the church."[78] For easy recall, it is necessary to view dispensationalism in this light: God's plan for humanity is within the framework of Israel and the church, fulfilled throughout different dispensations, or epochs, of time.

When the reader adopts this distinction, confusion is cleared up regarding the identification of those calling on the name of the Lord during the Tribulation. These are "Tribulation saints," not the church. Indeed, they are saints, but not church saints of present day. Tribulation saints are those who reject

Christ presently, but after the Rapture, realize the grave mistake of their denial and accept Christ during the Tribulation. These left behind will then call upon the name of the Lord, in the **last days**, and shall be saved **(Acts 2:17, 21)**. This answers another thought-provoking question: **"Can people still be saved after the Rapture?"** The answer most assuredly is yes.

The Bible gives many references to the "saving of men" during the Tribulation period. Further harmonization of Scripture concerning this is **Revelation 6:9** "And when he had opened the fifth seal, I saw under the altar the souls of them that were slain for the word of God, and for the testimony which they held." This denotes humanity will continually call upon Christ's name and thus, be saved. Sadly noted, many will be martyrs during the Tribulation.

Conclusion

This principle of distinction by no means exchanges the only door to the Father—Jesus. Every person, Jew and Gentile, must come by way of the cross.

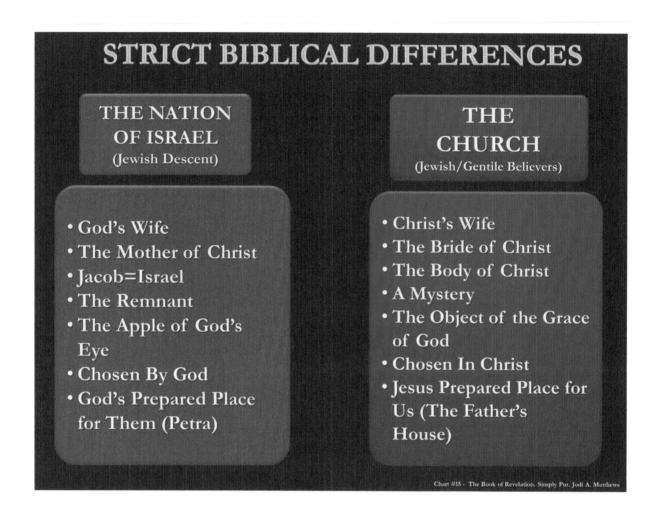

STRICT BIBLICAL DIFFERENCES

THE NATION OF ISRAEL (Jewish Descent)	THE CHURCH (Jewish/Gentile Believers)
• God's Wife • The Mother of Christ • Jacob=Israel • The Remnant • The Apple of God's Eye • Chosen By God • God's Prepared Place for Them (Petra)	• Christ's Wife • The Bride of Christ • The Body of Christ • A Mystery • The Object of the Grace of God • Chosen In Christ • Jesus Prepared Place for Us (The Father's House)

Chart #15 - The Book of Revelation. Simply Put. Jodi A. Matthews

STRICT BIBLICAL DIFFERENCES

There is a heresy active within Christendom not based according to the Scriptures. This heresy is called, "replacement theology." Much of what follows is drawn from an article entitled, "What Is Replacement Theology/Supersessionism." "Replacement theology essentially teaches that the church has replaced Israel in God's plan. Adherents of replacement theology believe the Jews are no longer God's chosen people, and God does not have specific future plans for the nation of Israel. All the different views of the relationship between the church and Israel can be divided into two camps: either the church is a continuation of Israel (replacement/covenant theology), or the church is completely different and distinct from Israel (dispensationalism/premillennialism)."[79] This book supports the latter statement.

A PIECE OF THE PUZZLE!

#15

Israel's Supernatural Protection

"If Israel has been condemned by God, and there is no future for the Jewish nation, how do we explain the supernatural survival of the Jewish people over the past 2,000 years despite the many attempts to destroy them? How do we explain why and how Israel reappeared as a nation in the 20th century after not existing for 1,900 years?"[80] The church will never replace Israel, nor is Israel ever forgotten **(Romans 11)**.

     Chart #15 unfolds the "strict biblical differences." This principle will be explained fully as further passages are studied.

Conclusion

In light of God's plan for Israel and the church, the focus should not center on "their plan" versus "our plan." One does not replace, supersede, or override the other. Each plan is uniquely distinct in the common thread of God's ultimate purpose: **one new man**.

> "Having abolished in his flesh the enmity, even the law of commandments contained in ordinances; for to make in himself of twain **one new man (Jew and Gentile),** so making peace..."
> (Ephesians 2:15)

REVELATION CHAPTER 2

Epistles to Ephesus, Smyrna, Pergamum, and Thyatira **Planet Chapter**

Revelation Chapters 2 and 3 record Jesus' messages to the seven churches in Asia Minor. It is here that Christ now dictates letters to the seven churches concerning "what is now" (Revelation 1:19). Each letter is addressed to the "angel" or "messenger" (pastors) of the church. "Jesus, in a special way, reveals an intimate knowledge of the church addressed, pinpoints the church's most serious flaw, and then conveys a command intended to correct the problem area."[81] As you read, notice that as Christ addresses His Body, He earnestly desires the church to **overcome** its sin.

"The letters addressed to each church have a remarkable agreement of structure. The seven epistles commences with, 'I know thy works.' Each contains a promise from Christ, 'To him that overcometh.' Each ends with, 'He that hath an ear, let him hear what the Spirit saith unto the churches.'"[82]

Map #16 exhibits the order of the churches addressed on the map. When one examines their arrangement, they are in chronological order geographically, forming a circuitous travel beginning with **Ephesus**, proceeding north to **Smyrna** and **Pergamous**, then venturing right-south to **Thyatira**, then further south to **Sardis**, and finally southern-most to **Philadelphia** and **Laodicea**. This represents another Divine order equal to the chronological order of Revelation itself.

The Sum and Substance

Let us first review independently the remarkable "agreement of structure" identified in each message, as these statements are repeated in each epistle:

"I know thy works"—Is there anything "hidden" from the One who sees all? "Neither is there any creature that is not manifest in his sight: but all things are naked and opened unto the eyes of him with whom we have to do" **(Hebrews 4:13)**. Christians are more apt to be visited by the LORD than a sinner; the profession of faith is a weighty proclamation, for Christians are clothed with the blood-stained banner of Christ.

The repeated statement of, **"I know thy works"** denotes Christ's penetrating examination of the seven churches. Revelation 5:6 bespeaks of His piercing vision: **"And I beheld, and, lo, in the midst of the throne and of the four beasts, and in the midst of the elders, stood a Lamb as it had been slain, having <u>seven horns</u> and <u>seven eyes</u>, which are the seven Spirits of God sent forth into all the earth."** Christ is beholding the "good" and "evil" transpiring not only in the world, but also in the churches.

"To Him that overcometh"—To overcome means, "to get to the top of" to "prevail over difficulty." This rehearsed phrase is annexed to the Body of Christ. The church is endowed with power from the Holy Ghost **(John 14:17)**. It is with this power alone that one can overcome temptations,

persecutions, and trials. There are many promises to the believer who builds aright **(1 Corinthians 3:12–14)**; who endures temptation **(James 1:12)**; and who shepherds the flock of God **(1 Peter 5:4)**, indicative of the larger focus that serving Christ is not for naught. "Therefore, my beloved brethren, be ye steadfast, unmoveable, always abounding in the work of the Lord, forasmuch as ye know that your labour is not in vain in the Lord" **(1 Corinthians 15:58)**.

"He that hath an ear, let him hear what the Spirit saith unto the churches." "Albeit, the letters are dictated by Christ, but ends with 'listen to the Spirit,' expressing that the Trinity **(Father, Son, Holy Spirit)** are One. This clause urges the deepest attention as to the most momentous truths."[83] The hearing ear must be open to hear the "applause" and "admonishment." The one who hears is the one who is considered a son and accepts chastisement from the Father **(Hebrews 12:5–11)**.

It is comforting to know the security of the salvation of the church, but it is also sobering to admit **"Judgement begins at the House of God."** "For the time is come that judgement must begin at the house of God: and if it first begin at us, what shall the end be of them that obey not the gospel of God?" **(1 Peter 4:17)**.

These seven churches have been chosen to represent the Universal Church of God throughout history. There will be an examination of **background**, **applause**, **admonishment,** and **stimulus–response** (solution to admonishment).

The Church at Ephesus

Revelation 2:1–7 *¹Unto the angel of the church of Ephesus write; These things saith he that holdeth the seven stars in his right hand, who walketh in the midst of the seven golden candlesticks; ²I know thy works, and thy labour, and thy patience, and how thou canst not bear them which are evil: and thou hast tried them which say they are apostles, and are not, and hast found them liars: ³And hast borne, and hast patience, and for my name's sake hast laboured, and hast not fainted. ⁴Nevertheless I have somewhat against thee, because thou hast left thy first love. ⁵Remember therefore from whence thou art fallen, and repent, and do the first works; or else I will come unto thee quickly, and will remove thy candlestick out of his place, except thou repent. ⁶But this thou hast, that thou hatest the deeds of the Nicolaitans, which I also hate. ⁷He that hath an ear, let him hear what the Spirit saith unto the churches; To him that overcometh will I give to eat of the tree of life, which is in the midst of the paradise of God.*

The Great Theatre of Ephesus

"They cried out saying, 'Great is Diana of Ephesians.' Now the whole city was filled with confusion…they rushed into the theatre having seized Paul's traveling companions."
(Acts 19:28, 29)

Ephesus (The Backslidden Church): The church at Ephesus was nearest to Patmos, where John received the epistle to the seven churches. It was the "church that John was especially connected with; he planted it (Acts 19). Ephesus was the largest and most influential of the cities in that area. Its population was 200,000. Although several temples stood in the city, the Temple of Diana dominated its religious culture (Acts 19:26–28).[84] During the first century, there was an annual month-long festival in honor of Diana, which drew as many as half a million people from all over the Mediterranean world."[85] "Diana was the twin sister of the god Apollo; she was the wild goddess of the hunt, and she assisted women at childbirth. The Temple of Diana was famed one of the seven wonders of the world during ancient times."[86] With the first-century Christians' surroundings of idol worship and activities, Christ applauds those who walk uprightly in spite of the environment of deep-rooted pagan gods.

Applause:	Works hard, perseveres; rejects the wicked; endures **(vv. 2–3)**
Admonishment:	Left its first love (Jesus) **(v. 4)**
Stimulus–Response:	Repent, remember from where fallen; return to first love **(v. 5)**
Reward if Obeyed:	Will eat from the tree of life **(v. 7)**

v. 6 "thou hatest the deeds of the Nicolaitans" Who are the Nicolaitanes? "The name means, 'conquerors of the people.'"[87] The Nicolaitanes are not a sect, but professing Christians who, like Balaam of old, tried to introduce into the church a false freedom, that is, licentiousness (disregarding sexual restraints). "These Nicolaitanes, or followers of Balaam, abused Paul's doctrine of the grace of God (Jude 1:4)."[88] This doctrine was found in and actively practiced at the church at Pergamum, which will be examined later.

v. 7 **"eat of the tree of life"** Involved those who "kept" the sayings of Christ just stated (Revelation 1:3). "They who refrain from the Nicolaitane indulgences (Revelation 2:6) and idol-meats (Revelation 2:14–15), shall eat of meat infinitely superior"[89] in the paradise of God.

The Church at Smyrna

Revelation 2:8–11 *[8]And unto the angel of the church in Smyrna write; These things saith the first and the last, which was dead, and is alive; [9]I know thy works, and tribulation, and poverty, (but thou art rich) and I know the blasphemy of them which say they are Jews, and are not, but are the synagogue of Satan. [10]Fear none of those things which thou shalt suffer: behold, the devil shall cast some of you into prison, that ye may be tried; and ye shall have tribulation ten days: be thou faithful unto death, and I will give thee a crown of life. [11]He that hath an ear, let him hear what the Spirit saith unto the churches; He that overcometh shall not be hurt of the second death.*

City of Smyrna - First Level Arches
"A gathering place in Smyrna"

Smyrna (The Persecuted Church): North of Ephesus. "It was the most beautiful of all cities.[90] Population 100,000 to 200,000. In addition to emperor worship, Smyrna worshipped numerous other gods.[91] The worship of mother of Sipylus, a form of 'Earth Mother' worship, was practiced there."[92] "Its name means 'myrrh.' Smyrna means 'crushed,' like the word myrrh, which was crushed to release its fragrant perfume."[93] Myrrh was first mentioned as a principal ingredient in the holy anointing oil **(Exodus 30:23)**. It formed part of the gifts brought by the wise men from the east, who came to worship the infant Jesus **(Matthew 2:11)**.

Applause:	Suffers, is in poverty, and endures persecution **(v.9)**
Admonishment:	None
Stimulus–Response:	Remain faithful; fear not of suffering; be faithful unto death **(v. 10)**
Reward if Obeyed:	Shall not be hurt of the second death **(v. 11)**

v. 9 **"the synagogue of Satan."** "These were Jews of national descent, but not spiritually of 'the true circumcision.'"[94] These Jews opposed Christianity and mightily persecuted Christians in Smyrna; it was considered the synagogue of Satan's activities.

Myrrh
"prized for its alluring frangrance,
often used for buriels, symbolizing death"

© Can Stock Photo Inc./marilyna

63

v. 10 "tribulation ten days:" The church at Smyrna was encamped with many Jews who were of the synagogue of Satan. These ten days parallel with the Beast recorded in Revelation 13, having ten heads and ten crowns, signifying that Smyrna's persecutions and martyrdom was at the hands of, and influenced by, Satan himself. The number ten here signifies the system, pattern, and order of the culture was the intense persecution of the saints. Many at Smyrna were **faithful until death.**

Again, Smyrna was known for emperor worship, which alludes to Christ's Word to remain faithful and to not fear suffering. "Polycarp, the Bishop of Smyrna, a martyr, blessed the God of heaven before he was bound and burned alive."[95] He suffered much. His narrative bears a reading by all Christians.

"Ten days" "Also is commonly called 'prophetic days,' each answering to a year, the ten years of tribulation may denote ten years of persecution; and this was precisely the duration of the persecution under Diocletian, during which all the churches were grievously afflicted."[96]

v. 11 "shall not be hurt of the second death." This refers to the lake of fire **(Revelation 20:14)**—the final abode of the wicked. It seems that they who die a persecuted death, although they might be hurt by it, would in no way be harmed by it *eternally*, for it is considered highly beneficial to them. "For our light affliction, which is but for a moment, worketh for us a far more exceeding and eternal weight of glory;" (**2 Corinthians 4:17**). "The living torments are in the 'second death.'"[97] For it is here the wicked dies but eternally commiserates the torments of death.

The Church at Pergamos

Revelation 2: 12–17 *[12] And to the angel of the church in Pergamos write; These things saith he which hath the sharp sword with two edges; [13] I know thy works, and where thou dwellest, even where Satan's seat is: and thou holdest fast my name, and hast not denied my faith, even in those days wherein Antipas was my faithful martyr, who was slain among you, where Satan dwelleth. [14] But I have a few things against thee, because thou hast there them that hold the doctrine of Balaam, who taught Balac to cast a stumbling block before the children of Israel, to eat things sacrificed unto idols, and to commit fornication. [15] So hast thou also them that hold the doctrine of the Nicolaitans, which thing I hate. [16] Repent; or else I will come unto thee quickly, and will fight against them with the sword of my mouth. [17] He that hath an ear, let him hear what the Spirit saith unto the churches; To him that overcometh will I give to eat of the hidden manna, and will give him a white stone, and in the stone a new name written, which no man knoweth saving he that receiveth it.*

The Pergamum Acropolis

as viewed from Asclepium below
"a healing god"

Pergamos (The Licentious Church): "The political capital of Asia under the Romans. This city had a population approaching 200,000.[98] In the city were five palaces, an amphitheater seating 15,000, and a library with 200,000 volumes. Pergamum was also a city given over to a wide spectrum of worship.[99] Dionysus, the god of wine, joy, theater, and agriculture was revered at his temple. Sick people from all regions of Asia came to the Temple of Aesculapius (god of medicine who was represented by a snake symbol), hoping to be cured."[100] "Asclepius was worshipped under the 'serpent' form; and Satan is considered, 'the old serpent' **(Revelation 12:9).**"[101] It was through the supreme magistracy at Pergamos, the man of God, Antipas, was persecuted and his life ended (v. 13).

Applause:	Has not denied the faith; remained true **(v. 13)**
Admonishment:	Tolerates immorality; hold doctrine of Nicolaitans; evil ways **(vv. 14–15)**
Stimulus–Response:	Repent **(v. 16)**
Reward if Obeyed:	Will eat hidden manna; given white stone, and new name **(v. 17)**

v. 14 "the doctrine of Balaam who . . . cast a stumbling block " "Balaam was a diviner. Through his counsel, he gave wicked counsel to the Moabite women urging them to seduce the men of Israel, causing them to indulge in sexual practices with foreign women, which God forbade. The effect of this is recorded in Numbers 25."[102] The young women of Moab seduced the Hebrews to the impure and idolatrous worship of Baal-Peor, for which 24,000 Israelites were slain (Numbers 31:16).

An Asclepium
snake on column

v. 15 "doctrine of the Nicolaitanes, which thing I hate." The church of Ephesus withstood this teaching. The name means, "conquerors of the people." The Nicolaitanes, again, were not a sect, but professing Christians who tried to introduce into the church a false freedom of licentiousness (disregarding sexual restraints). "These Nicolaitanes abused Paul's doctrine of the grace of God (Jude 1:4)."[103] This heinous teaching was held in high esteem here.

v. 16 "Repent; or else I will come unto thee quickly " Although others may be silent in the church, Christ is not, regarding these issues.

v. 17 "the hidden manna" "The heavenly food of Israel, in contrast to idol meats."[104]

Pergamum inscription
on "white stone"

"a white stone" "A precious stone. The people in this area were familiar with precious stones, for in New Testament times, in the Temple of Zeus was a magnificent thronelike altar.[105] This marble altar was 112 by 118 feet."[106]

"The white stone is a glistening diamond, the Urim, meaning 'light,' answering to the color white. None but the high priest knew the name written upon it, probably the incommunicable name of God, (YHVH). The high priest consulted it in some divinely appointed way to get direction from God when needful. The Lord is steadfastly ready to "reward" those who choose to return to Him."[107]

The Church at Thyatira

Revelation 2:18–29 *[18]And unto the angel of the church in Thyatira write; These things saith the Son of God, who hath his eyes like unto a flame of fire, and his feet are like fine brass; [19]I know thy works, and charity, and service, and faith, and thy patience, and thy works; and the last to be more than the first. [20]Notwithstanding I have a few things against thee, because thou sufferest that woman Jezebel, which calleth herself a prophetess, to teach and to seduce my servants to commit fornication, and to eat things sacrificed unto idols. [21]And I gave her space to repent of her fornication; and*

Didyma Temple of Apollo
didyma, meaning "twin"

"the most significant sanctuary"

she repented not. [22]Behold, I will cast her into a bed, and them that commit adultery with her into great tribulation, except they repent of their deeds. [23]And I will kill her children with death; and all the churches shall know that I am he which searcheth the reins and hearts: and I will give unto every one of you according to your works. [24]But unto you I say, and unto the rest in Thyatira, as many as have not this doctrine, and which have not known the depths of Satan, as they speak; I will put upon you none other burden. [25]But that which ye have already hold fast till I come. [26]And he that overcometh, and keepeth my works unto the end, to him will I give power over the nations: [27]And he shall rule them with a rod of iron; as the vessels of a potter shall they be broken to shivers: even as I received of my Father. [28]And I will give him the morning star. [29]He that hath an ear, let him hear what the Spirit saith unto the churches.

Thyatira (The Lax Church): "South of Pergamos, a Macedonian colony.[108] Lydia, the purple-seller of this city, having been converted at Philippi, a Macedonian city with which Thyatira had much interaction, was probably the instrument of first carrying the Gospel to her native town. This city was a center of trade in textiles and leather. Thyatira was a prosperous, commercial city. In the city, several divinities were worshipped, above all, Apollo (god of music, prophecy, and intellect) in whose honor games were instituted.[109] The church there is criticized for tolerating a woman, symbolically named Jezebel, who promotes false teaching and also immorality."[110]

Applause:	Has charity, service, faith, patience; the last works more than the first **(v. 19)**
Admonishment:	Tolerates immorality; seduces servants; false doctrine of Jezebel **(v. 20)**
Stimulus–Response:	Repent; hold fast until Christ comes **(v. 21)**
Reward if Obeyed:	Will give power over the nations; will have morning star **(vv. 26, 27, 28)**

v. 20–23 "a few things against thee . . . Jezebel" "The symbolical Jezebel was to the church of Thyatira what Jezebel, Ahab's wife, was to him. Jezebel was swift to shed blood, wholly given to Baal worship, and seduced the weak Ahab and Israel beyond calf worship. Her spiritual counterparts lured God's servants by pretended utterances of inspiration to fornication and eating of idol meats as the Balaamites and Nicolaitanes did."[111]

v. 26–27 "power over nations . . . rule with a rod of iron" "This promise is to those that "overcome." At Christ's coming the saints shall possess the kingdom under the whole heaven; therefore over this earth"[112] **(Daniel 7:22; Luke19:17)**.

v. 28 "the morning star" That is Christ, the Morning Star, Himself **(Revelation 22:16)**.

REVELATION CHAPTER 3

Epistles to Sardis, Philadelphia & Laodicea

Planet Chapter

The final address to the last three churches of Asia. The Spirit speaks explicitly to the seven churches of Asia and the Spirit speaks expressly to the churches today. The admonishments, nonetheless shameful, grueling, and disgracing are not left without remedy of the path in which one should take. **"May he that hath an ear, let him hear what the Spirit saith unto the churches" (Revelation 3:6).**

The Church at Sardis

<u>**Revelation 3:1–6**</u> *¹And unto the angel of the church in Sardis write; These things saith he that hath the seven Spirits of God, and the seven stars; I know thy works, that thou hast a name that thou livest, and art dead. ²Be watchful, and strengthen the things which remain, that are ready to die: for I have not found thy works perfect before God. ³Remember therefore how thou hast received and heard, and hold fast, and repent. If therefore thou shalt not watch, I will come on thee as a thief, and thou shalt not know what hour I will come upon thee. ⁴Thou hast a few names even in Sardis which have not defiled their garments; and they shall walk with me in white: for they are worthy. ⁵He that overcometh, the same shall be clothed in white raiment; and I will not blot out his name out of the book of life, but I will confess his name before my Father, and before his angels. ⁶He that hath an ear, let him hear what the Spirit saith unto the churches.*

A Sardis Gymnasium Marble Court

The area of Sardis produced the "sardius" stone found in Revelation 21:20

Sardis (The Dead Church): "The ancient capital of Lydia. It had a population in the first century estimated at 120,000.[113] Sardis had many temples, including one dedicated to the emperor Augustus.[114] The most impressive temple, however, was that of Athena.[115] Sardis had a name, that is 'a reputation.'" "It was the ancient residence of the kings of Lydia, among them Croesus, known for his immense wealth.[116] Its productive soil continued as a source of wealth."[117] "It was famed among the churches for spiritual vitality"[118]; yet the "One who has seven eyes and seven horns, pronounced her dead. One has not the life of God when he has not walked consistently and steadily before God, his Spirit has been grieved, and He has withdrawn much of His light and power."[119] Albeit, even when much of His light and power is withdrawn, His Spirit remains until the end of the age **(Matthew 28:20)**.

Applause: No Applause; full of rebuke
Admonishment: Considered dead **(v. 1)**
Stimulus–Response: Be watchful, strengthen what remains; repent **(v. 2–3)**
Reward if Obeyed: White raiment, name not blotted out; will confess name **(v. 5)**

v. 3 "come on thee as a thief" "The Greek proverb was that the feet of the avenging deities are shod with wool, expressing the noiseless approach of the divine judgements, and their possible nearness at the moment when they were supposed the farthest off."[120] This is a possible meaning of Christ coming on thee as a thief.

v. 5 "and I will not blot out his name" "A register was kept in ancient cities of their citizens: the names of the dead were erased.[121] Does this means

A Sardis Synagogue, 4ᵗʰ Century

one's name can be blotted out of Heaven's roll? The answer, 'No.' In sense of 'the call,' many are enrolled among **the called** to salvation, who shall not be found among **the chosen**. Salvation is open to all and is pending (humanly speaking) upon the acceptance of man. But Revelation 20:15 exhibits the book of the elect alone, after the erasure of the others' non-acceptance of the gift of salvation."[122]

The Church at Philadelphia

> <u>**Revelation 3:7–13**</u> *⁷And to the angel of the church in Philadelphia write; These things saith he that is holy, he that is true, he that hath the key of David, he that openeth, and no man shutteth; and shutteth, and no man openeth; ⁸I know thy works: behold, I have set before thee an open door, and no man can shut it: for thou hast a little strength, and hast kept my word, and hast not denied my name. ⁹Behold, I will make them of the synagogue of Satan, which say they are Jews, and are not, but do lie; behold, I will make them to come and worship before thy feet, and to know that I have loved thee. ¹⁰Because thou hast kept the word of my patience, I also will keep thee from the hour of temptation, which shall come upon all the world, to try them that dwell upon the earth. ¹¹Behold, I come quickly: hold that fast which thou hast, that no man take thy crown. ¹²Him that overcometh will I make a pillar in the Temple of my God, and he shall go no more out: and I will write upon him the name of my God, and the name of the city of my God, which is new Jerusalem, which cometh down out of heaven from my God: and I will write upon him my new name. ¹³He that hath an ear, let him hear what the Spirit saith unto the churches.*

Philadelphia (The Favored Church): "This church is twenty miles east of Sardis and has not been thoroughly excavated because the modern Turkish city of Alasehir (the city of God) is

Philadelphia – "Brotherly Love"
The Church of St. John Columns

built over it.[123] The city's temples merited it a prosperous stream of pilgrims."[124] "Philadelphia suffered grievously from earthquakes like its neighboring town, Sardis."[125] It and Smyrna alone of the seven received applause exclusively.

Applause: Had little strength but kept God's Word; did not deny Christ's name **(v. 8)**
Admonishment: None
Stimulus–Response: Hold fast; let no man take thy crown **(v. 11)**
Reward if Obeyed: A pillar in God's Temple; God's name on forehead **(v. 12)**

v. 8 "thou hast a little strength" The littleness of Philadelphia's strength led to Christ keeping the door open unto them where no man or enemy was able to prevail against them.

v. 9 "I will make them to come and worship before thy feet" A continuation of Christ giving this church Divine protection, and her enemies would come and worship and be prostrate before her.

v. 10 "the hour of temptation" Most take this as a time of serious, worldwide divine judgment. "Some premillennialists see here evidence that the Rapture of Christians will take place before the Tribulation" **(1 Thessalonians Chapter 4)**.[126]

The Church at Laodicea

<u>**Revelation 3:14–22**</u> [14]*And unto the angel of the church of the Laodiceans write; These things saith the Amen, the faithful and true witness, the beginning of the creation of God;* [15]*I know thy works, that thou art neither cold nor hot: I would thou wert cold or hot.* [16]*So then because thou art lukewarm, and neither cold nor hot, I will spue thee out of my mouth.* [17]*Because thou sayest, I am rich, and increased with goods, and have need of nothing; and knowest not that thou art wretched, and miserable, and poor, and blind, and naked:* [18]*I counsel thee to buy of me gold tried in the fire, that thou mayest be rich; and white raiment, that thou mayest be clothed, and that the shame of thy nakedness do not appear; and anoint thine eyes with eyesalve, that thou mayest see.* [19]*As many as I love, I rebuke and chasten: be zealous therefore, and repent.* [20]*Behold, I stand at the door, and knock: if any man hear my voice, and open the door, I will come in to him, and will sup with him, and he with me.* [21]*To him that overcometh will I grant to sit with me in my throne, even as I also overcame, and am set down with my Father in his throne.* [22]*He that hath an ear, let him hear what the Spirit saith unto the churches.*

Laodicea (The Lukewarm Church): "The seventh city on the circuitous Roman road in Asia Minor was Laodicea, about sixty miles southeast of Philadelphia."[127] "It was destroyed by an earthquake, AD 62, and rebuilt by its wealthy citizens without the help of the state. This wealth arose from the excellence of its wools.[128] Its world-renowned 'black glossy wool' and well-known 'eye remedy' was popularly known as Phrygian powder.[129] Its coins and inscriptions show evidence of the worship of Zeus, Aesculapius, Apollo, and the emperors."[130] "Its wealth led to a self-satisfied, lukewarm state in spiritual things."[131] Their love of money or their riches blinded their spiritual eyes to self-examination **(1 Timothy 6:10)**. Again, Laodicea was also famous for medicines, particularly the eye ointment.

Applause:	No applause
Admonishment:	Neither hot nor cold; materialistic; trusted in wealth **(v. 16–17)**
Stimulus–Response:	Buy of Christ; anoint thine eyes; be zealous, repent **(v. 18–19)**
Reward if Obeyed:	Will sit with Christ **(v. 21)**

v. 16 "spue thee out of my mouth" "Physicians used lukewarm water to cause vomiting. Cold and hot drinks were common at feasts, but never lukewarm. There were hot and cold springs near Laodicea."[132] "Hierapolis, a neighboring city, was famed for its hot mineral water believed to be medicinal, while Colossae, also near at hand, was noted for cold, pure water. Laodicea's water had to be delivered by aqueduct, and therefore arrived lkewarm."[133]

Laodicea – "The Lukewarm Church"
Architectural Fragments of Laodicea

"Laodicea had to use a long viaduct for its water, which was not only tepid but impure and sometimes foul, making people sick."[134] "Referring to the well-known fact that tepid water tends to produce sickness at the stomach and an inclination to vomit."[135] "The image is intensely strong, and denotes deep disgust and loathing at the indifference, which prevailed in the church at Laodicea."[136]

v. 20 "I stand at the door, and knock:" Here is the relentless pursuit of Christ to His wife (the church); He stands knocking upon the door of one's heart to let Him back in.

Laodicea Double Aqueduct Pipe
"Carried hot and cold waters to Laodicea"

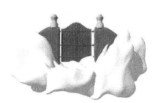

REVELATION CHAPTER 4

Worship in Heaven   **Paradise Chapter**

Worship in Revelation! There are two chapters betoken of worship in Revelation (chaps. 4–5). One would scarcely picture the thought of "praise" in this book due to the excessive chatter of the Antichrist, 666, or the Tribulation commencing in Chapter 6. When you don't "jump ahead" but <u>chronologically</u> study Revelation relative to its arrangement, you will see the marvelous beauty of praise and the Rapture of believers before the wrath of God is poured upon an unbelieving earth (chaps. 6–19).

Herein is the transition from earth to heaven. "This marks the opening of the next vision in the succession from **'the things which are,'** the existing state of the seven churches in John's time, to **'the things which shall be hereafter.'"**[137]

Chapters 4 and 5 will be explained in the power of the Scriptures speaking for themselves.

An Open Door

> **Revelation 4:1–2** *¹After this I looked, and, behold, a door was opened in heaven: and the first voice which I heard was as it were of a trumpet talking with me; which said, Come up hither, and I will shew thee things which must be hereafter. ²And immediately I was in the spirit: and, behold, a throne was set in heaven, and one sat on the throne.*

v. 2 "behold, a throne was set in heaven" John is "raptured" to heaven where he sees One sitting on the throne. **Artwork #17** gives as best a visual view of this throne; yet, the appearance of Christ and the throne is beyond human comprehension.

Another Vision of Christ

"I will worship toward thy holy temple, and praise thy name for thy loving kindness and for thy truth: for thou hast magnified thy word above all thy name."
(Psalm 138:2)

Revelation 4:3–5 *³And he that sat was to look upon like a jasper and a sardine stone: and there was a rainbow round about the throne, in sight like unto an emerald. ⁴And round about the throne were four and twenty seats: and upon the seats I saw four and twenty elders sitting, clothed in white raiment; and they had on their heads crowns of gold. ⁵And out of the throne proceeded lightnings and thunderings and voices: and there were seven lamps of fire burning before the throne, which are the seven Spirits of God.*

v. 3 "he that sat" The multifaceted visual of Christ is vastly different than Revelation 1:14–15, confirming the glorified form of Christ cannot be condensed to any one ethic race of people upon the earth. Chapter 5 gives yet another description of Christ.

v. 4 "I saw four and twenty elders sitting" "These are not angels, for they have white robes and crowns of victory, implying conflict and endurance. These represent the Heads of the Old and New Testament churches respectively:"[138] The twelve patriarchs comprise the nation of Israel, and twelve apostles comprise the church. This verse can comfortably reiterate God's single plan concerning two **distinct** groups of people—Israel and the church—culminating into God's ultimate purpose: one new man (Ephesians 2:15).

FIT THE MISSING PIECES!

See **Chart #18** for further explanation of Verse 2, The Secret Coming -vs- The Second Coming

REVELATION CHAPTER 4

Artwork provided courtesy of David Miles – davidmiles.net

Artwork #17 - The Book of Revelation. Simply Put. Jodi A. Matthews

Beasts as Worship Leaders

Revelation 4:6–8 *⁶And before the throne there was a sea of glass like unto crystal: and in the midst of the throne, and round about the throne, were four beasts full of eyes before and behind. ⁷And the first beast was like a lion, and the second beast like a calf, and the third beast had a face as a man, and the fourth beast was like a flying eagle. ⁸And the four beasts had each of them six wings about him; and they were full of eyes within: and they rest not day and night, saying, Holy, holy, holy, Lord God Almighty, which was, and is, and is to come.*

v. 6 "four beasts full of eyes" These magnificent creatures are there for one purpose: **Praise**, rendering laudation of God's first attribute, "Holy, holy, holy." **Psalm 148** shouts to humanity that **all** are created to praise the Lord!

Beasts as Worship Instructors

Revelation 4:9–11 *⁹And when those beasts give glory and honor and thanks to him that sat on the throne, who liveth for ever and ever, ¹⁰The four and twenty elders fall down before him that sat on the throne, and worship him that liveth for ever and ever, and cast their crowns before the throne, saying, ¹¹Thou art worthy, O Lord, to receive glory and honor and power: for thou hast created all things, and for thy pleasure they are and were created.*

v. 9 "those beasts give glory and honor and thanks to him that sat on the throne" Included in the gathering of believers in the universal church, transcending denominations, is the segment devoted to **"worship,"** for praise is comely among the saints **(Psalm 33:1, 147:1)**.

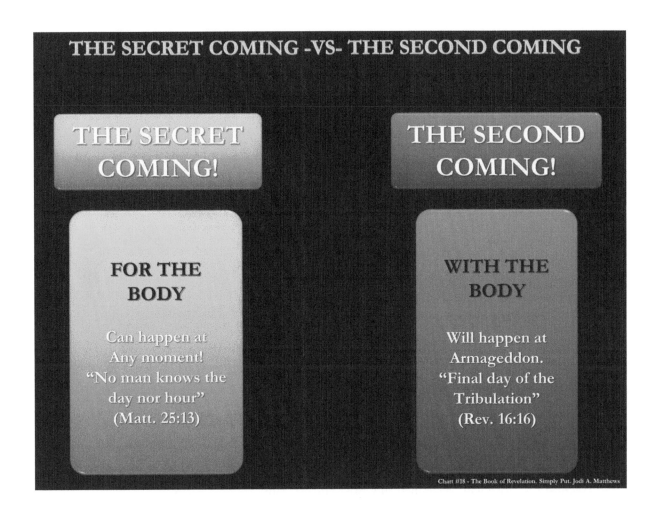

THE SECRET COMING -VS- THE SECOND COMING

THE SECRET COMING!

FOR THE BODY

Can happen at
Any moment!
"No man knows the
day nor hour"
(Matt. 25:13)

THE SECOND COMING!

WITH THE BODY

Will happen at
Armageddon.
"Final day of the
Tribulation"
(Rev. 16:16)

Chart #18 - The Book of Revelation. Simply Put. Jodi A. Matthews

THE SECRET COMING VS THE SECOND COMING

According to Jesus' promise in John 14:1–3, there will be a rapture of the church to the Father's house; there is, however, a disagreement as to the exact timing of the Rapture. Let us get a more thorough understanding concerning the **"Two Phases of His One Coming."** Refer back to **Chart #3**, *"The Four Rapture Views"* for additional review.

Jesus was the first to discuss a rapture (John 14:1–3). In fact, He promised to come back and receive the church unto Himself. Paul tells how the Rapture will come about (1 Thessalonians 4:13–18). Again, the English word *rapture* comes from the Latin word *raptus*, which in Latin Bibles translates the Greek word *harpazo*, used fourteen times in the New Testament. The idea of the word means, "to suddenly remove or snatch away" . . .

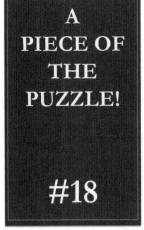

A PIECE OF THE PUZZLE!

#18

75

"to steal or plunder" (The Popular Encyclopedia of Bible Prophecy, p. 311).

Except putting the pieces together, most will confuse these two events alluded to most often in the modern world as the: **end of the world**. *Revelation, Simply Put* relates it as "The Secret Coming" and "The Second Coming." **Chart #18** distinguishes these two events.

The Difference Between the Two

The Secret Coming (a meeting in the air)—Concerns believers only. This event of the "snatching away" or "millions missing" is one of the events that will commence the seven-year Tribulation period (chaps. 6–19). This event is imminent, meaning, it can happen at any moment, for no man knows the day nor hour this will occur. Not everyone will "hear" this trumpet of God **(1 Thessalonians 4:16)**, only believers. Not everyone will "see" Christ, only believers. Paul further stated, **"So Christ was once offered to bear the sins of many; and unto them that look for him shall he appear the second time without sin unto salvation"** **(Hebrews 9:28)**. The Secret Coming is Christ

FIT THE MISSING PIECES!

See **Chart #19** for an explanation of what happens to the church after the Rapture

fulfilling His promise in John 14:1–3. It is a most blessed event for the believer, for there will be a resurrection of those who have died in Christ and we who are alive shall meet Christ in the air. Those who have buried loved ones will be united again in the air at this meeting after many years of separation.

The Second Coming (a meeting on earth)—Concerns unbelievers only. This event takes place at the end of the seven-year Tribulation. It is here that "every eye" shall see Christ coming in the clouds **(Revelation 1:7)**. It is safe to conjecture that those living upon the earth at this time will figure out the day of Christ's coming to earth, wherein the Tribulation is a "fixed" period of seven years precisely. This is why the prophet Daniel stated, regarding the **end of days**, "many shall run to and fro, and knowledge shall be increased" **(Daniel 12:4)**. This knowledge is not technological, but the knowledge of Christ and His Second Coming. Daniel further stated in this regard that, "none of the wicked shall understand; but the wise shall understand" **(Daniel 12:10)**. This denotes there will be a searching of the Scripture amongst the Jews and those dwelling on the earth in the last days. The searching is so intense such that one will know the precise day of the Second Coming of the Lord from the searching of Scriptures, for knowledge will increase concerning His Second Coming **(Daniel 9:2)**.

With this afterthought of the Scriptures, how is it that Christ will "appear to *some* a second time" **(Hebrews 9:28)** versus "<u>Every</u> eye shall see him . . ." **(Revelation 1:7)**? Are the Scriptures contradictory? God forbid. But herein **two** events will occur. Simply put, it is the two phases of His one coming. The first phase of His coming occurs *before* the Tribulation (the Rapture); the second phase of His coming befalls at the *end* of the seven-year Tribulation, final day of the 1,260 days, whichever date it may be. Those enduring the Tribulation and searching the Scriptures will be cognizant of this day.

Conclusion

After reading the first four chapters of this blessed book, the shaping and snapping of the pieces of the puzzle should fit together properly. I encourage you to review the Revelation timeline at this point to help you visualize the timing of these chronological events.

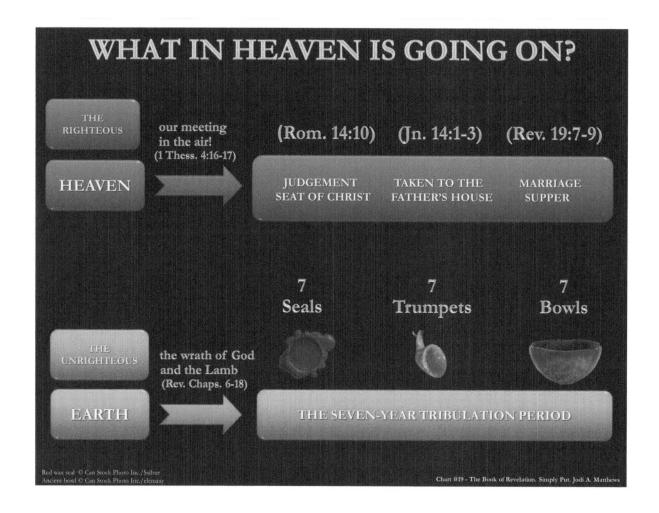

WHAT IN HEAVEN IS GOING ON?

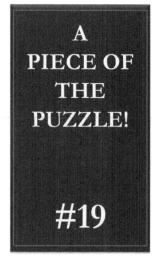

"Will the church endure the tribulation?" With careful deduction of the Scriptures, the answer is no. Revelation 4:1 is figurative of the Rapture of the church. Herein, the apostle John, who comprises the Body of Christ, is "taken up" to heaven and shown the things to take place, "hereafter."

If you do not "jump ahead" but chronologically study Revelation relating to its arrangement, you will see the beauty of the Rapture of believers *before* the wrath of God is poured upon an unbelieving earth (chaps. 6–19). **Chart #19** divulges a picture of the whole derivative of the Rapture and the Tribulation and how this will occur.

What Happens After the Rapture?

In further comprehension on this subject, this question will not involve commentary explanation, but simply Scripture shall interpret Scripture. The Tribulation (chaps 6–19) is defined in Scripture as, "The wrath of the Lamb" **(Revelation 6:17)**; "The wrath of God" **(Revelation 19:15)**; and "The wine of the wrath of God" **(Revelation 14:10, 18:6)**. **Romans 1:18** discloses "The wrath of God is revealed from heaven against all <u>ungodliness</u> and <u>unrighteousness</u> of men, who hold the truth in unrighteousness . . ." (underline added). The Bible clearly declares that God's wrath is stored up for the **wicked**, not the righteous.

FIT THE MISSING PIECES!

See <u>Chart #20</u> for explanation on the Judgement Seat of Christ and Rewards

2 Corinthians 5:21 bespeaks the righteousness concerning the church: "For he hath made him to be sin for us, who knew no sin; that we might be made <u>the righteousness</u> of God in him" (underline added). According to **Romans 4:25**, it was Christ who was, "delivered for our offences, and was raised again for our justification." And through the pouring out of Himself upon the cross Christ "delivered us from the <u>wrath to come</u>" **(1 Thessalonians 1:10, underline added)**. Wherein Paul refers to this deliverance as a "Great Salvation" **(Hebrews 2:3)**.

It bears repeating; the church will not experience the Tribulation. Scripture doesn't harmonize with the view of believers enduring the Tribulation partially, midway, neither altogether. **Chart #19** exhibits where the church will appear during this duration of time. The church will appear at the judgment seat of Christ **(2 Corinthians 5:10)**. This judgment doesn't involve one's salvation; it is a judgment of "rewards." It is at this judgment that Christians will receive rewards of their earthly deeds when on earth **(1 Corinthians 3:11–15)**; sadly, some will lose their reward.

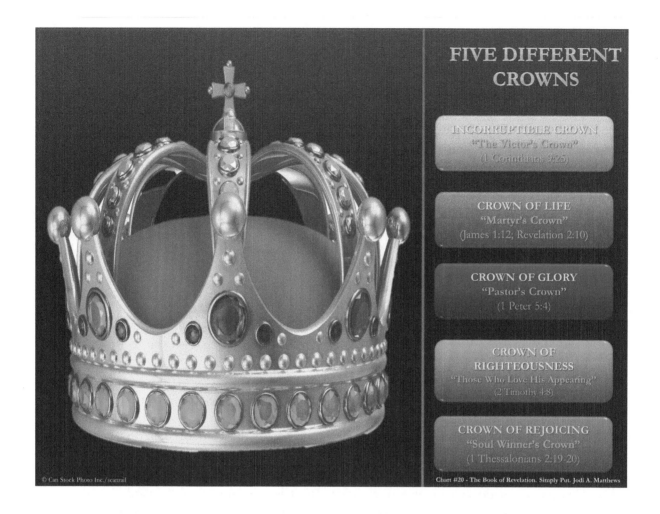

FIVE DIFFERENT CROWNS

INCORRUPTIBLE CROWN
"The Victor's Crown"
(1 Corinthians 9:25)

CROWN OF LIFE
"Martyr's Crown"
(James 1:12; Revelation 2:10)

CROWN OF GLORY
"Pastor's Crown"
(1 Peter 5:4)

CROWN OF RIGHTEOUSNESS
"Those Who Love His Appearing"
(2 Timothy 4:8)

CROWN OF REJOICING
"Soul Winner's Crown"
(1 Thessalonians 2:19-20)

© Can Stock Photo Inc./scanrail

Chart #20 - The Book of Revelation. Simply Put. Jodi A. Matthews

THE JUDGMENT SEAT OF CHRIST AND REWARDS

"For we must all appear before the judgement seat of Christ; that every one may receive the things done in his body, according to that he hath done, whether it be good or bad."
(2 Corinthians 5:10)

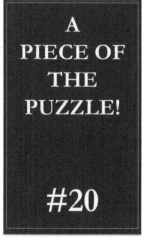

A PIECE OF THE PUZZLE!

#20

Most Christians are unaware of the judgment seat of Christ. Some assume this is Christ's judgment on the wicked. The Bible speaks to several judgments that will take place in regards to humanity. We will focus on the saints. For the wicked will not be judged until the completion of the thousand years **(Revelation 20:11–15)**. These are two separate judgments concerning "the believing" and "the unbelieving."

Will Christians Be Judged?

After the Rapture of the Body of Christ, one should not assume the church walks around heaven all day; there is a Divine order to events occurring in heaven. After the meeting in the air with our loved ones and our meeting face to face with the Savior, the body of believers will appear at the "bema" seat or judgment seat of Christ. Scripture tells why. "That every one may receive the things done in his body, according to that he hath done, whether it be good or bad" **(2 Corinthians 5:10)**.

There are several "crowns" and/or "rewards" given at this judgment. Here, at the judgment seat of Christ, the sea of believers will witness the veracity, truthfulness, and sincerity of each other's walk with the Lord when on earth. "An abiding conviction that each individual will stand at the judgment seat of Christ, and receive according to the deeds done in the body, is adapted to make men circumspect, and lead them most earnestly to desire and diligently to labor to walk uprightly."[139]

Conclusion

With so much emphasis on award shows today, it is evident the receiving of honor and recognition is esteemed in the world and churches. Yet, it will not compare to the award ceremony that will take place in heaven before God. **Will you receive a reward? Chart #20** divulges the crowns, for there are "crowns" and "rewards" reaped; also below are the various deeds that reap a reward:

REWARDS

"For God is not unrighteous to forget your work and labour of love, which ye have shewed toward his name..."
(Hebrews 6:10)

Alms/Giving	(Matt. 6:4)
Fasting	(Matt. 6:16)
Prayer	(Matt. 6:6)
Prophet's Reward	(Matt. 10:41)
Persecution Reward	(Lk. 6:23)
Loving Enemies Reward	(Lk. 6:35)
Serving The Lord	(Col. 3:24)
Not Losing Confidence	(Heb. 10:35)

REVELATION CHAPTER 5

Paradise Chapter

There is not only "worship" in heaven, but there is the "business" of heaven. Chapter 5 zeros in on the paperwork of heaven. John sees a scroll, Christ in earthly and heavenly form, and additional worship. This scroll reveals the "hereafter events" commencing in Chapter 6. John witnesses the call to heaven and earth to worship the Lamb of God who is worthy to open the seven seals.

The Lamb and the Scroll

Revelation 5:1–5 *¹And I saw in the right hand of him that sat on the throne a book written within and on the backside, sealed with seven seals. ²And I saw a strong angel proclaiming with a loud voice, Who is worthy to open the book, and to loose the seals thereof? ³And no man in heaven, nor in earth, neither under the earth, was able to open the book, neither to look thereon.*

Old Ancient Scroll

In ancient times, documents were sealed by rulers to keep those unauthorized from handling the document.

Each sealed scroll unfolds another of God's plan.

© Can Stock Photo Inc./inxti

⁴And I wept much, because no man was found worthy to open and to read the book, neither to look thereon. ⁵And one of the elders saith unto me, Weep not: behold, the Lion of the tribe of Juda, the Root of David, hath prevailed to open the book, and to loose the seven seals thereof.

v. 1 "a book written within and on the backside, sealed with seven seals." "This accords with the ancient form of books, and with the writing on the backside, 'a roll.' The writing on the back implies fullness and completeness."[140]

The Lamb, The Lion, The Root

Revelation 5:6–8 *⁶And I beheld, and, lo, in the midst of the throne and of the four beasts, and in the midst of the elders, stood a Lamb as it had been slain, having seven horns and seven eyes, which are the seven Spirits of God sent forth into all the earth. ⁷And he came and took the book out of the right hand of him that sat upon the throne. ⁸And when he had taken the book, the four beasts and four and twenty elders fell down before the Lamb, having every one of them harps, and golden vials full of odours, which are the prayers of saints.*

v. 6 "a Lamb as it had been slain, having seven horns and seven eyes" This is another vision of the Christ. John sees the Lamb who has paid the price for the sins of the world **(John 1:29).** This is the Lamb who was slain upon the cross. He is the only One worthy to open the scroll. "Thus, the opening of the seals will mean the successive steps by which God, in Christ, clears the way for the final opening and reading of the book at the visible setting up of the kingdom of Christ."[141]

"Horns." "The horn is often a symbol of strength, honor, and dominion."[142] The many horns denote Christ's tremendous power. His seven eyes renders nothing is hid from His vision, which is seven times in strength. Nothing in all of creation can hide from Him. "Everything is naked and exposed before his eyes. This is the God to whom we must explain all that we have done" **(Hebrews 4:13, NLT).**

Artwork provided courtesy of David Miles – davidmiles.net   Artwork #21 · The Book of Revelation, Simply Put, Jodi A. Matthews

More Worship in Revelation

Revelation 5:9–14 *⁹And they sung a new song, saying, Thou art worthy to take the book, and to open the seals thereof: for thou wast slain, and hast redeemed us to God by thy blood out of every kindred, and tongue, and people, and nation; ¹⁰And hast made us unto our God kings and*

priests: and we shall reign on the earth. [11] *And I beheld, and I heard the voice of many angels round about the throne and the beasts and the elders: and the number of them was ten thousand times ten thousand, and thousands of thousands;* [12] *Saying with a loud voice, Worthy is the Lamb that was slain to receive power, and riches, and wisdom, and strength, and honour, and glory, and blessing.* [13] *And every creature which is in heaven, and on the earth, and under the earth, and such as are in the sea, and all that are in them, heard I saying, Blessing, and honour, and glory, and power, be unto him that sitteth upon the throne, and unto the Lamb for ever and ever.* [14] *And the four beasts said, Amen. And the four and twenty elders fell down and worshipped him that liveth for ever and ever.*

FIT THE MISSING PIECES!

See **Chart #22** for further explanation of Evil, The Sealed Scroll and The Lamb

v. 9 "they sung a new song" One can imagine the "worship" currently taking place in heaven. This worship is loud. This worship is uniform. This worship is pure. The Bible displays a pattern of worship in the presence of God; hence, no one can stand in His presence without praising who He is.

EVIL, THE SCROLL, & THE LAMB

"The Lamb"
Executor of The Will
'Scroll'

7
Seals

7
Trumpets

7
Bowls

"The Scroll"
Sent forth to eradicate
evil from the earth
(Zech. 5; Rev. 5)

EVIL EXPELLED!

"What do you see? So I answered, I see a flying scroll . . . This is the curse that goes out over the face of the whole earth: 'Every <u>thief</u> shall be expelled,' according to this side of the scroll; and, 'Every <u>perjurer</u> shall be expelled,' according to that side of it. I will send out the curse," says the LORD of hosts; "It shall enter the house of the thief And the house of the one who swears falsely by My name . . ." (Zechariah 5:2-4) (NKJV)

Red wax seal © Can Stock Photo Inc./Ssilver
Ancient bowl © Can Stock Photo Inc./elenarav

Chart #22 - The Book of Revelation. Simply Put. Jodi A. Matthews

EVIL, THE SEALED SCROLL, AND THE LAMB

Why, Lord?

"The world's population reached 7 billion on October 31, 2011."[143] In spite of the growth of the world's population, there is also the vivid decline of humanity due to mortality (death). Man continues to die from infectious and parasitic diseases, STD's, childhood diseases, malignant neoplasms (cancers), respiratory infections, premature death (newborns); these are just communicable and noncommunicable conditions that have taken the lives of humanity.

Moreover, death is multiplied extensively with "murders, suicides, car accidents, drowning,

A PIECE OF THE PUZZLE!

#22

fires, wars, and natural disasters."[144] This leaves the anger of many toward God in their search for answers of lives lost. Man continuously asks the question, **why?** Why does man have to die? Will the earth remain in this wicked state of death and violence? Each question furthers the inquisition.

There is no ultimate answer in this life. But Scripture reveals the cause of death is not at the hands of God but there is another entity at work in the earth: **Satan**. There are various reasons for fatalities, but it is Satan that lies at its source. "He is mentioned fifty-seven times in Scripture by this name. Unbeknownst to many, he is also called, **'the prince of this world' (John 12:31); 'the prince of the power of the air' (Ephesians 2:2); 'the god of this world' (2 Corinthians 4:4)**."[145] These titles are distinctly misread, for many in the modern world disbelieve he exists or he is located beneath the earth, which is quite opposite of Scripture's description of him.

In fact, "Scripture declares his power is very great in the world, for he excites and seduces man to evil in every possible way."[146] "Men are said to be taken captive by him **(2 Timothy 2:26)**. He is the author of that evil, both physical and moral, by which the human race is afflicted. Satan is represented as soliciting men to commit sin. He is the source of impediments, which are thrown in the way of the Saint. Christians are warned against his devices **(2 Corinthians 2:11)**."[147] "He is also, most highly, described as the one who had the power of death . . . **"that through death he might destroy him that had the power of death, that is, the devil (Hebrews 2:14)**. Satan has the power of death, not as lord, but simply as executioner."[148] Above all, he is known as a **"thief" (John 10:10)** and a **"liar" (John 8:44)**. Keep these terms in mind.

The Sealed Scroll

Christ's supreme purpose for manifesting in the flesh is provided in **1 John 3:8, "For this purpose the Son of God was manifested, that he might destroy the works of the devil."** "How does this connect to the Book of Revelation? **Revelation 5:1** zooms in on the hand of God to show a scroll which no one can open and that only Jesus is able to take and open the scroll."[149] "The ancient form of books, with the writing on the backside, was considered a 'roll' or a 'scroll.' The roll or book appears from the context to be the title-deed of man's inheritance redeemed by Christ, and contains the successive steps by which He shall recover it from its usurper (Satan) and obtain actual possession of the kingdom already purchased for Himself and His elect saints."[150]

This scroll in the hand of the Father, to be executed by the Son, has garnered much speculation as to its nature. Of the suggestions that have been advanced, two are especially noteworthy: **1)** that it is a double inscribed contract deed; the other **2)** a testament or will. "The former goes back to ancient times when contracts were written on tablets, wrapped round with clay. . . and the document was sealed with seven seals.[151] This procedure follows that of a **will**, in that a will was sealed by seven witnesses, and after the death of the testator, it was opened."[152]

"A 'will,' by legal expression, is the declaration of a person's mind or wishes as to the disposition of his property, to be performed or to take effect after his death."[153] A will must have a **testate** (one who dies and leaves a will) and an **executor** (a person appointed by the testator to carry out the requests in his will). Since God cannot die, He sent His Son in the flesh to die and execute His will in the earth. "For none in heaven, in the earth, neither beneath the earth could loose the seven seals" (Revelation 5:3), for it could only be opened by the one appointed as "executor" when the testator dies. It is then John sees "a Lamb <u>as it had been slain</u> . . ." (Jesus) ". . .came and took the book out of the right hand of him that sat upon the throne"**(Revelation 5:7)**.

The Lamb

The Lamb is the One who will prevail to loose the seven seals. The result of these seven seals is revealed in Revelation 6. These seven seals unleash a behemoth of destruction upon the earth. Is this utter destruction due to God's hatred toward humanity? God forbid! The Father loves mankind immensely. A further study of reason for the loosing of the scroll is revealed in **Zechariah 5:1–5**.

The study of Zechariah Chapter 5 will explain the purpose of the "Tribulation Period" described in Revelation 6. Although this will be discussed thoroughly in Chapter 6, it garners discussion here. "The 'flying scroll' in Zechariah 5 correlates with the 'scroll' of Revelation 5. Zechariah 5 has something to say about how God deals with sin."[154] As earlier studied, the world is ridden with sin, murders, and dishonesty. This is inherently led by Satan himself through the tool of human participation.

The prophet Zechariah sees a vision of a "flying scroll." This scroll concerns the purifying of the land by the removal of sin. **Zechariah 5:3** states, "This is the curse that goeth forth over the face of the whole earth . . ." The creation presently groans for its redemption **(Romans 8:22)**. It further states, "for everyone that **stealeth** shall be cut off . . . and every one that **sweareth** shall be cut off." Herein is revealed a curse ready to fall on all who might come under it by their transgression. "Thieves and perjurers are especially mentioned as incurring the curse."[155] It justly tells the future destination of the chief liar and thief (Satan). God has not forgotten evil. All wickedness will be judged at its due time.

"Then the vision of the woman in a measuring basket taken to Babylon **(Zechariah 5:5–11)** was a prophecy that sin and wickedness would be removed from Israel"[156]; that it would be destroyed and its power removed from the land. This is why **Revelation 14:8** bespeaks, **"Babylon is fallen, is fallen, that great city, because she made all nations drink of the wine of the wrath of her fornication."** Babylon is known as the origin of wickedness and sin from ancient times to presently. The seat of wickedness of all humanity will be destroyed in one hour.

The Removal of Evil Eternally

Simply put, **how will evil be removed from the world?** With the judgments of God enumerated in Revelation 6 and Zechariah 5, executed by the Lamb. This is one of the central purposes of the Tribulation, **"to remove wickedness, sin, and defilement from the earth,"** returning it to its original possessor, Christ, who will reinstate its original design of utopia during the millennial kingdom on earth.

During this epoch, "perfect peace" will reign, for the <u>thief</u>, the <u>liar</u> and all <u>transgressors</u> of the Law will be eradicated from the earth through the sealed judgments sent forth in the earth to seek out he who steals, he who lies, and he who contrives wickedness, to destroy its power over creation and humanity.

This is a **signature** reason the church (the righteous) will not be present during the Tribulation; not because one has escaped, but one has been **delivered** through the blood of Christ Himself who will execute judgment on the unrighteous, not the righteous, and expel evil from the land **(Romans 1; Zechariah 5)**.

"And he said to me, What do you see? And I said, A roll **(scroll)** going through the air; it is twenty cubits long and ten cubits wide. **3** Then he said to me, This is the curse which goes out over the face of all the land: for long enough has every **thief** gone without punishment, and long enough has **every taker of false oaths** gone without punishment. **4** And I will send it out, says the Lord of armies, and it will go into the house of the thief and into the house of him who takes a false oath by my name: and it will be in his house, <ins>**causing its complete destruction**</ins>, with its woodwork and its stones."
(Zechariah 5:2-4)
(Bible in Basic English)

AN INTRODUCTION TO CHAPTER

"So God created man in his own image, in the image of God created he him; male and female created he them . . . and the evening and the morning were the sixth day."
(Genesis 1:27, 31)

3D silver six © Can Stock Photo Inc./Erasion

AN INTRODUCTION TO CHAPTER SIX

Chapter 6 marks the second pivotal chapter in Revelation. Revelation 1 is the first cardinal chapter. In spite of the fact every chapter in this blessed book is important as a whole, within the whole, you will find pinnacles (or high points of development) structured throughout its pages. These "high points" display an erratic turn of events. Some argue these things happened in the past; others argue Revelation is about Christ and His Revelation, spiritualizing the other chapters into nonexistence. One must remember, there are no *wasted* words in Scripture. In fact, the writer John expounds eleven chapters' worth of the workings, happenings, and occurrences of **the Tribulation** (chaps. 6–16).

Chapter 6: The Beginning of the End

The next chapters of study will give vivid details concerning what will take place during the Tribulation. Chapters 6 through 16 are the series of "Sevens:" **The Seven Seals, The Seven Trumpets, and The Seven Bowls.** The three sevens unfold judgments upon the earth. These combined judgments are unveiled as the Tribulation and Great Tribulation.

The Framework

You should have the "border," so to speak, of the prophetic puzzle assembled. What lies before you are the missing center pieces to complete this picture. The proceeding chapters will fit many pieces together; therefore, it is important that **"Fit the Missing Pieces"** sections are reviewed when called upon. Once more, these important pieces are placed at the end of each chapter read in which the puzzle piece will fit. This is done to keep the continuity of reading each chapter as a whole, succeeded by **"A Piece of the Puzzle"** to aid in making the connection.

The Number "6": Chapter 6, Happenstance?

Chapter 6 is pivotal because it moves the reader back to earth to witness earth-shattering events. "It seems quite obvious that the Bible uses numbers in patterns."[157] "Whether or not numbers really do have a significance is still debated in many circles. In fact, the division into chapters and verses was not made until comparatively modern times."[158] "The division of the Bible into chapters and verses were designed to facilitate reference to it. There are times the division is not always wisely made, yet it is very useful."[159] It is amazing to see where the division lines lie concerning humanity and the earth, **Chapter 6**. Man was created on the sixth day; man labors six days only. It is also the number of the man of lawlessness, six hundred and sixty-six (666) (Revelation 13:18); this will be examined later.

REVELATION CHAPTER 6

Planet Chapter

The four horses of the apocalypse marks a new event occurring in history. In review, see **Chart #13**, "The Dispensations," in lieu of understanding the epoch active during this time. The dispensation of grace has closed with the Rapture of the church and the next dispensation, so to speak, of Tribulation, will begin.

Although the Tribulation is not deemed a dispensation or epoch, it stands strong as a period of time in which unnatural things take place in the heavens and upon the earth before the eyes of humanity. This temporary time period occurs before the final epoch, the "kingdom dispensation" (the Millennium). Jesus states as to this epoch of time (Tribulation), **"There will be signs in sun, moon, and stars; and on earth anguish among the nations in their bewilderment at the roaring of the sea and its billows; while men's hearts are fainting for fear, and for anxious expectation of what is coming on the world. For the forces which control the heavens will be disordered and disturbed" (Luke 21:25–26, Weymouth's N.T. Translation)**.

FIT THE MISSING PIECES!

See **Chart #24** for further explanation of the Purpose of the Tribulation Period

Apocalypse. "This is the Greek name of the Book of Revelation;"[160] in addition, "apocalyptic thought was dominated by the conviction that no matter how bad circumstances might be at any given moment, God and His people would ultimately triumph over their enemies.[161] Apocalyptic writing always envisions a cosmic catastrophe prior to the final, decisive victory of God.[162] It is not a fatalistic conviction, but hope in a sovereign God who causes His people to triumph over evil.[163] The book of Daniel is the only apocalypse in the Old Testament canon of Scripture, and the book of Revelation is the only apocalypse within the New Testament canon of Scripture."[164] Highlighting its credentials once more, **". . . the Bible explains itself."[1]** Chapter 6 marks the genesis of catastrophe by the four horses of the apocalypse foreseen by Daniel the prophet **(The seventieth week)** and detailed by John the Revelator **(chaps. 6–16)**.

"The opening of the first four seals is followed by judgments in preparation for His coming."[165]

The First Seal: The Antichrist

> <u>**Revelation 6:1–2**</u> *¹And I saw when the Lamb opened one of the seals, and I heard, as it were the noise of thunder, one of the four beasts saying, Come and see. ²And I saw, and behold a white horse: and he that sat on him had a bow; and a crown was given unto him: and he went forth conquering, and to conquer.*

---

[1] Daymond R. Duck and Larry Richards, ed., *The Book of Revelation: The Smart Guide to the Bible Series,* Introduction iii (Nashville, TN: Nelson Reference, a Division of Thomas Nelson, Inc., 2006).

The White Horse = "Conqueror"

Horses in the O.T. were an emblem of war

© Can Stock Photo Inc/Mariait

v. 2 "and behold a white horse: and he that sat on him" This man on the white horse is identified as the Antichrist. Many commentators differ as to who this is, but with careful deduction of the Scriptures, one can clearly see it is an imposter of Christ, the Antichrist.

"he that sat on him" "His significance is due to his arms, his crown, and the white horse he rides."[166] There is a sharp contrast in the weaponry and crown of this rider to the Rider on the white horse in Revelation 19:11, which is the Christ!

"and a crown was given unto him" "There was a crown given to him. This crown is not 'the diadem' (diadema) in Revelation 19:12, but the 'garland crown' (stephanos)."[167] The True Christ adorns **"the diadem"** versus the Antichrist who bears the **"stephanos,"** garland crown.

"had a bow" He is armed with a usual weapon of war in that age. "Take note; there may be a special significance in the fact that he is armed with a bow instead of a sword."[168] The Rider in Revelation 19:15 has a "sharp sword." The Word of God is consistently identified in Scripture as **a Sword** (Hebrews 4:12; Revelation 19:13–15).

"went forth conquering, and to conquer" It is enough to state here that he represents either some conqueror but not *the* Conqueror. Herein is the pseudo-Christ that has *yet* to conquer but must go forth to conqueror. This pseudo-Christ is granted power to conquer for a limited time, forty-two months **(Revelation 13:5)**; Christ is the conqueror of all time!

FIT THE MISSING PIECES!

See **Chart #25** for further details on the Antichrist

The Second Seal: Wars

Revelation 6:3–4 *³And when he had opened the second seal, I heard the second beast say, Come and see. ⁴And there went out another horse that was red: and power was given to him that sat thereon to take peace from the earth, and that they should kill one another: and there was given unto him a great sword.*

v. 3 "I heard the second beast say, Come and see." The heavenly creatures are at work, assisting John in the next order of events. The second beast would be that creature possessing the face of an ox (Revelation 4:7). When the seer arrives at this vision, he immediately begins to write that vision, which he sees before him at that time.

v. 4 "And there went out another horse that was red " "The color of blood. The color of the horse in each case answers to the mission of the rider."[169] "Its rider represents war and bloodshed. During the Tribulation, **war** will characterize the world situation."[170] The nations will indulge in nuclear warfare as depicted in the seven trumpets, where trees, green grass, and rivers will either become burned or contaminated **(Revelation 8:7, 10)**.

The Red Horse = "Wars"

Great conflict and mass killings on earth
© Can Stock Photo Inc/Mariait

The Third Seal: Famine

> **Revelation 6:5–6** *⁵And when he had opened the third seal, I heard the third beast say, Come and see. And I beheld, and lo a black horse; and he that sat on him had a pair of balances in his hand. ⁶And I heard a voice in the midst of the four beasts say, A measure of wheat for a penny, and three measures of barley for a penny; and see thou hurt not the oil and the wine.*

v. 5 "I heard the third beast say" John is now aided by the heavenly creature whose face is that of a man bespeaking, "Come and see."

v. 6 "And I beheld . . . lo a black horse" "Black implies sadness and want.[171] This is the black horse of famine. The pair of balances symbolizes the scarcity of provision, the bread being doled out by weight."[172] "During the Tribulation, the economy of the world will be in a situation where it will require a day's pay to buy a loaf of bread."[173]

The Black Horse = "Famine"

Scarcity of provision. It will require a day's pay ($60 approx.) to purchase a loaf of bread
© Can Stock Photo Inc/Krisdog

The Pale Horse: Death

> **Revelation 6:7–8** *⁷And when he had opened the fourth seal, I heard the voice of the fourth beast say, Come and see. ⁸And I looked, and behold a pale horse: and his name that sat on him was Death, and Hell followed with him. And power was given unto them over the fourth part of the earth, to kill with sword, and with hunger, and with death, and with the beasts of the earth.*

v. 7 "I heard the fourth beast say" The fourth beast form was like a flying eagle (Revelation 4:7). This heavenly creature is the benefactor in introducing John to the next vision seen.

v. 8 "a pale horse" "The last of the horses is the pale horse representing death."[174] "Sword, famine, pestilence, and wild beasts causes a depopulation"[175] in the world in which one-quarter of the world's population would have perished from the judgments of God; sadly, many are not ready to meet their fate for ". . . Death, and Hell followed with him" (v. 8).

The Pale Horse = "Death"

Death toll of human race rises 90% during the time of Tribulation

© Can Stock Photo Inc/Mariait

These four seals are marked off from the last three seals. This demonstrates the severe calamities of the first four horses of the apocalypse. These four live up to their name, "apocalypse," signifying great disaster.

Revelation 6:9–11 *⁹And when he had opened the fifth seal, I saw under the altar the souls of them that were slain for the word of God, and for the testimony which they held: ¹⁰And they cried with a loud voice, saying, How long, O Lord, holy and true, dost thou not judge and avenge our blood on them that dwell on the earth? ¹¹And white robes were given unto every one of them; and it was said unto them, that they should rest yet for a little season, until their fellow servants also and their brethren, that should be killed as they were, should be fulfilled.*

v. 6 "the fifth seal, I saw . . . them that were slain" Here, the souls of martyred saints are unveiled. These saints are "Tribulation saints" not saints of the "Church Age."

FIT THE MISSING PIECES!

See Chart #29 for further explanation of the World's Mortality Rate in Tribulation

The question is posed and debated: **"Can people be saved during the Tribulation?"** Yes, but sadly, many Tribulation saints will be martyred for their faith (v.5). May it be noted, there is a dichotomy between Tribulation saints, (Gentiles and Jews who are not divinely protected, but martyred because of their faith) *versus* the 144,000 (men of Jewish descent divinely protected during the Tribulation).

This passage of Scripture demonstrates the strength of those being saved after the Rapture. Chapter 7 tells us that there will be 144,000 **Jewish men evangelists** saved—12,000 from each tribe—in addition to the saving of their Jewish brethren (nation of Israel). Then there are Gentiles and Jews who are also saved; this number forms "a great multitude" that no one can number, from all nations, coming out of the Great Tribulation **(7:1–8, 14)**.

THE FOUR HORSES OF THE APOCALYPSE

Artwork provided courtesy of David Miles – davidmiles.net

Artwork #23 - The Book of Revelation. Simply Put. Jodi A. Matthews

A Preview to Armageddon

> <u>Revelation 6:12–17</u> *[12] And I beheld when he had opened the sixth seal, and, lo, there was a great earthquake; and the sun became black as sackcloth of hair, and the moon became as blood; [13] And the stars of heaven fell unto the earth, even as a fig tree casteth her untimely figs, when she is shaken of a mighty wind. [14] And the heaven departed as a scroll when it is rolled together; and every mountain and island were moved out of their places. [15] And the kings of the earth, and the great men, and the rich men, and the chief captains, and the mighty men, and every bondman, and every free man, hid themselves in the dens and in the rocks of the mountains; [16] And said to the mountains and rocks, Fall on us, and hide us from the face of him that sitteth on the throne, and from the wrath of the Lamb: [17] For the great day of his wrath is come; and who shall be able to stand?*

v. 12 "when he had opened the sixth seal" A preview to Armageddon. The seer sees the end of the present age, and the dawning of the next—Christ's Second Advent to earth. Although this seal is opened, it does not occur until the end of the Tribulation epoch.

One must note, John writes these visions in the order that he sees them, accounting for some passages resuming in other chapters, as the continuation of this vision resumes in Chapters 11:15–18, 19:11–19. Many wicked men in the earth loathe Christ's coming.

May it be highlighted during the Tribulation epoch, those who are wise will understand right down to the precise day of His coming; in sharp contrast to the Rapture of the church, in which no man knows the day nor hour **(Matthew 25:13)**. Yet, in the last days, ". . . the wise shall understand" **(Daniel 12:10)**. Specifically designated in the wise are Jews who, in the time of the end, will search the Scriptures and their knowledge shall increase concerning Christ's Second Coming **(Daniel 12:4)**.

The Second Coming of Christ during the Tribulation will become more **pronounced** than ever during these days, with the mighty aid of the two witnesses prophesying the last forty-two months of the Great Tribulation **(Revelation 11:2)**.

THE PURPOSE OF THE TRIBULATION PERIOD

By: Arnold Fruchtenbaum – www.ariel.org

1. To make an end of wickedness. **(Is. 13:9; 24:19; Matt. 24:37-39)**

2. To bring about world revival. **(Rev. 7:1-17; Matt. 24:14)**

3. To prepare Israel for its conversion and restoration (to break their power). **(Dan. 9:24; 12:7)**

Chart #24 - The Book of Revelation. Simply Put. Jodi A. Matthews

THE PURPOSE OF THE TRIBULATION

As duly explained in **Chart #24**, the purpose of the Tribulation period is not God exhibiting hatred toward humanity; there is an ultimate, Divine purpose. Dr. Arnold Fruchtenbaum, a Messianic Jew of Ariel Ministries, firmly articulates three specific reasons for these judgments exhibited in Revelation Chapters 6–19. The purpose of the seven seals, seven trumpets, and seven bowls is to: **1)** "Make an end of wickedness"; **2)** "Bring about world revival"; and **3)** "Prepare Israel for its conversion and restoration."

Let's examine each reason individually:

1. **To make an end of wickedness:** The earth is ridden with many unsolved murders. The sex trafficking of children is widespread. The depravity of the human heart is wicked without Christ the King reigning within. Although laws are in place, numerous good people are dying at the hands of wicked men.

A PIECE OF THE PUZZLE!

#24

Man's heart is so deprived that he takes the life of one only to subsequently kill himself to avoid prosecution or punishment. Since the fall of Adam and at the behest of these things is the executer of sin, evil, wickedness, and death—**Satan**. Satan is represented as soliciting men to commit sin. He is the author of that evil, both physical and moral, by which the human race is afflicted. The human race is said to be taken captive by him (2 Timothy 2:26).

Who will stop this great wickedness in the earth? Isaiah 13:9 bespeaks, "Behold, the day of the LORD cometh, cruel both with wrath and fierce anger, to lay the land desolate: and he shall destroy the sinners thereof out of it" (underline added). How will God destroy Satan and wickedness from the earth? Wickedness will be dispelled by way of "the scroll" in **Zechariah 5:1–5**, loosed by the Lamb in **Revelation 5:5**, and exhibited through the Tribulation described in Revelation Chapters 6–16, recognized as the "Wrath of the Lamb" and the "Wrath of God" **(Revelation 6:17, 14:10, 14:19, 15:7, 16:1)**. (Review Chart #22, "Evil, The Scroll, The Lamb" for full explanation)

"The earth is the Lord's and the fullness thereof . . ." **(Psalm 24:1)** and the Tribulation is the onset of God recompensing evil its due reward, ridding the **earth** of Satan, sin, wickedness, and all **unjust** men who take part in Satan's wickedness. "And a third angel followed them, saying with a great voice, If anyone worships the Beast and its image, and receives a mark in his forehead or in his hand, **he also** will drink of the wine of the anger of God, having been mixed undiluted in the cup of His wrath. And he will be tormented by fire and brimstone before the holy angels, and in the presence of the Lamb" **(Revelation 14:9–10, emphasis added)**.

Reiterating, when one accepts Christ, Scripture declares he has been made righteous in Him. And through the pouring out of Himself upon the cross Christ "delivered us from the wrath to come" **(1 Thessalonians 1:10)**. This wrath of God is, ". . . revealed from heaven against all ungodliness and unrighteousness of men . . ." **(Romans 1:18)**. This is why "the church," who is in Christ, will **not** be present during the Tribulation, for that is not its purpose. The Bible clearly declares God's wrath is stored up for the wicked, not the righteous **(Romans 1:18; Zechariah 1–5)**. Although the church may endure tribulation presently, it is never subject to the "Wrath of God."

2. **To bring about world revival:** During the Tribulation all is not lost; many men will call upon the name of the Lord and be saved! **(Joel 2:32; Acts 2:21)**. This is also exhibited in the opening of the fifth seal: "And when he had opened the fifth seal, I saw under the altar the souls of them that were slain for the word of God, and for the testimony which they held . . ." **(Revelation 6:9)**. These under the altar do not embody those of the church; rather they are the ones at the onset of the Tribulation who will be left behind, realizing the truth of Scripture, call upon the name of the Lord, and are saved. Simply put, these are "Tribulation saints."

Revelation 7:9 bespeaks of a "great multitude" of all nations, kindreds, people, and tongues. This great multitude is *not* the church. The appearance of this great multitude is due to the world revival of the 144,000 Jewish witnesses proclaiming the Gospel after the Rapture of the church. Sadly admitted, many Tribulation saints will be martyred during this epoch of Tribulation. But unto those who remain alive, most honorably, God will "rapture" this great multitude out of the earth equally before the Great Tribulation **(Revelation 7:14)**. For no righteous person is subject to His wrath. (More explanation of this will follow in Chapter 7.)

3. To prepare Israel for its conversion and restoration (to break their power): Israel, the nation, has rejected the Savior at present; although, a few are being saved as a result of God's kindness in choosing them **(Romans 11:5).** Therefore, many Jews (Israel, the nation) will also be left behind to endure the Tribulation, but this is not to pronounce hatred upon the Jews, rather to prepare Israel for its conversion and restoration.

Scripture declares, "Some of the Jews have hard hearts, but this will last only until the complete number of Gentiles comes to Christ" **(Romans 11:25, NLT).** It further speaks regarding Israel, "Did God's people stumble and fall beyond recovery? Of course not! His purpose was to make his salvation available to the Gentiles . . ." **(Romans 11:11, NLT).** The restoration of Israel will come when Israel's power is broken during the Time of Jacob's Trouble **(Jeremiah 30:7)** titled the "Tribulation" in Revelation and when they accept Christ as their King as He delivers them from annihilation of the Antichrist during the seven-year Tribulation **(Zechariah 12 and 13)**. This, too, awaits its final fulfillment.

DETAILS ABOUT THE ANTICHRIST

- Identity obscured as the rider of the White Horse (Rev. 6:1-2)
- He is human (Dan. 7:8)
- He will rise to power in the last days (Dan 8:19, 23)
- He will arise out of a Revived Roman Empire (Dan. 7:7, 23; 9:26-27)
- He is intelligent, persuasive, multi-lingual (Dan. 7:20)
- He has an exceptional-looking face (Dan. 7:20)
- He is a master mathematician (mark of beast) (Rev. 13:16-18)
- He will rule by deception (Dan. 8:24)
- He will come from a Godly family (Dan. 11:37)
- He will not desire women (Dan. 11:37; Rev. 11:7-8)
- He will move his kingdom to Jerusalem (2 Thess. 2:4; Rev. 11:2, 7-8)
- He will make a peace treaty (agreement) with Israel (Dan. 9:27)
- He will try to annihilate the Nation of Israel (Matt. 24:15-21; Rev. 12:15)
- He will claim to be God (Dan. 11:36; 2 Thess. 2:4; Rev. 13:15)
- Will not be revealed until the Body of Christ is removed (2 Thess. 2:3-8)

Chart #25 - The Book of Revelation. Simply Put. Jodi A. Matthews

DETAILS ABOUT THE ANTICHRIST

Antichrist. This word has garnered much fear; however simply stated, "Anti is 'one that is opposed;' Christ means 'Anointed.'[176] Strictly, Antichrist means one opposed to the Anointed one. In this sense, John says there were already in his time many Antichrists, many having the spirit of an Antichrist; unbelievers, heretics, and persecutors."[177] **Chart #25** furnishes great details on the person of the Antichrist. Albeit, presently his identity is cloaked, yet Scripture unveils vivid descriptions of his **person**.

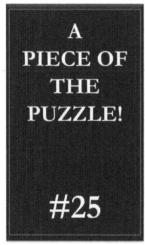

A PIECE OF THE PUZZLE!

#25

Now, there is the **"Spirit"** of Antichrist and there is the **"Person"** of Antichrist. The **spirit of Antichrist** existed even in John's day and is heavily propagated today, wherein there are many religions who deny the Christ and the fullness of His deity, in spite of professing love for Him.

His Person

However, Daniel, the prophet, bespeaks of the **person of Antichrist**. The prophet unveils that he is "human," giving credence to John, the revelator, stating, "the dragon gave **him** his power . . .,"(Revelation 13:4, emphasis added) denoting this man will receive authority from Satan himself. He will be the embodiment of Satan in the flesh; he is in sharp contrast to Jesus ". . . the Word made flesh" (John 1:14), God incarnate. The apostle Paul further concurs with Daniel and John concerning this wicked man's humanity calling him the ". . .man of sin," "the son of perdition" **(2 Thessalonians 2:3)** and ". . . that Wicked one" **(2 Thessalonians 2:8)**. Scripture clearly declares this Wicked One, who will arise in the last days, is far beyond a "spiritual working" in the earth but will be in the earth physically.

The physical manifestation of Satan in the flesh is so acutely evident Daniel utters his making of a peace treaty (agreement) with Israel for seven years **(Daniel 9:27)**. These seven years are split into two halves of 1,260 days, expressed by John the seer **(Revelation 11:3)**. John further states the Beast, Antichrist, shall have authority for forty-two months (1,260 days) **(Revelation 13:5)**. These evil descriptions portrays the rider of the white horse **(Revelation 6:2)**. He appears as one coming in peace; however, he comes with war and to conquer, claiming himself to be God **(2 Thessalonians 2:4)**.

His Purpose

In this light, one must recollect Satan's ultimate desire **". . . to be God" (Isaiah 14:12; Ezekiel 28:13–14)**. Satan desires worship, praise, to sit upon the mount of the congregation, and to be like the Most High **(Isaiah 14:12–14)**. Everything he forges today stems from his desire to build a kingdom where all will worship him **(Revelation 13:4, 14–15)**. It is no wonder this rider on the white horse resembles Christ in its form, less the proper weaponry: *arms, crown, limited authority*. One can rightfully respond in the affirmative to Swete's words of contrast: **"It is tempting to identify him with the Rider on the white horse in 19:11, whose name is 'the Word of God.' Tempting. But the two riders have <u>nothing</u> in common beyond the white horse"**[2] (emphasis added).

FIT THE MISSING PIECES!

See **Chart #26** for further explanation of Daniel's 70th Week

The Antichrist encompasses the wrath of the Lamb. His purpose is to set the stage for the restoration of Israel accepting its True Messiah, Jesus Christ. Reaffirming Fruchtenbaum's words: "One of the purposes of the tribulation is to prepare Israel for restoration" **(Daniel 12:7)**. There is wisdom in how God deals with His people, Israel. Scripture exhibits the tumultuous relationship the nation of Israel has had with God, even present-day rejection of its Messiah.

---

[2] Henry Barclay Swete, *Robertson, A. T. Word Pictures in the New Testament* (Nashville, TN: Broadman Press, 1933).

His Part

The assimilation of Israel's history can be best described in brief summary commencing in the book of Judges; In Israel's disobedience, God delivered them into the hands of their enemies. Their adversaries, in close and rapid succession, befell them. "But all these calamities were designed only as chastisements, a course of correctional discipline by which God brought His people to see and repent of their errors; for as they returned to faith and allegiance, He raised up judges."[178]

As stated throughout the book of Judges, as in ancient times, so shall it be in the last days for Israel. The Antichrist, Israel's adversary, shall stand in the glorious land (Jerusalem) in hopes of consuming its people (the Jews) **(Daniel 11:16, 41; 2 Thessalonians 2:4)**. Zechariah the prophet proclaimed, "And it shall come to pass, that in all the land, saith the LORD, two parts therein shall be cut off and die; but the third shall be left therein" **(Zechariah 13:8)**, meaning many Jews will perish during the Tribulation at the hands of the Antichrist, but those left will call upon the LORD **(Zechariah 13:9)**. The LORD, hearing their cry once more, will not send a judge, but **the King of the Jews** to deliver His people and the LORD shall fight against the Antichrist and those nations who fought against Israel **(Zechariah 14:1–4)**.

Conclusion

The Antichrist is **a tool** for restoration and the overthrow of himself **(Revelation 19:20)**. Satan, conjecturing he is succeeding at his plan, in hindsight is accomplishing the plan of God in the final course of the age.

There is solace in knowing one does not fear the Antichrist when his hope is in Christ! May you be reintroduced to the truth: ". . . Jesus . . . delivered us from the wrath to come" **(1 Thessalonians 1:10)**. Therefore, one does not await the arrival of the Antichrist—but the Christ! **(Titus 2:13)**. Those placing their hope in Christ will not be disappointed **(Romans 10:11)** but ". . . shall be caught up to meet the Lord in the air: and so shall we ever be with the Lord" **(1 Thessalonians 4:17)**.

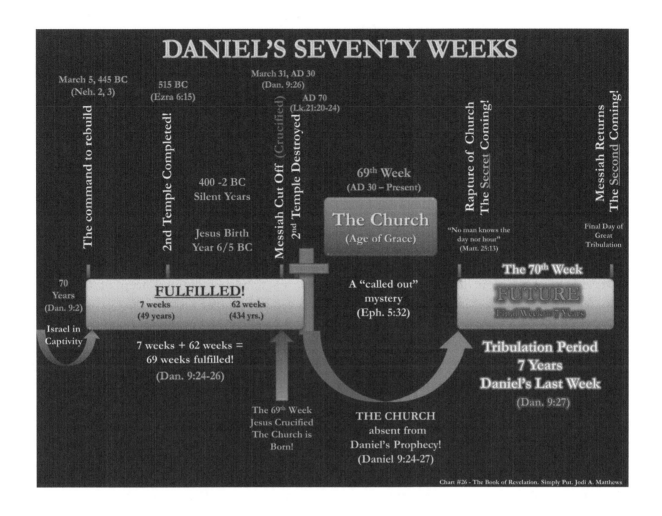

DANIEL'S SEVENTY WEEKS

March 5, 445 BC
(Neh. 2, 3)

515 BC
(Ezra 6:15)

March 31, AD 30
(Dan. 9:26)

AD 70
(Lk.21:20-24)

The command to rebuild

2nd Temple Completed!

400 -2 BC
Silent Years

Jesus Birth
Year 6/5 BC

Messiah Cut Off (Crucified)
2nd Temple Destroyed

69th Week
(AD 30 – Present)

Rapture of Church
The Secret Coming!

Messiah Returns
The Second Coming!

The Church
(Age of Grace)

"No man knows the
day nor hour"
(Matt. 25:13)

Final Day of
Great
Tribulation

70
Years
(Dan. 9:2)

FULFILLED!

7 weeks
(49 years)

62 weeks
(434 yrs.)

A "called out"
mystery
(Eph. 5:32)

The 70th Week

FUTURE
Final Week = 7 Years

Israel in
Captivity

7 weeks + 62 weeks =
69 weeks fulfilled!
(Dan. 9:24-26)

The 69th Week
Jesus Crucified
The Church is
Born!

THE CHURCH
absent from
Daniel's Prophecy!
(Daniel 9:24-27)

Tribulation Period
7 Years
Daniel's Last Week
(Dan. 9:27)

Chart #26 - The Book of Revelation. Simply Put. Jodi A. Matthews

DANIEL'S SEVENTY WEEKS
(Daniel 9:24–27)

A
PIECE OF
THE
PUZZLE!

#26

Daniel's message of the seventy sevens is one of the greatest prophecies in the Bible. Leupold calls it **"the divine program for the ages."**[179] "The first part, consisting of the first six chapters, is chiefly historical; and the second part, consisting of the remaining six chapters, is chiefly prophetical.[180] The historical part of the book treats the period of the Captivity. Daniel is the historian of the captivity.[181] The prophetical part consists of three visions and one lengthened prophetical communication."[182]

"The Book of Daniel is a commentary to Revelation. Again, Daniel is the only apocalypse in the Old Testament canon of Scripture, and the Book of Revelation is the only apocalypse within the New Testament canon of Scripture."[183] Highlighting its credentials once more, ". . . the Bible explains itself." In relation to this important Scripture, this manual will expound upon this text with a fine-tooth comb and with the substantial aid of *The New American Commentary Volume 18* by Stephen R. Miller.

Chart #26 outlays, in picture form, the charting of Daniel's seventy weeks. Against this backdrop, I will reference it often during the explanation of this imperative text. In keeping with continuity and the historical context, begin your study in Daniel 9:1.

The Circumstance

Gabriel declared that the time involved was **seventy weeks**. "This word *weeks* means 'sevened' (specifically of years). It refers to periods of sevens.[184] Most scholars hold that they refer to periods of seven years each. Years fit the context well. The Jews were familiar with the concept of sevens of years as well as of days because the Sabbatical Year was based on this premise.[185] Every seventh year, there was to be a Sabbath of rest for the land **(Leviticus 25:1–7)**. God promised that if Israel did not keep these Sabbath years, they would be driven from the land and scattered among the nations **(Leviticus 26:33–35; Jeremiah 34:12–22)**.[186] According to 2 Chronicles 36:21, one result of the seventy-year Babylonian captivity was that the land was allowed to rest in order to make up for the Sabbath years, which the Jews had failed to keep."[187]

The seventy years decreed upon Israel and prophesied by Jeremiah were literal years **(Jeremiah 34:12–22)**. It is in this light Daniel writes concerning the diaspora (dispersion of Israel) and desolation of the city (Jerusalem).That judgment is not finished **(Daniel 9:24–27)**. **Chart #26**, depicts at the onset that Daniel understood, by the reading of Jeremiah's prophecy **(Daniel 9:2)**, the number of years Israel would remain in captivity is **seventy years**. These years of captivity were nearing its end when Daniel read this prophecy, signifying Israel would soon be released to return to Jerusalem and rebuild the Temple. When the Jews were dispersed to Babylon and other nations, the land laid "desolate" or was abandoned and neglected for seventy years.

"Thereupon, after its reading, Daniel turned his face to God in prayer. He uses that kind of prayer prescribed by Solomon in his prayer at the dedication of the Temple.[188] Daniel offered confessions according to God's promises in Leviticus 26:39–42, that if Israel, in exile for sin should repent and confess, God would remember for them His covenant with Abraham.[189] The covenant with Abraham was a 'Land Covenant.' Daniel takes his countrymen's place for confession of sin, identifying himself with them, and as their representative and intercessory priest, accepts the punishment of their iniquity. Thus, he typifies the Messiah, the Sin-bearer and great Intercessor.[190] As a result of this prayer, in fact, while Daniel was speaking, God sent an answer to Daniel's prayer" **(Daniel 9:3–21)**.

The Period of Time

Here, Gabriel swiftly flies with the answer declaring that the time involved is seventy sevens. Each week signifies seven years; thus, the number of weeks involved is 490 years. Employed is definite numbers to represent these periods. To reiterate, "the Jews had Sabbatical years, Leviticus 25:8, by which their years were divided into weeks of years, as in this important prophecy, each week contains seven years. The seventy weeks therefore here spoken of amount to four hundred and ninety years."[191] "If the seventieth seven is the **future tribulation** (as this manual holds), there should be evidence in other Scriptures that the duration of that period will be seven literal years **(Revelation chaps. 6–19)**."[192]

"In Daniel 9:24, there are six events mentioned, which would be the consequences"[193] of these 490 years upon "the people and holy city" **(Daniel 9:24)**. The identification of the people and the city are clear from the context. "Daniel's people were the **Jews**, and his holy city was **Jerusalem**.[194] For these reasons, the majority of scholars rightly understand this prophecy to refer to the nation of Israel and the city of Jerusalem.

The six events are:

1. To finish the transgression
2. To make an end of sins
3. To make reconciliation for iniquity
4. To bring in everlasting righteousness
5. To seal up the vision and prophecy
6. To anoint the most holy"

The Beginning of the Seventy Sevens

"The text divides the seventy sevens into three groups. Gabriel states that the first two groups total 483 years **(vv. 25–26)**, and will conclude with the coming of 'the Anointed One,' the ruler (Jesus). Gabriel told Daniel to pay especial attention, 'to know' and 'to understand' are synonymous here to the very important information that he was about to receive, partially because here was the answer to Daniel's prayer for an end to Jerusalem's desolation. The starting point of the seventy sevens will commence with a **decree to restore and rebuild Jerusalem**, which were destroyed by the Babylonians in 586 BC."[195] There are various dates given in close proximity; this manual stands with the date of March 5, 445 BC, according to Nehemiah.

In a survey of the events contained in the first sixty-nine weeks, a number of significant events would transpire. Jerusalem would be restored, but most importantly the "Anointed One" (Jesus) would come, who would be "cut off" **(Daniel 9:25–26)**. To be cut off signified Christ's crucifixion. The coming of the Messiah at the end of sixty-nine sevens could refer to Christ's birth, His baptism, and His presentation to Israel as its promised Messiah on Palm Sunday.[196] Understand that after the reconstruction of Jerusalem in the first "seven sevens" (forty-nine years), another "sixty-two sevens" (434 years) would pass and the momentous event of the birth of Christ and His killing would take place.[197] Daniel is privy to the *timing* of these events.

At the rejection of the Messiah and upon crucifixion, the church is born, not to replace Israel, but as a called-out mystery (Jews and Gentiles). Mystery, in its context denotes it was not revealed unto the prophets of old, but Paul received this revelation that God's program extends to the Gentiles. All who believe in "the Christ" are grafted in this great plan of salvation (Romans 11). The church, birthed in the sixty-ninth week, is absent from Daniel's prophecy, wherefore Daniel is given the prophecy concerning **"his people"** and **"his city" (Daniel 9:25–26)**.

The Completion of 490 Years

In light of the death, burial, and resurrection of the Christ, upon the Anointed One's coming, the dispensation of "law" ended and the dispensation of "grace" began AD 30. This age of grace continues presently, where a number of Gentiles are accepting the Christ and being joined to His Body where He is the head. Though there are a few select Jews who accept Him, many have been blinded until the fullness of the Gentiles is complete **(Romans 11:25)**. This age of grace will end with the Rapture of His Body (the church) to heaven.

Consequently, on the other hand, in light of Daniel's prophecy for **the Jews**, the seventieth week will commence with a covenant (agreement) by the Antichrist at the onset of the Tribulation era **(Daniel 9:27)**, shifting God's focus back to His beloved nation (Israel) to fulfill its prophecies historically and nationally. Thus, fulfilling the prophecy, God hid His face from Israel and turned His face toward a foolish nation (Gentiles) **(Deuteronomy 32:16–43)**.

The Seventieth Seven and the Antichrist

With this understanding of God hiding His face from Israel, this calls forth the affirmation of **"the gap"** between the sixty-ninth and seventieth weeks, which entail the age of grace where many foolish

FIT THE MISSING PIECES!

See **Chart #27** for further explanation of the Roman Empire

nations (Gentiles) are accepting the Messiah **(see Chart #26)**. At this juncture, when God turns His face back to Israel, there remains one week left to complete God's purposes for His people **(Daniel 9:27)**. This week will engulf tribulation and Great Tribulation, not only for Israel (who has rejected her Messiah) but all humanity who follows accordingly in its rejection of the Christ. Hence, John reveals what will happen during the final seven years of God's dealings with Israel **(Revelation 6–19)**.

The events of the last seven will begin with a covenant. This covenant is produced by a man, the Antichrist. Historically, the destruction of Jerusalem and the Temple after the Babylonian period was perpetrated by the Romans in AD 70; Titus Vespasianus led the Roman legions against Jerusalem and utterly destroyed both the city and the Temple. "Yet, verse 27 makes clear there is another 'ruler' prince of the Roman people; this ruler will be the future persecutor of Israel during the seventieth seven (v. 26). 'The people of the ruler' does not mean that the people belong to the ruler, but rather that the ruler will come from these people. If the text is to be taken literally at this point, this future ruler will come out of the peoples and nations that make up the **ancient Roman Empire**. Daniel already had divulged in Chapter 7 that the Antichrist's origin will be from the fourth empire, Rome."[198] **(See Chart #27)**

This agreement will be made with "many." The many is best taken as a description of the Jewish people as a group, the nation of Israel. "This agreement probably entails a promise of protection[199] and a rebuilding of the Temple. It is easy to understand why Israel would enter into such an arrangement with the powerful forces of Antichrist. With such protection, Israel will feel safe and secure. The term of the treaty will be 'for one seven,' that is, seven years."[200]

"In the midst of the week, verse 27 reveals the Antichrist will put an end to sacrifice and offering. The seventieth seven is commonly referred to as the tribulation period, and the second half of this seven is known as the great tribulation **(Revelation 7:14; Matthew 24:21)**. It is in the midst of the week that Jesus tells the Jews to read Daniel **(Matthew 24:15)**, for the Antichrist, at that time, will break his agreement with them and attempt, at force, worship of himself **(2 Thessalonians 2:4; Revelation 13:8, 14–17)**."[201] He will lay the Temple **desolate** again.

Conclusion

This will be a terrible period in the world's history, but the Lord has "decreed" that these atrocities will not continue forever. The Antichrist's wickedness will last only **"until the end that is decreed is poured upon him" (Revelation 19:19–21)**.

Again, Daniel's message of the seventy weeks is one of the greatest prophecies in the Bible.

Lion, Bear, Beast © Can Stock Photos/jmhite, openlens, derocz
Leopard © klauspiwi – Fotolia.com - Statute designed by Copyartwork
Chart #27 - The Book of Revelation. Simply Put. Jodi A. Matthews

ROME: WHAT'S THE BIG DEAL?

"**Rome.** The capital of Italy with over 2.7 million residents. Called the Eternal City, it is one of the world's richest cities in history and art.[202] The rise of Rome, from an insignificant pastoral settlement to perhaps the world's most successful empire"[203], aids in its imprint in history records. Many may conjecture, what's the significance of this city in light of other beautiful, artistic, and powerful cities in the world? It is not, per se, the "city" but the "empire."

The Roman Empire has notoriety in the historical books, but most importantly biblical books. It was a dominant power in Western Europe and in the days of Jesus.

A PIECE OF THE PUZZLE!

#27

Daniel advises that this "Ancient Empire" will be revived in the last days and play a prominent role in the end times. Both Daniel and Jesus give credence to this empire and its significance **(Daniel 2:41–43, 7:7–25; Luke 21:20–24)**. The Roman Empire was in power during the time of Christ and His disciples. This exhibits the great history of Rome, which spans over two thousand years to present day.

The earlier chapter of Daniel expounded upon and exhibited in **Chart #26** (Daniel 9) is preparatory to the chapters that will be discussed here. These next two chapters **(Daniel 2 and 7)** fit together the location in which the Antichrist will arise from and the position he will assume in the last days. Take note; his *location*, not identity, is revealed. His expressed identity (facial features, name, height, ethnic descent) will not be revealed until the church is taken out of the way. Wherefore, the Antichrist is part of the seven seals mentioned in Revelation 6:1–2, which is the **wrath** of the Lamb, under which none who trusts in the Lamb is subject to **(Revelation 6:12–17; 1 Thessalonians 1:10, 5:9)**.

The Dream and Interpretation

"In Daniel Chapter 2, King Nebuchadnezzar had a dream that troubled him. The dream was interpreted by Daniel as representing four coming Gentile world powers.[204] This dream remains prophetically significant to us today. In Daniel Chapter 7, Daniel has a vision of four beasts that symbolize four great world empires. These parallel the parts of the image in Nebuchadnezzar's dream in Chapter 2."[205] **Chart #27** displays this image, showing the four world empires accordingly.

Although there have been many great empires in world history, none were as distinct as these four: **The Babylonian Empire**, **The Medo-Persian Empire**, **The Greek Empire**, and **The Roman Empire**. Merriam-Webster dictionary defines *empire* as, "A major political unit having a territory of great extent or a number of territories or peoples under a single sovereign authority." Simply put, **an empire is one that has great territory (land) and its citizens in the land are under one ruler; thus, one has an empire.**

"History records these four empires' vast territory. In fact, these four empires would <u>control Israel</u> and her destiny in the future."[206] This is the bulls-eye that severs these empires from other world empires, not just its territory but its dominion over a particular group of people—**Israel**. Studying **Chart #27**, you will see that each denoted empire was overthrown by its successor. **Babylon** was subdued by the **Medo-Persians**; the **Medo-Persians** were conquered by the **Greeks**; the **Greeks** were overpowered by the **Romans**; and the **revived Roman Empire** will be crushed by the **Kingdom of Christ**! This is just a recitation of history in short order, but we will focus our attention, as Daniel does, on the fourth empire: **Rome**.

The Fourth Empire: Rome

The importance of the Roman Empire is spoken of by Daniel mentioning the "iron" **(Daniel 2:40)** and "the beast" **(Daniel 7:23)**. Just to reiterate, these two are parallel. The first was fulfilled in AD 70 when the Roman Empire destroyed Jerusalem and the Temple; the other speaks of one who will arise from **this same people** who first destroyed the Temple in AD 70 (Roman Empire), and he will defile the Temple once again in hopes of annihilating the Holy people (Israel) **(Daniel 7:19–25; 9:27; Zechariah 13:8; Revelation 12:14, 15)**.

Daniel further states, ". . . in the days of these kings shall the God of heaven set up a kingdom, which shall never be destroyed. . ." **(Daniel 2:44)**. Simply put, in the days of the revived Roman Empire, there shall be no other empires to arise after, except the **Kingdom of Christ**. The Kingdom of Christ will arrive in the days of the "ten toes," "the Beast," and "the revived Roman Empire."

The Last Days

Are we in the last days? The answer is two-fold. The last days began at the crucifixion of Christ, AD 30, and continues in **present day**. Simply put, the last days have been progressing for over 1,900 years. The book of Hebrews shares with the modern world: "God . . . hath in these last days spoken unto us by his Son" **(Hebrews 1:2)**. This means since the crucifixion, God no longer requires animal sacrifice, but **trust** in His Son, Jesus Christ, who was the perfect sacrifice. Throughout the last days, the Father speaks through Christ only.

However, there is a *last* of the last days, so to speak. The "last" of the last days is depicted in Daniel's seventieth week. This will consist of the last seven years of world history before Christ's Second Advent and the start of the millennial kingdom. In <u>those days</u>, Christ prophesied, ". . . then shall be great tribulation, such as was not since the beginning of the world to this time, no, nor ever shall be" **(Matthew 24:21)**.

The Fourth Beast: Antichrist

"The fourth beast is a monster, 'dreadful and terrible' **(Daniel 7:7)**. This beast symbolized Rome[207] or the Revived Roman Empire. The monster had ten horns, signifying ten kings or divisions of the empire. These horns correspond to the ten toes on the metallic image in Daniel 2. Out of the ten horns of this fourth empire comes a 'little horn' **(Daniel 7:8)**.[208] This represents the Antichrist, who will come to power during the Tribulation."[209]

When you reference a topographical map, you can clearly see the "empire" or territory of the Old Roman Empire **(See Map #28)**. Daniel reveals the Antichrist will arise from a revived Roman Empire. What is the revived Roman Empire? This empire will consist of the **exact** countries that the ancient Roman Empire controlled in AD 70. Simply put, there will be a "union" of nations coming together in the "last days." These nations must comprise the precise nations of the ancient Roman Empire to fulfill the prophecy of Daniel 7.

The European Union

Is the revived Roman Empire reviving itself today? Let's focus on the European Union. "The European Union is a group of nations uniting under a common management. The ideas behind the European Union were first put forward on May 9, 1950, by French foreign Minister Robert Schulman.[210] Based on Schulman's plan, six countries signed a treaty to run their heavy industries— coal and steel—under a common management.[211] In this way, none can on its own make the weapons of war to turn against the other, as in the past. The six are: **Germany, France, Italy, the Netherlands, Belgium** and **Luxembourg**."[212]

Note that these six countries were also located in the ancient **Roman Empire (See Maps #28 and #28b)**. Daniel states in the last days the cooperation or "unity" of ten toes will take place in countries that comprised the ancient Roman Empire **(Daniel 2:41)**. Hence, in the last days, there will be much conversation politically concerning "one world order," in which the nations of the world can better track *one* currency, *one* religion, and *one* world government. Daniel prophesied this unity will not mix **(Daniel 2:41, 42)**. Meaning, many nations will not agree to it. But the "iron"— iron represents Rome—in the mix of the miry clay will be strong (European Union) **(Daniel 2:41, 42; 7:7, 19)**.

Presently, the EU has grown to over twenty-seven member countries; **all** are countries found formerly in the ancient Roman Empire. The same countries that formed the ancient Roman Empire union, thus, are forming a present-day union. "he EU has continually expanded since European integration first began in 1951, and it continues to expand with additional countries pending approval. Even so, the additional countries pending, when approved, further forms the ancient Roman Empire. These European countries are cooperating economically."[213] Daniel reveals that from this union of nations, the (revived Roman Empire) the Antichrist shall arise **(Daniel 7:24)**.

Conclusion

It is amazing to behold the forming of the EU before one's eyes, for its exact location is the location of the former ancient Roman Empire. The EU's motto is **"United in Diversity."** "It signifies how Europeans have come together, in the form of the EU, to work for **peace** and prosperity."[214] It is of no wonder Daniel foretold, **"And through his policy also he shall cause craft to prosper in his hand; and he shall magnify himself in his heart, and by peace shall destroy many . . ." (Daniel 8:25)**.

Although we may witness these things currently, it should be clearly understood that "these things" are paving the road for the "last" of the last days and will not take effect until the Tribulation.

SEE THE MISSING PIECES!

See **Maps #28 & #28b** to view a comparison of Old Roman Empire and Present-Day European Union

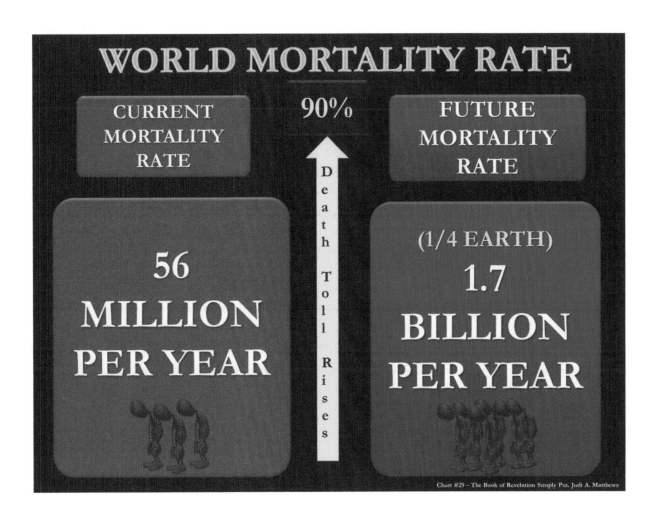

WORLD MORTALITY RATE

CURRENT MORTALITY RATE

90%

FUTURE MORTALITY RATE

56 MILLION PER YEAR

Death Toll Rises

(1/4 EARTH) 1.7 BILLION PER YEAR

Chart #29 – The Book of Revelation Simply Put, Jodi A. Matthews

THE WORLD'S MORTALITY RATE

"According to the world's population in 2002, wherein the world was 6.7 billion people,[215] it reached 7 billion on October 31, 2011.[216] Out of 6.7 billion persons, 57 million of humanity's population dies each year, on average, due to communicable diseases, maternal and perinatal conditions, nutritional deficiencies, noncommunicable conditions, accidents, drownings, fires, etc."[217]

Chart #29 displays the brutal truth of man's mortality rate during the Tribulation. It rises to a disproportionate number. At the onset of the Tribulation, Revelation 6:8 states, under the pale horse's mission, **one-fourth** of the earth shall die. This one-fourth, in lieu of 6.7 billion people in the earth calculates to 1.7 billon persons to die during the initial onslaught of the Tribulation. Those who are left behind will have a fifty-fifty chance of

A PIECE OF THE PUZZLE!

#29

survival; though some will survive. In this light and context, Jesus stated, **"And except those days should be shortened, there should no flesh be saved: but for the elect's sake those days shall be shortened" (Matthew 24:22).**

Conclusion

The book of Acts, which is 13 percent prophecy, offers a magnificent hope in the last days. Peter preached, **"And it shall come to pass in the last days . . . I will shew wonders in heaven above, and signs in the earth beneath; blood, and fire, and vapour of smoke: The sun shall be turned into darkness, and the moon into blood, before that great and notable day of the Lord come: And it shall come to pass, that whosoever shall call on the name of the Lord <u>shall be saved</u>" (Acts 2:17a, 19–21).**

"These days are the 'last days,' the time of the Messiah, so the phrase was understood among the Jews."[218] These verses compliment Revelation 6:12–16, denoting the coming of Christ to the earth will cause great ecological signs in the heavens, where neither the sun nor moon will shine. Hence, in *these days*, people will call upon the name of the Lord and He shall **save** them.

REVELATION CHAPTER 7

Spotlight Chapter

This is the first "Spotlight Chapter." If you recall, Spotlight Chapters alert you to broad insight on a person, place, or event in heaven or earth. It gives details of how, who, and what. It enlarges upon people and personalities bringing into focus their role in the end-time drama. Chapter 7 relates, in detail, how many will be saved during the Tribulation and a particular group of people who will carry the Gospel to the world during the Tribulation.

Also, keep in mind the beauty of Revelation's chronological order. Certain passages cease, only to resume in a later chapter (i.e., the facts concerning the 144,000 ceases from **Chapter 7:1–8** and further details resume in **Chapter 14:1–5**). It must be understood that the chronological order of this book relates to "chapter events" not "chapter passages."

Chapter events, in arranged order, are **Chapters 1–3,** the Church Age division; **Chapters 4–5,** the scene in heaven portion and is indicative of the Rapture of the church; **Chapters 6–18,** the seven-year Tribulation that follows the Rapture; and **Chapters 19–22,** the return of Christ, one thousand-year reign, final judgment, and new heaven and earth. Chapter passages will cease and resume in the chronological divisions referenced; wherefore, the seer wrote the visions that appeared before him forthwith. This manual will reference this as these accounts occur, as previously experienced in Chapter 6.

The 144,000

> **Revelation 7:1–4** *¹And after these things I saw four angels standing on the four corners of the earth, holding the four winds of the earth, that the wind should not blow on the earth, nor on the sea, nor on any tree. ²And I saw another angel ascending from the east, having the seal of the living God: and he cried with a loud voice to the four angels, to whom it was given to hurt the earth and the sea, ³Saying, Hurt not the earth, neither the sea, nor the trees, till we have sealed the servants of our God in their foreheads. ⁴And I heard the number of them which were sealed: and there were sealed an hundred and forty and four thousand of all the tribes of the children of Israel.*

v. 4 "there were sealed an hundred and forty and four thousand" Herein a definite number is announced. Although quite a large number, it is definite. Numbers in the Bible deserve better than the landscape of "a long period of time" when its literal enumeration is given. The seer, John, gives details concerning his nation, the nation of Israel.

FIT THE MISSING PIECES!

See **Piece #30** for further explanation of will ALL Israel be saved?

What is the purpose of the sealing of these 144,000? Through careful deduction of the Scriptures, it can be positively inferred their job is to save Israel. This brings to the forefront the burning question, **"Will all Israel be saved?"**

FIT THE MISSING PIECES!

See **Piece #31** for further explanation of the meaning of the Missing Tribes

"of all the tribes of the children of Israel." "Attempts have been made to identify the 12 tribes here with the church;[219] this book cannot join in that argument. Most want to avoid the implication that this is literally **Israel**.[220] The fact that specific tribes were mentioned and specific numbers from each tribe were indicated would seem to remove this from the symbolic and to justify literal interpretation."[221]

Take special notice to the exclusion of two tribes: **Dan** and **Ephraim**. In light of the tribe of Ephraim missing, this reveals an important truth and justifies the distinction of God's plan for Israel and God's plan for the church. For further explanation, see "Fit the Missing Piece #32" at the end of this chapter.

The Great Multitude

> **Revelation 7:9–12** *⁹After this I beheld, and, lo, a great multitude, which no man could number, of all nations, and kindreds, and people, and tongues, stood before the throne, and before the Lamb, clothed with white robes, and palms in their hands; ¹⁰And cried with a loud voice, saying, Salvation to our God which sitteth upon the throne, and unto the Lamb. ¹¹And all the angels stood round about the throne, and about the elders and the four beasts, and fell before the throne on their faces, and worshipped God, ¹²Saying, Amen: Blessing, and glory, and wisdom, and thanksgiving, and honour, and power, and might, be unto our God for ever and ever. Amen.*

v. 9 "lo, a great multitude, which no man could number" The evangelistic ministry of the 144,000 saves not only Israel, but a great multitude of people, and tongues have received the Gospel on earth during the Tribulation; wherefore many shall be martyred in light of their profession of faith.

The nonenumeration of this "great multitude" demonstrates the weakness of such arguments that the numbers stated in Revelation are "symbolic." Scripture clearly denotes and declares when its numbers signify an innumerable account; thus, here stated, John could not enumerate this number, for it could not be numbered.

"of all nations, and kindreds, and people, and tongues" depicting the sharp contrast of ethnicity. This group contains all ethnicities; the 144,000 renders one ethnicity (Jewish men).

Another Rapture?

> **Revelation 7:13–17** *¹³And one of the elders answered, saying unto me, What are these which are arrayed in white robes? And whence came they? ¹⁴And I said unto him, Sir, thou knowest. And he said to me, These are they which came out of great tribulation, and have washed their robes,*

and made them white in the blood of the Lamb. ¹⁵Therefore are they before the throne of God, and serve him day and night in his Temple: and he that sitteth on the throne shall dwell among them. ¹⁶They shall hunger no more, neither thirst any more; neither shall the sun light on them, nor any heat. ¹⁷For the Lamb which is in the midst of the throne shall feed them, and shall lead them unto living fountains of waters: and God shall wipe away all tears from their eyes.

v. 13 "What are these which are arrayed in white robes? And whence came they?" There is the sudden appearance of a "great multitude" in heaven. One of the elders in heaven, wherein John had been translated in Chapter 4, asks a Socratic[3] question of John, being fully aware of its answer. Where did these people come from?

v. 14 "These are they which came out of great tribulation" This statement is important, as it relates the richness and validity of another Rapture. The great multitude previously mentioned in verse 9 has been caught away to heaven at the onset of the Great Tribulation. In fact, there will be a total of three raptures throughout the duration of the Great Tribulation period. These raptures occur post-church Rapture. (See Master Timeline: Rapture Groups highlighted in **blue**)

FIT THE MISSING PIECES!

See Chart #32 for further explanation of Two Distinct Events: Three Additional Raptures?

---

[3] Named after the Greek philosopher, Socrates, this is a form of debate meant to stimulate critical thinking and encourage personal illumination.

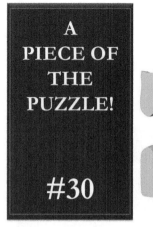

A
PIECE OF
THE
PUZZLE!

#30

WILL ALL ISRAEL BE SAVED?

**"Are Jews saved because
they are God's chosen people?"**

**"Do Jews have to believe
in Jesus Christ to be saved?"**

Jesus said, **"I am the way, the truth, and the life; no one comes to the Father but by Me" (John 14:6)**. The "no one" He referred to includes Jews and Gentiles. Jews are not saved because they are God's chosen people but because they believe in Jesus Christ as their true Messiah. "There are many Messianic Jews who have accepted Yeshua (the Hebrew word for 'Jesus') as their Messiah."[222]

"However, there is no doubt that the Jews are still God's *chosen* people."[223] As a nation collectively, Israel has rejected their Savior. This occurred in AD 30 when Pilate addressed the Jews in the midst of releasing one prisoner at the celebratory feasts of the Jews, he asked, **". . . will ye therefore that I release unto you the King of the Jews?"** Then Jesus' brethren **(the Jews)** cried, "Not this man, but Barabbas. Now Barabbas was a robber." At this behest, Jesus, King of the Jews, was rejected by His brethren, scourged, and crucified **(Matthew 27:26)**. Thus, Peter, speaking to the Jews, after Christ's ascension, reiterated their rejection speaking, ". . . ye denied the Holy One and the Just, and desired a murderer to be granted unto you; And killed the Prince of life, whom God hath raised from the dead; whereof we are witnesses" **(Acts 3:14–15)**.

Not by DNA

Albeit, every person is born a sinner and accounts for the death of Christ upon the cross; however, it was by the hands of His brethren that crucifixion was executed. Justifying **Revelation 1:7**, "Behold, he cometh with clouds; and every eye shall see him, and they also which pierced him **(the Jews)**, his brethren: and all kindreds of the earth shall wail because of him" (emphasis added).

John, the seer, writes of the specific connection of Israel nationally and historically to their brother, the Christ, whom they've rejected throughout the ages. This demonstrates many Jews will not accompany the Rapture; hence, the Rapture is for believers (the church), those who accept Christ as the Messiah. Wherefore a great number of the nation of Israel will be in the Tribulation (Review Chart #24 for Purpose of the Tribulation).

It's All "Jewish" to Me

Romans 11:26 says:

> **"And so all Israel shall be saved: as it is written,**
> **There shall come out of Sion the Deliverer, and shall turn away**
> **ungodliness from Jacob:"**

In order to comprehend the complete context of the word *all*, look to Zechariah 12 and 13. The prophet Zechariah prophesied the future salvation of this nation; but he first stated, "And it shall come to pass, that in all the land, saith the LORD, **two parts therein shall be cut off** and die; but **the third** shall be left therein. And I will bring **the third** part through the fire, and will refine them as silver is refined, and will try them as gold is tried: they shall call on my name, and I will hear them: I will say, It is my people: and they shall say, The LORD is my God" **(Zechariah 13:8–9, emphasis added).** This passage expounds upon the Tribulation period that many Jews will die. In fact, two-thirds will expire. Whether the two-thirds that expire has accepted the Christ remains to be known. But this passage of Scripture clearly denotes not all Israel is saved because of ethnicity.

The fact remains, a third shall be left. This **"third,"** experiencing the Tribulation, is **all** that will remain of Israel, the nation. This third will be refined, accepting the Messiah; wherefore, **ALL** Israel, in this context, shall be saved **(Zechariah 13:8–9, 12:8–12).** Further exposition on this third and their supernatural protection during the last three-and-a-half years of Tribulation will be examined thoroughly in Revelation 12.

Conclusion

The restoration of Israel will come when Israel's power is broken during the time of Jacob's trouble **(Jeremiah 30:7),** and when they accept Christ as their King as He delivers them from annihilation of the Antichrist during the seven-year Tribulation. This, too, awaits its final fulfillment.

MEANING OF THE MISSING TRIBES
IN REVELATION 7

"Why are 'Dan' and 'Ephraim' missing
from the tribes of the 144,000?"[4]

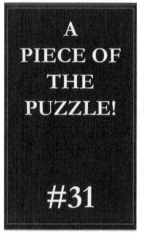

Revelation Chapter 7 unveils a group of people totaling a specific number of 144,000. This group of people listed are clearly of Jewish descent, for Scripture indicates these persons are from "**. . . all the tribes of the children of Israel" (Revelation 7:4).** The nation of Israel descends from the twelve Sons of Jacob. Before the adoption of Joseph's two sons, Ephraim and Manasseh, Joseph stood as his own tribe. After the adoption, Ephraim and Manasseh represented Joseph's lot in the land of Canaan (see Genesis 48:5–6).

It is interesting to note the inclusion of the tribes of Ephraim and Manasseh, representative of the tribe of Joseph continuously throughout Scripture. Even so, during the primitive stages of land allotment by Joshua to the tribes, he did not assign Joseph an inheritance, but conveyed it to Joseph's sons, Ephraim and Manasseh (Joshua 16:4).

Revelation 7:1–8 notes a new and interesting fact concerning the twelve tribes of Israel; two tribes are missing (Dan and Ephraim) and Joseph, who was absent, is now numbered among the twelve again. What is the meaning of this?

The Tribe of Dan

"As relates to the tribe of Dan. Much speculation has arisen about why the tribe of Dan is omitted.[224] Perhaps, Dan was omitted here because it was one of the first tribes to go into idolatry **(Judges 18:30; 1 Kings 12:28–29)**. However, Dan is mention in Ezekiel 48:2 in the millennial land distribution."[225]

The Tribe of Ephraim

As relates to the tribe of Ephraim. The name *Ephraim* means, "double fruit." Furthermore, Ephraim was prophesied by Jacob to become a multitude of nations (Genesis 48:19). This phrase is important, for it describes the Gentile peoples of the world. Let us examine this Scripture and phrase in its original context, according to Strong's Hebrew Lexicon:

---

[4] Donald P. Moss, Joseph, Ephraim and Manasseh—A Foreshadow of God's Agenda for Jew and Gentile, "For the Eyes of Your Understanding," http://www.biblebigpicture.com/biblelessons/spiritualinheritanceofephraim.htm (March 29, 2012).

Multitude = (*malo*): meaning "fullness"
Of Nations = (*gowy*): "a foreign nation; a Gentile"

Simply put, the tribe of Ephraim is the tribe from which the Gentiles descend. His tribe depicts the "fullness of Gentiles." The apostle Paul stated firmly that, "For I would not, brethren, that ye should be ignorant of this mystery, lest ye should be wise in your own conceits; that blindness in part is happened to Israel, **until the fullness of the Gentiles be come in**" (Romans 11:25). Presently, the church, the Body of Christ, is predominately Gentile, with a few Jews accepting the Messiah. This is prophecy fulfilled, spoken by Jacob under the guidance of the Holy Spirit.

However, a question remains about Manasseh, why is he still mentioned in this list of Revelation 7? This answer is derived from the same prophecy, which was bestowed upon his brother in **Genesis 48:19**. As relates to Manasseh, his grandfather Jacob prophesied, ". . . he also shall become a people" (v.19). This phrase, in its original context is the word *am*, signifying, "a tribe as those of Israel." Manasseh's tribe is considered a Jewish tribe as the others; thus, he joins the 144,000 Jewish evangelists, who are supernaturally protected to carry the Gospel to its brethren, Israel, during the Tribulation, saving many others along the way (Revelation 7:9).

The Missing Factor

Against this backdrop, Revelation Chapter 7 verifies an important truth. **Could Ephraim (the Gentile tribe) be missing from this list in light of the fact he has been raptured from the earth before the Tribulation?** When one has placed his faith in the Lamb, he does not endure the wrath of the Lamb during the Tribulation (1 Thessalonians 1:10; Revelation 6:16). This justifies Paul's expressed distinction between the calling of Israel and the church. That many of his brethren are blind and reject the Savior during this dispensation (Romans 11:25). Moreover, God's agenda for Israel was spoken long ago in **Deuteronomy 32:20–21**:

> **And he said, I will hide my face from them {Israel}, I will see what their end shall be: for they are a very froward generation, children in whom is no faith. They have moved me to jealousy with that which is not God; they have provoked me to anger with their vanities: and I will move them to jealousy with those which are not a people; I will provoke them to anger with <u>a foolish nation</u> {The Gentiles}.**

The foolish nation is described as those Gentile nations that readily accept the Christ. For John states, "He came unto his own, and his own received him not. But as many as received him, to them gave the power to become the sons of God, even to them that believe on his name:" **(John 1:11–12)**. This "as many" is the Gentile peoples of the earth. This fact supports our adoption as sons and daughters of God. "But when the fullness of the time was come, God sent forth his Son, made of a woman, made under the law, to redeem them that were under the law, that we might receive the **<u>adoption</u>** of sons" **(Galatians 4:4–5)**.

This is a credible answer that strengthens the pretribulation argument of the Rapture of the church before the seven-year tribulation period begins.

> "For I would not, brethren, that ye should be ignorant of this mystery, lest ye should be wise in your own conceits; that blindness in part is happened to Israel, until the fulness of the Gentiles be come in."
> **(Romans 11:25)**

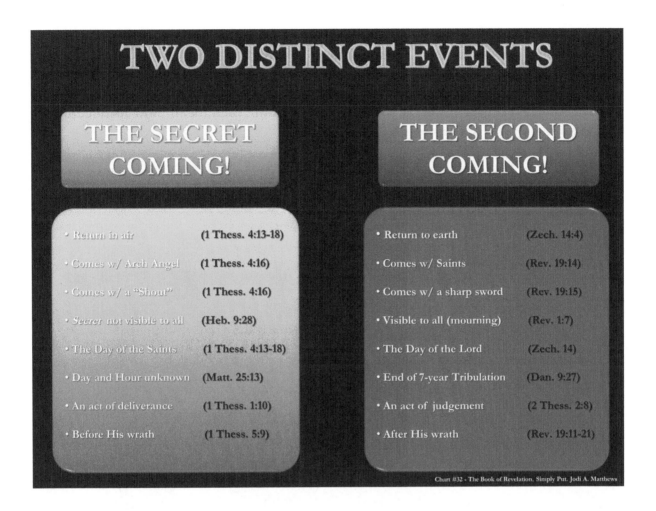

TWO DISTINCT EVENTS	
THE SECRET COMING!	**THE SECOND COMING!**
• Return in air (1 Thess. 4:13-18)	• Return to earth (Zech. 14:4)
• Comes w/ Arch Angel (1 Thess. 4:16)	• Comes w/ Saints (Rev. 19:14)
• Comes w/ a "Shout" (1 Thess. 4:16)	• Comes w/ a sharp sword (Rev. 19:15)
• *Secret* not visible to all (Heb. 9:28)	• Visible to all (mourning) (Rev. 1:7)
• The Day of the Saints (1 Thess. 4:13-18)	• The Day of the Lord (Zech. 14)
• Day and Hour unknown (Matt. 25:13)	• End of 7-year Tribulation (Dan. 9:27)
• An act of deliverance (1 Thess. 1:10)	• An act of judgement (2 Thess. 2:8)
• Before His wrath (1 Thess. 5:9)	• After His wrath (Rev. 19:11-21)

Chart #32 - The Book of Revelation. Simply Put. Jodi A. Matthews

TWO DISTINCT EVENTS
(Three Additional Raptures?)

"Almost all agree that the rapture is to be distinguished from the Second Coming in the sense that the former is when Christ comes for His own people, and the latter is His coming with them in triumph and glory."[226] **Chart #32** enumerates distinctions of the raptures in Scripture.

A PIECE OF THE PUZZLE!

#32

Frequent note is taken in Revelation of the disappearance and reappearance of certain peoples throughout the reading of this blessed book. Scripture clearly signifies there will be further raptures occurring during the Tribulation. Reason being, although there will be many who remain obstinate toward Christ, many will accept Christ. This is demonstrated in the "great multitude" **(Revelation 7:9)**. The great multitude, who are Tribulation saints, are caught away in light of the Great Tribulation, the last three-and-a-half years of Tribulation to come upon the earth.

Scanning the Christian pilgrimage throughout the course of the Bible and history, believers are not the object of God's wrath **(1 Thessalonians 1:10, 5:9)**. Slightly after the Great Tribulation begins (last three-and-a-half years), if one has not been martyred because of his profession of faith, the Father raptures to heaven those who remain alive and whose faith is in Christ, for none of the righteous endures His wrath. **Romans 5:9** says, **"Much more then, being now justified by his blood, we shall be saved from wrath through him."**

The Church Is Not the First

The believer should not be bewildered at these multiple events of raptures. If you recall, the word *rapture* is the catching up or translation of the church—to "remove suddenly" or "carry away." In the study of Scripture, there are seven raptures recorded. There could possibly be more, but these recorded are most evident.

Seven Raptures Recorded In Scripture:

1. **Enoch** (Genesis 5:24)
2. **Noah** (Genesis 7:16-18)
3. **Elijah** (2 Kings 2:11)
4. **The Church** (1 Thess. 4:17)
5. **Great Multitude** (Revelation 7: 14)
6. **144,000** (Revelation 14:1-3)
7. **Two Witness** (Revelation 11:12)

Examining the Rapture Chronicles, one can easily see that the church is not the first entity to experience a rapture; in fact, three have already occurred. Taking note, this manual adopts Noah as a type of rapture—being shut in the Ark and carried away upon the floods of water. The Ark was specifically "lifted up above the earth" **(Genesis 7:17)**. Noah and his family were divinely protected.

Conclusion

In light of the numerous raptures to occur, the fact is supported that the Tribulation is a different epoch of time. The Tribulation epoch will demonstrate indescribable happenings, disturbances, disappearances, and calamities in the heavens, earth, and seas. Jesus emphatically said, **"Men's hearts failing them for fear, and for looking after those things which are coming on the earth: for the powers of heaven shall be shaken"** (Luke 21:26).

REVELATION CHAPTER 8

Planet Chapter

The Number 8 usually signifies
"New Beginnings"

Noah and his family "8 souls" were the
beginning of a new human existence after
the flood (1 Peter 3:20)

The number eight is commonly referenced in the Bible as the number of "new beginnings." "It seems quite obvious that the Bible uses numbers in patterns."[227] Whether or not numbers really do have significance is still debated in many circles. Revelation 8 continues the history of the seven seals, with the seventh being opened. The opening of the seventh seal conveys a genesis of *new* judgments. These judgments come under the guise of the seven trumpets. The trumpet judgments bring ecological disasters. The calamities evoked upon the eco system affect humanity, wherefore many men shall die under this judgment too. The Scriptures in Chapter 8 explain themselves; therefore, this chapter will be reviewed in brevity in this light.

Silence in Heaven

Revelation 8:1 *And when he had opened the seventh seal, there was silence in heaven about the space of half an hour.*

v. 1 "there was silence in heaven" Scripture declares "great noises" in heaven. There are the twenty-four elders around the throne offering praise; four creatures crying, "Holy, holy, holy"; there are Seraphim angels above the throne proclaiming His Holiness; and there is the redeemed of ages rendering laudation—in heaven is a "great noise" of praise. The praise, worship, and glorious shouts all come to an abrupt silence.

Revelation 8:2–5 *²And I saw the seven angels which stood before God; and to them were given seven trumpets. ³And another angel came and stood at the altar, having a golden censer; and there was given unto him much incense, that he should offer it with the prayers of all saints upon the golden altar which was before the throne. ⁴And the smoke of the incense, which came with the prayers of the saints, ascended up before God out of the angel's hand. ⁵And the angel took the censer, and filled it with fire of the altar, and cast it into the earth: and there were voices, and thunderings, and lightnings, and an earthquake.*

Trumpets, in biblical times,
were known as
"Shofars"

Shofars were blown at special
festivals, and to herald the arrival of
special seasons
(Leviticus 23:24)

v. 2 "to them were given seven trumpets." Praise, worship, and holy cries end at the behest of the seven trumpets. Each trumpet unleashes a behemoth of catastrophe upon the earth for there were, "voices, and thunderings, and lightnings, and an earthquake."

The First Trumpet

> **Revelation 8:6–7** *⁶And the seven angels which had the seven trumpets prepared themselves to sound. ⁷The first angel sounded, and there followed hail and fire mingled with blood, and they were cast upon the earth: and the third part of trees was burnt up, and all green grass was burnt up.*

v. 7 "the third part of trees . . . and all green grass" Jesus stated, "And ye shall hear of wars and rumours of wars" **(Matthew 24:6)**. At the sounding of the first trumpet, one-third of the earth's greenery is burned. This possibly is the result of wars happening upon the earth. The choice weaponry of the battle will be nuclear weapons. During the Tribulation, the heart of man reaches utter depravity.

The Second Trumpet

> **Revelation 8:8–9** *⁸And the second angel sounded, and as it were a great mountain burning with fire was cast into the sea: and the third part of the sea became blood; ⁹And the third part of the creatures which were in the sea, and had life, died; and the third part of the ships were destroyed.*

v. 8 "as it were a great mountain burning with fire was cast into the sea" The word *as* signifies John's loss of words to describe the visions he is seeing; thus, he uses images familiar to what he knows to describe end-time events. In this, the saltwater environments and oceans are turned to blood and one-third of the sea creatures die. Take note; this is not all marine life but one-third. It seems these trumpet judgments are ecological in nature.

The Third Trumpet

> **Revelation 8:10–11** *¹⁰And the third angel sounded, and there fell a great star from heaven, burning as it were a lamp, and it fell upon the third part of the rivers, and upon the fountains of waters; ¹¹And the name of the star is called Wormwood: and the third part of the waters became wormwood; and many men died of the waters, because they were made bitter.*

v. 10 "and there fell a great star from heaven" "This star can be liken to a 'shooting star' or 'meteor.' Meteors are commonly called falling stars or shooting stars.[228] There is a wide range of space rocks in our solar system. Most of them are not on orbital paths that bring them anywhere near Earth"[229]; however, during the Tribulation this "star" called Wormwood enters into earth's atmosphere and the waters are poisoned. From this poison many men die. Interesting to note is the propagation to drink water presently, in fact, eight glasses a day; consequently, the overwhelming number of dying men with this judgment can be acutely realized.

The Fourth Trumpet

Revelation 8:12 *And the fourth angel sounded, and the third part of the sun was smitten, and the third part of the moon, and the third part of the stars; so as the third part of them was darkened, and the day shone not for a third part of it, and the night likewise.*

v. 12 "and the third part of the sun was smitten, and . . . moon, and . . . stars" The solar system refuses to give its light to the earth a third part of the day. A twenty-four-hour day is divided into eight hours, three divisions. Against this backdrop of the sun, moon, and stars devoid of light, with an estimated sunrise of 7:00 a.m., the earth descends into utter darkness by 3:00 p.m. each day after this judgment is pronounced. Whereas, what should be its highest and brightest emulates the midnight hour during the three o'clock hour of the day.

Revelation 8:13 *And I beheld, and heard an angel flying through the midst of heaven, saying with a loud voice, Woe, woe, woe, to the inhabiters of the earth by reason of the other voices of the trumpet of the three angels, which are yet to sound!*

v. 13 "Woe, woe, woe" "A lamentable prediction or foretelling of those parts of the divine execution which yet are behind."[230]

REVELATION CHAPTER 9

Planet Chapter

Chapter 9 opens and furnishes details of the cause of the "woe" mentioned in Revelation 8:13. Additional destruction pours upon the earth and its inhabitants. The prophet sees demonic-like creatures unleashed and its affect. These woes pierce man directly. St. John further sees an army coming from the east, bringing with it utter destruction. Chapter 9 vocalizes humanity's resistance to the One of heaven. As in the former chapter, this chapter will be reviewed with brevity.

The Fifth Trumpet

Revelation 9:1–2 [1]*And the fifth angel sounded, and I saw a star fall from heaven unto the earth: and to him was given the key of the bottomless pit.* [2]*And he opened the bottomless pit; and there arose a smoke out of the pit, as the smoke of a great furnace; and the sun and the air were darkened by reason of the smoke of the pit.*

v. 1 "a star fall from heaven unto the earth" Another star from heaven. This star denotes an angel. "An angel encompassed with light suddenly descends and seemed like a star falling from heaven."[231]

v. 1 "key of the bottomless pit." "This angel has power to inundate the earth with a flood of temporal calamities and moral evils."[232] Earth has not felt, nor can man comprehend, the evils withheld from them. Even nowadays the earth is wicked and violent with beasts turning against man ravaging him; however, upon God's present mercy, total evil is constrained **(2 Thessalonians 2:6)**.

Star = Angelic Being

Stars in the Bible can denote constellations, persons, or angelic hosts.

"Where wast thou . . . When the morning stars {angelic host} sang together, and all the sons of God shouted for joy?"
(Job 38:4a, 7)

© Can Stock Photo Inc./Ancello

Demonic Locusts

Revelation 9:3–6 [3]*And there came out of the smoke locusts upon the earth: and unto them was given power, as the scorpions of the earth have power.* [4]*And it was commanded them that they should not hurt the grass of the earth, neither any green thing, neither any tree; but only those men which have not the seal of God in their foreheads.* [5]*And to them it was given that they should not kill them, but that they should be tormented five months: and their torment was as the torment of a scorpion, when he striketh a man.* [6]*And in those days shall men seek death, and shall not find it; and shall desire to die, and death shall flee from them.*

v. 3 "there came out of the smoke locusts upon the earth" Commentators disagree as to whether this is literal or spiritual; wherefore, remaining true to its literal interpretation, these are literal locusts with the exception of a demonic trait to them. "These locusts are from the Abyss, home of demons **(Luke 8:31)**"[233], and are reserved for end times. These locusts, however, do not eat vegetation but have the power to torment man for five months **(Revelation 9:10)**. This bears weight to its literal interpretation of locusts.

A Modern-Day Locust
© Can Stock Photo Inc./yio

v. 4 "And it was commanded them that they should not hurt the grass of the earth" These locusts have purpose, direction, and intention. Evidently, the 144,000 are still upon the earth and are supernaturally protected from these heinous creatures; however, the rest of the men are tormented unmercifully.

v. 6 "in those days shall men seek death, and shall not find it" What an insurmountable period of time the Tribulation shall be. Presently, the great enemy of man is "death" **(1 Corinthians 15:26)**. Loved ones are painfully separated in this age by way of death and dying. Throughout this five-month duration death—man's great enemy—takes an intermission; ergo, man shall try to end his life but supernaturally is unable to die for five months.

A Vivid Description

> **Revelation 9:7–11** *⁷And the shapes of the locusts were like unto horses prepared unto battle; and on their heads were as it were crowns like gold, and their faces were as the faces of men. ⁸And they had hair as the hair of women, and their teeth were as the teeth of lions. ⁹And they had breastplates, as it were breastplates of iron; and the sound of their wings was as the sound of chariots of many horses running to battle. ¹⁰And they had tails like unto scorpions, and there were stings in their tails: and their power was to hurt men five months. ¹¹And they had a king over them, which is the angel of the bottomless pit, whose name in the Hebrew tongue is Abaddon, but in the Greek tongue hath his name Apollyon.*

v. 10 "And they had tails like unto scorpions " John uses the term *like* denoting these locusts are beyond the scope of a natural habitat locust, and are demonic. Again John, the seer, uses the word *like* in giving his best description of end-time events. John is a first-century being describing possibly twenty-first century events; thus, his vernacular consists most commonly of objects of his day.

Revelation 9:12 *One woe is past; and, behold, there come two woes more hereafter.*

v. 12 "Woe" "An exclamation denoting pain or displeasure. It occurs as a noun denoting a disaster or calamity."[234]

Revelation 9:13–16 *[13] And the sixth angel sounded, and I heard a voice from the four horns of the golden altar which is before God, [14] Saying to the sixth angel which had the trumpet, Loose the four angels which are bound in the great river Euphrates. [15] And the four angels were loosed, which were prepared for an hour, and a day, and a month, and a year, for to slay the third part of men. [16] And the number of the army of the horsemen were two hundred thousand thousand: and I heard the number of them.*

v. 13 "I heard a voice from the four horns of the golden altar" "The voice seems to come from the very presence of the Deity, from the place where offerings are made to God."[235]

The Euphrates River Near Halabiya (Syria)

It is by far the largest and most important of all the rivers of Western Asia. The Euphrates is first mentioned in Genesis 2:14 as one of the rivers of Paradise.

v. 14 "Saying . . . Loose the four angels which are bound in the great river Euphrates." "The river where Babylon, the ancient foe of God's people, was situated."[236] These angelic beings are symbolic, in the sense they will influence the gathering of a great army to cause destruction in the earth by the hands of men (vv. 15–17). The ruin is so significant, a third part of humanity dies (v. 18). "The four angelic ministers of God's judgements shall go forth, assembling an army of horsemen throughout the four quarters of the earth to slay a third of men. The brunt of the visitation shall be on Palestine."[237]

v. 15 "prepared for an hour, and a day, and a month, and a year" The appointed timing of God is to be celebrated. One can rest assure evil shall be recompensed, yet, at the appointed time. **Habakkuk 2:3**, "For the vision is yet for an appointed time, but at the end it shall speak, and not lie: though it tarry, wait for it; because it will surely come, it will not tarry." Such events in Revelation are identified for yet an appointed time.

v. 16 "the army of the horsemen were two hundred thousand thousand" "John hears the actual number of 200 million. This number could not be reached in John's day, for the world was not as populous. Currently, with the world's population reaching 7 billion in 2011"[238], this number can easily be reached, particularly amongst the eastern nations.

Revelation 9:17–19 *^{17}And thus I saw the horses in the vision, and them that sat on them, having breastplates of fire, and of jacinth, and brimstone: and the heads of the horses were as the heads of lions; and out of their mouths issued fire and smoke and brimstone. ^{18}By these three was the third part of men killed, by the fire, and by the smoke, and by the brimstone, which issued out of their mouths. ^{19}For their power is in their mouth, and in their tails: for their tails were like unto serpents, and had heads, and with them they do hurt.*

v. 17 "thus I saw the horses in the vision, and them that sat on them" The seer further states he sees who this army is and its weaponry, and identifies them using the best description of a first-century writer.

v. 17 "having breastplates of fire, and of jacinth, and brimstone" An army of this magnitude can only arise from one location of the earth—**China.** "China is the most populace nation in the world with 1.3 billion"[239] humans, compared to America's 311 million. China, and its neighboring Asian countries situated in the far east of the map topographically, can easily produce a 200 million-man army.

Albeit China was not known in John's day, but John identified (very strongly) possibly China as **"the kings of the east"** in **Revelation 16:12**: "And the sixth angel poured out his vial upon the great river Euphrates; and the water thereof was dried up, that the way of the kings of the east might be prepared." These "kings of the east" include China and its neighboring counterparts.

It is interesting to note that the seer identified specific "colors"; these colors match that of China's color palettes today: **"breastplates of fire"** = red; **"jacinth"** = deep blue; **"brimstone"** = sulphur, bright yellow.

v. 18 "the third part of men killed, by . . . fire . . . by . . . smoke, and by . . . brimstone, which issued out of their mouths." Fire-breathing dragons with large heads are a favorite Chinese symbol. Also take note; China is commonly called "the Yellow Pearl." The weaponry strength of China surpasses that of normal weapons; again, this war and destruction is waged with nuclear weapons.

Revelation 9:20–21 *^{20}And the rest of the men which were not killed by these plagues yet repented not of the works of their hands, that they should not worship devils, and idols of gold, and silver, and brass, and stone, and of wood: which neither can see, nor hear, nor walk: ^{21}Neither repented they of their murders, nor of their sorceries, nor of their fornication, nor of their thefts.*

v. 20 "the rest . . . which were not killed . . . yet repented not" The utter depth of human depravity during the Tribulation reaches its height, validating the truth of Scripture: "Men loved darkness rather than light, because their deeds are evil" **(John 3:19)**. The conjecture that men will repent in calamities fails to hold true. The unrepentant heart is even harder toward the Almighty when catastrophe envelopes. It is not a "calamity issue" but a "heart issue."

v. 21 "Neither repented they of their murders" One has insight into the sins of the Tribulation: *murders, sorceries, fornication,* and *thefts.* The etymology of the word *sorceries* denotes pharmaceutical drugs. This sin has magnified in the twenty-first century, and will be more pronounced throughout the duration of the Tribulation. This pharmaceutical drug abuse is possibly induced by deep depression, anxiety, and suicidal thoughts caused by wives, children, friends, and close family members who have been raptured at the onset of the Tribulation leaving unbelieving loved ones distraught.

Take note; **"thefts"** is also a chief sin. This sin is possibly induced by the millions who have "gone missing" (the church) according to modern vernacular; albeit, the rise of **identity theft** is preeminent throughout this epoch as it relates to forsaken bank accounts, homes, private possessions, and creature comforts of saints who have been raptured.

REVELATION CHAPTER 10

Spotlight Chapter

This chapter discloses a magnificent vision of a mighty angel coming down from heaven. This mighty angel conveys an especial message enfolded in seven thunders. Hence, Chapter 10 unveils the accounts of future visions of Revelation **(Chapters 11–22)**. It is a **Spotlight Chapter**, enlarging upon or giving details of a specific person, place, or thing in the Revelation literature. At this juncture, a mighty angel discloses further apocalyptic visions to John.

A Mighty Angel

Revelation 10:1–2 *¹And I saw another mighty angel come down from heaven, clothed with a cloud: and a rainbow was upon his head, and his face was as it were the sun, and his feet as pillars of fire: ²And he had in his hand a little book open: and he set his right foot upon the sea, and his left foot on the earth,*

v. 1 "And I saw another mighty angel" "This angel is not of the seven blowing the seven trumpets, for the seventh trumpet does not sound till Revelation 11:15. But this angel is liken unto the other strong angels in **5:2** and **18:21** or the other angel in **14:6, 15**."[240]

The Seven Thunders

Revelation 10:3–4 *³And cried with a loud voice, as when a lion roareth: and when he had cried, seven thunders uttered their voices. ⁴And when the seven thunders had uttered their voices, I was about to write: and I heard a voice from heaven saying unto me, Seal up those things which the seven thunders uttered, and write them not.*

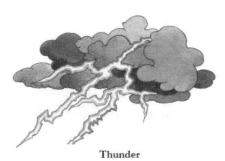

Thunder

Thunder is poetically called
"the voice of the Lord"
(Psalm 29:3)

© Can Stock Photo Inc./Palych

v. 4 "I was about to write" Professor Stuart has remarked that this proves that "John wrote down what he saw and heard as soon as practicable (forthwith), and in the place where he was and that the supposition of many modern critics, that the Apocalyptic visions were written at Ephesus a considerable time after the visions took place, has no good foundation."[241]

v. 4 "Seal up those things" "These are the only things, in light of all John heard, that he is commanded to keep secret; so something peculiarly secret was revealed to the beloved John, besides all

133

the secrets that are written in this book."[242] "Though heard by John, they were not to be imparted by him to others in this book of Revelation."[243]

v. 4 "seven thunders" Job speaks of the mystery of God's thunder: "Lo, these are parts of his ways: but how little a portion is heard of him? but the thunder of his power who can understand?" **(Job 26:14)**. "What we know or can know of the ways of God is but little, very little, compared with what remains to be known."[244] The seven thunders are not for revelation or unveiling, as the events disclosed thus far.

The Ceasing of Time

> **Revelation 10:5–6** [5] *And the angel which I saw stand upon the sea and upon the earth lifted up his hand to heaven,* [6] *And sware by him that liveth for ever and ever, who created heaven, and the things that therein are, and the earth, and the things that therein are, and the sea, and the things which are therein, that there should be time no longer:*

v. 6 "that there should be time no longer" "This has no reference to the Day of Judgement."[245] This relates that the martyrs shall no longer have a time to wait for the accomplishment of their prayers for the purgation of the earth by the judgments, which shall remove theirs and God's foes from it. (See the article "Evil, The Scroll & The Lamb" Chart #22).

The Mystery of God

> **Revelation 10:7** *But in the days of the voice of the seventh angel, when he shall begin to sound, the mystery of God should be finished, as he hath declared to his servants the prophets.*

v. 7 "the mystery of God should be finished" "What this mystery refers to who knows."[246] **"as he hath declared to his servants the prophets"** denotes "it is most likely that this trumpet belongs to the Jewish state."[247]

There is a wisdom compiled in the "mysteries of God" throughout Scripture. Some are disclosed, such as the mystery of resurrection **(1 Corinthians 15:51; Ephesians 5:32)**. Others remain within the sovereignty of God Himself to be revealed in its time, such as: "the mystery of iniquity" **(2 Thessalonians 2:7)**; explaining the existence of evil; "the mystery of Godliness" **(1 Timothy 3:16)**; and representing how God came in the flesh manifesting Himself wholly deity and wholly human, never ceasing to exist as God the Father. Such truths are too great for man to comprehend.

The voice of the seventh angel, or the blowing of the seventh trumpet is established in **Revelation 11:15**. This trumpet is **not** representative of the Rapture of the church mid-Tribulation. It is not that of the Rapture trump of God **(1 Thessalonians 4:16)** as some suppose but a different trump. It is the completion to the wrath of God trumpets that began in Revelation 8:6.

A Strict Charge

<u>**Revelation 10:8–11**</u> *⁸And the voice which I heard from heaven spake unto me again, and said, Go and take the little book which is open in the hand of the angel which standeth upon the sea and upon the earth. ⁹And I went unto the angel, and said unto him, Give me the little book. And he said unto me, Take it, and eat it up; and it shall make thy belly bitter, but it shall be in thy mouth sweet as honey. ¹⁰And I took the little book out of the angel's hand, and ate it up; and it was in my mouth sweet as honey: and as soon as I had eaten it, my belly was bitter. ¹¹And he said unto me, Thou must prophesy again before many peoples, and nations, and tongues, and kings.*

v. 8 "Go and take the little book" John is instructed to take the book found in the mighty angel's hand.

v. 9 "Take it, and eat it up" Indicative of one reading the Word of the Lord through study, as to prepare to preach. There must be an "ingestion" of the Living Word personally before speaking, teaching, and/or preaching publically.

v. 10 "it was in my mouth sweet as honey . . . my belly was bitter" The consuming (studying) of God's Word strengthens one's being. The fellowship is sweet, in contrast to the "message" given among the people that may contain judgments **(v. 11)**. This is exhibited in Christ's letter to the seven churches where applause and admonishments were proclaimed **(Chapters 2 and 3)**.

REVELATION CHAPTER 11

Spotlight Chapter

Chapter 11 is pivotal. This is a transitional chapter because many changes have taken place and the introduction of **two ancient persons** are revealed in the earth throughout the duration of the Great Tribulation. Much information is relayed in this centermost chapter; thus, it is titled a Spotlight Chapter.

Photo of Present-Day Temple Mount

The Dome of the Rock currently sits in the
middle, occupying or close to the area where the
Bible mandates the Holy Temple be rebuilt.

Model of Jewish Temple on Temple Mount

Temple Mount served as the resting place of the First and
Second Jewish Temples. It will also serve as the future location
of the Third Temple to be rebuilt by the Jewish Nation.
(Revelation 11:1-2)

This Spotlight Chapter "arrays the focus on the Temple and its morally reprehensible control under Gentile dominion for forty-two months. There is one region God chose to place His name, here in the location where the Temple was built."[248] In this, you can see the strict devotion and ties of the Jews to this mountain of Holiness, Mt. Moriah, the location wherein the first and second Temples stood on its surface. "At the present time, the Dome of the Rock (a shrine in Jerusalem at the site from which Muhammad ascended through the seven heavens to the throne of God) is built on the site of the Jewish Temple."[249] Thus, the Jewish people are in the land (May 1948), less a place to worship.

Chapter 11 highlights a future Temple to be rebuilt on its historical grounds, Mt. Moriah. This Temple will be the third of its kind since AD 70. The fact Jews are forbidden to worship there presently has not stopped the plans to rebuild a third Temple. Rabbi Chaim Richman, International Director of the Temple Institute in Jerusalem confirms, "The Temple Institute is actively engaged in research and preparation for the resumption of the service in the Holy Temple, to preparing operational blueprints for the construction of the Temple according to the most modern standards."[250]

These plans by the Jewish people are not happenstance but prophecy. It is paving the way for the instantaneous construct of the Temple at the onset of the Tribulation. "Many of the items pertaining to the Temple, such as the Menorah, priests' garments, vessels of copper, gold, and silver are primed for the next Temple.[251] Piece by piece, the Third Temple is taking shape"[252]; accordingly, the Jews presently have **"a Temple in waiting."**

The truth of Scripture shows that the apostle John was given this vision (Revelation 11) over 1,900 years ago (AD 95/96). The seer writes the outcry of circumstances surrounding this third Temple, rebuilt by his Jewish brethren, only to be inhabited by the Antichrist at the end of history **(2 Thessalonians 2:3–4)**.

The Third Temple

Revelation 11:1–2 *¹And there was given me a reed like unto a rod: and the angel stood, saying, Rise, and measure the temple of God, and the altar, and them that worship therein. ²But the court which is without the temple leave out, and measure it not; for it is given unto the Gentiles: and the holy city shall they tread under foot forty and two months.*

Model of Herod's Temple

King Herod brought substantial modifications to the Second Temple, expanding and enlarging its area. This Temple stood during the time of Jesus' ministry on earth. (St. Matthew 24:1)

© Can Stock Photo Inc. /compuinfoto

v. 1 "Rise, and measure the temple of God" This refers to the future Tribulation Temple (third Temple) to be built by the Jewish nation at the onset of the Tribulation.

v. 2 "the holy city shall they tread under foot forty and two months." These forty-two months is a prophetical time, the same period as Daniel's "time, times, and an half"[253] **(Daniel 12:7).** For forty-two months or 1,260 days (last half of the Tribulation) the Holy City and Temple will be inhabited and ruled by the Gentiles (v.2). The arch-Gentile to rule for these forty-two months is the Antichrist—"and power was given unto him to continue forty and two months" **(Revelation 13:5)**. In fact, he will inhabit the Most Holy Place (the place where God was enthroned between the Cherubim in ancient times) and then declare himself God **(2 Thessalonians 2:3–4)**.

This declaration by the Antichrist proves to be sacrilegious (gross irreverence toward a hallowed person, place, or thing) in the eyes of the Jewish people; therefore, the Antichrist defiles the Temple committing this **abomination of desolation** spoken of by Jesus and Daniel **(Matthew 24:15; Daniel 9:27, 12:11)**.

The Two Candlesticks

Revelation 11:3–6 *³And I will give power unto my two witnesses, and they shall prophesy a thousand two hundred and threescore days, clothed in sackcloth. ⁴These are the two olive trees, and the two candlesticks standing before the God of the earth. ⁵And if any man will hurt them, fire proceedeth out of their mouth, and devoureth their enemies: and if any man will hurt them, he must in this manner be killed. ⁶These have power to shut heaven, that it rain not in the days of their prophecy: and have power over waters to turn them to blood, and to smite the earth with all plagues, as often as they will.*

v. 3 "power unto my two witnesses" "These seem to be two prophets, two select eminent instruments. Some have supposed (though without foundation) that they are Moses and Elijah, whom they resemble in several respects."[254]

There is another aspect to be considered, of which this manual adopts. The two witnesses could possibly be Enoch and Elijah—based upon Scripture interpreting Scripture: "it is appointed unto men once to die, but after this the judgement" (Hebrews 9:27). One can respond in the affirmative Enoch and Elijah failed to experience physical death on the earth, whereas both were taken (raptured) **(Genesis 5:24; 2 Kings 2:11)**. At the end of 1,260 days, these two ancient witnesses will be killed by the Beast (Revelation 11:7), which could account for their physical death appointed unto all men once to die. Of course, this theory is based upon positive conjecture, not fact.

v. 3 "and they shall prophesy a thousand two hundred and threescore days" These 1,260 days are equivalent to the forty-two months bespoken of in the duration of time the Antichrist will rule during the times of the Gentiles, forty and two months of power **(Revelation 11:7, 13:5)**. Spiritualization of numbers breeds infidelity to biblical authority, as it relates to specific numbers enumerated consecutively.

There is not a large discrepancy on the appearance of these two witnesses. Some commentators place their prophecy at the first half of the 1,260 days of Tribulation, others at the last half. This book supports the latter, due to the 144,000 witnesses whom, at the onset of Tribulation, are sealed to prophesy to Israel and the world the first half of the Tribulation, then being raptured to heaven at the midpoint of the Tribulation **(Revelation 14:1–5)**; the astonishing appearance of two ancient men (two witnesses) are thus assigned to prophesy the final duration of the Great Tribulation **(v. 3)**. The two witnesses are expressly located in one domain, the Holy City, the place that will be trodden underfoot by Gentile dominion during the last half of the Tribulation **(2 Thessalonians 2:3–4)** **(Revelation 11:2, 13:5)** (Reference Master Time Line).

v. 5 "And if any man will hurt them, fire proceedeth out of their mouth" These men have supernatural powers over nature; wherefore the heavens will obey their voice to produce miracles in nature on the earth. Many of the Gentile powers (Antichrist) will try to kill them, to no avail, for these men will not die until after the prophesying of 1,260 days or forty-two months— **Malachi 4:5** "Behold, I will send you Elijah the prophet before the coming of the great and dreadful day of the LORD."

The Beast and Two Witnesses

> **Revelation 11:7–10** *⁷And when they shall have finished their testimony, the beast that ascendeth out of the bottomless pit shall make war against them, and shall overcome them, and kill them. ⁸And their dead bodies shall lie in the street of the great city, which spiritually is called Sodom and Egypt, where also our Lord was crucified. ⁹And they of the people and kindreds and tongues and nations shall see their dead bodies three days and an half, and shall not suffer their dead bodies to be put in graves. ¹⁰And they that dwell upon the earth shall rejoice over them, and make merry, and shall send gifts one to another; because these two prophets tormented them that dwelt on the earth.*

v. 7 "And when they shall have finished their testimony" At the conclusion of the 1,260 days of prophesying.

v. 7 "the beast . . . shall overcome them, and kill them." The Antichrist finally succeeds after 1,260 days with the murder of the two witnesses during his duration of dominion in the Holy City (great city).

v. 8 "their dead bodies shall lie in the street of the great city" Take note; the Antichrist's genesis begins or arises in Rome (the revived Roman Empire); however, during the midpoint of the Tribulation, the epoch in which he is granted power for forty-two months **(Revelation 13:5)**, he shall make war with the Jewish people **(Matthew 24:15)**, cease their Temple worship **(Daniel 9:27)**, move his hierarchy to the Temple **(2 Thessalonians 2:3–4)**, and turn the great city (Jerusalem) into a place of debauchery and evil for 1,260 days.

v. 8 "which spiritually is called Sodom and Egypt" The great debauchery of sins found in the Holy City, administered by the Antichrist, is heinous and against all things sacred.

"Sodom" "Sodom was distinguished for its wickedness and especially for that vice to which its abominations have given name."[255] "It would be necessary to find in the Holy City such abominations as characterized in Sodom, or so much wickedness that it would be proper to call it Sodom."[256] It can be rightfully stated the Antichrist's sexual preference will be that of men, whether openly professed or, the coined term, "on the down low" **(Daniel 11:37; Revelation 11:8)**. It is under his dominion of forty-two months that the great city spiritually becomes titled, "Sodom." The present-day word *sodomy* is derived from its root word of ancient times, Sodom.

"and Egypt" That is to say, it would have such a character that the name Egypt might be properly given to it. "Egypt is known in the Scriptures as the land of oppression—the land where the Israelites, the people of God, were held in cruel bondage."[257] Egypt is also known as the land of many idols, under which the Jewish nation created a golden calf (Egyptian worship) shortly after their deliverance from Egypt **(Exodus 32:1–8)**. This too will dominate the great city, Jerusalem, the place where our Lord was crucified in the last days.

v. 10 "And they that dwell upon the earth shall rejoice over them, and make merry" In light of the two witnesses' murder, the men of the earth shall rejoice, for the preaching of the two witnesses caused great torment. "And this is the condemnation, that light is come into the world, and men loved darkness rather than light, because their deeds were evil" **(John 3:19)**.

A Third Rapture

> **Revelation 11:11–12** [11]*And after three days and an half the spirit of life from God entered into them, and they stood upon their feet; and great fear fell upon them which saw them.* [12]*And they heard a great voice from heaven saying unto them, Come up hither. And they ascended up to heaven in a cloud; and their enemies beheld them.*

v. 11 "after three days and an half the spirit of life from God" The breath of the Almighty enters the two witnesses, standing them to their feet before the eyes of all men.

v. 12 "Come up hither. And they ascended up to heaven" At this juncture, the two witnesses are raptured before the eyes of all men. Through the infrastructure of technology (camera phones, YouTube, satellite TV), "all eyes" shall behold this ascending to heaven, naturally leaving one's eyes affixed on the heavens.

The Earthquake

Revelation 11:13 *And the same hour was there a great earthquake, and the tenth part of the city fell, and in the earthquake were slain of men seven thousand: and the remnant were affrighted, and gave glory to the God of heaven.*

v. 13 "And the same hour was there a great earthquake" This earthquake is the quake spoken of in **Revelation 6:12–17**. It is its continuation, signifying the coming of the Son of man in the clouds, which causes a great earthquake, including the third "woe," which shall quickly come to pass in verses 15–18 **(See Chapter 7 for chronological order explanation)**.

v. 13 "and the remnant were affrighted, and gave glory to the God of heaven." In light of thousands losing their lives, those who remain believe and give glory to the God of heaven.

The Third Woe

Revelation 11:14 *The second woe is past; and, behold, the third woe cometh quickly.*

v. 14 "the third woe cometh quickly." "Of the three woes which were announced (Revelation 8:13) the first was described in Revelation 9:1–12, the second in Revelation 9:13–21, 'And, behold, the third woe cometh quickly,' the last of the series. The meaning is that that which was signified by the third 'woe' would be the next and final event."[258]

The Seventh Trumpet Sounded

Revelation 11:15–19 *[15]And the seventh angel sounded; and there were great voices in heaven, saying, The kingdoms of this world are become the kingdoms of our Lord, and of his Christ; and he shall reign for ever and ever. [16]And the four and twenty elders, which sat before God on their seats, fell upon their faces, and worshipped God, [17]Saying, We give thee thanks, O Lord God Almighty, which art, and wast, and art to come; because thou hast taken to thee thy great power, and hast reigned. [18]And the nations were angry, and thy wrath is come, and the time of the dead, that they should be judged, and that thou shouldest give reward unto thy servants the prophets, and to the saints, and them that fear thy name, small and great; and shouldest destroy them which destroy the earth. [19]And the temple of God was opened in heaven, and there was seen in his temple the ark of his testament: and there were lightnings, and voices, and thunderings, and an earthquake, and great hail.*

v. 15 "And the seventh angel sounded" The vision of the seven trumpets are concluded, thus, making way for the seven bowl judgments. This is not the winding up of time, but the next vision seen of the seer written.

v. 15 "The kingdoms of this world are become the kingdoms of our Lord" The proclamation to the earth of Christ's millennial kingdom, for the earth is no longer under Gentile rule as it has been in ages past. The stone cut without hands, His kingdom shall reign upon the earth never to be destroyed as the previous kingdoms **(Daniel 2:44–45)**.

v. 18 "And the nations were angry" Not all will love the appearing of Christ from the heavens with His saints **(Revelation 19:11–21)**; the wicked loathe His visible coming at the end of the Great Tribulation.

REVELATION CHAPTER 12

Spotlight Chapter

Israel is a unique nation, and Revelation 12 is a unique chapter. This chapter contains the **history** of Israel from its genesis to its finale in the theocratic chronicle of the Jewish aggregation. None of the interpretations teaching Chapter 12 as the history of the church is satisfactory; this manual does not hold that view. In honor of the history of Israel, this manual displays a **World History Timeline** exhibiting the especial providence, protection, and prophecy concerning this nation.

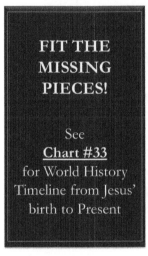

FIT THE
MISSING
PIECES!

See
Chart #33
for World History
Timeline from Jesus'
birth to Present

This Spotlight Chapter comprises the **"past,"** **"present,"** and **"future"** of the nation of Israel. Its history stretches far beyond its genesis, into eternity, with war in heaven. In order to highlight Chapter 12's uniqueness, its text will be **"highlighted"** in response to its past, present, and future. Against this backdrop, it will be most convenient to explain "how to read" Chapter 12.

Remember, the seer wrote the visions that appeared before him. Certain passages cease, only to resume in a further chapter. Chapter 12 Scripture passages cease and resume within itself; thus, in order to maintain continuity in reading this unparalleled chapter, it should be read according to

its **"Highlighted Colors,"** giving a solid footing to the historicity contained in this chapter. This chapter will be expounded upon with the aid of *The Bible Knowledge Commentary* by John F. Walvoord and Roy B. Zuck.

It must be understood that the chronological order of this book relates to "chapter events" not "chapter passages." Chapter events, in arranged order, are: **Chapters 1–3**, the Church Age division; **Chapters 4–5**, the scene in a portion of heaven and is indicative of the Rapture of the church; **Chapters 6–18**, the seven-year Tribulation that follows the Rapture; and **Chapters 19–22**, the return of Christ, one thousand-year reign, final judgment, and the new heaven and earth. Chapter passages will cease and resume in the chronological divisions referenced.

HIGHLIGHT INDICATORS OF ISRAEL'S HISTORY

ETERNITY (timeless/aeon) = **GREEN**
PAST (past/present) = **PINK**
FUTURE (future) = **YELLOW**

<u>**Revelation 12:1–17**</u> *¹And there appeared a great wonder in heaven; a woman clothed with the sun, and the moon under her feet, and upon her head a crown of twelve stars: {wonder or sign} ²And she being with child cried, travailing in birth, and pained to be delivered. ³And there appeared another wonder in heaven; and behold a great red dragon, having seven heads and ten horns, and*

seven crowns upon his heads. {wonder or sign} ⁴And his tail drew the third part of the stars of heaven, and did cast them to the earth: and the dragon stood before the woman which was ready to be delivered, for to devour her child as soon as it was born. ⁵And she brought forth a man child, who was to rule all nations with a rod of iron: and her child was caught up unto God, and to his throne. ⁶And the woman fled into the wilderness, where she hath a place prepared of God, that they should feed her there a thousand two hundred and threescore days. ⁷And there was war in heaven: Michael and his angels fought against the dragon; and the dragon fought and his angels, ⁸And prevailed not; neither was their place found any more in heaven. ⁹And the great dragon was cast out, that old serpent, called the Devil, and Satan, which deceiveth the whole world: he was cast out into the earth, and his angels were cast out with him. ¹⁰And I heard a loud voice saying in heaven, Now is come salvation, and strength, and the kingdom of our God, and the power of his Christ: for the accuser of our brethren is cast down, which accused them before our God day and night. ¹¹And they overcame him by the blood of the Lamb, and by the word of their testimony; and they loved not their lives unto the death. ¹²Therefore rejoice, ye heavens, and ye that dwell in them. Woe to the inhabiters of the earth and of the sea! for the devil is come down unto you, having great wrath, because he knoweth that he hath but a short time. ¹³And when the dragon saw that he was cast unto the earth, he persecuted the woman which brought forth the man child. ¹⁴And to the woman were given two wings of a great eagle, that she might fly into the wilderness, into her place, where she is nourished for a time, and times, and half a time, from the face of the serpent. ¹⁵And the serpent cast out of his mouth water as a flood after the woman, that he might cause her to be carried away of the flood. ¹⁶And the earth helped the woman, and the earth opened her mouth, and swallowed up the flood which the dragon cast out of his mouth. ¹⁷And the dragon was wroth with the woman, and went to make war with the remnant of her seed, which keep the commandments of God, and have the testimony of Jesus Christ.

VERSES 1–2, 5 (past/present) The woman symbolizes Israel, as indicated by **Genesis 37:9–11**, where the sun and the moon refers to Jacob and Rachel, Joseph's parents. "The stars in the woman's crown clearly relate to the twelve sons of Jacob and identify the woman as Israel fulfilling the Abrahamic Covenant."[259]

"Many commentaries are so intent on attempting to identify Israel as the church that they ignore these plain indications that the woman is Israel.[260] The fact is supported that the church does not birth Christ, but Christ has birthed the church. The symbolism, while not referring specifically to Mary the mother of Christ, points to Israel as the source of Jesus Christ."[261]

v. 5 "she brought forth a man child" This man child is the Christ, Jesus, who will rule all nations during the Millennial Reign with a rod of iron **(Zechariah 14)**. "The catching up of the Child references the Ascension, not to the later Rapture of the church, though the same word for "snatched up" is used of the Rapture **(1 Thessalonians 4:17; Acts 8:39; 2 Corinthians 12:2–4)**."[262]

VERSES 3–4, 7–10, 12 (eternity/timeless) "From similar descriptions, in Daniel 7:7 and Revelation 13:1, this beast represents Satan's control over world empires.[263] Revelation 12:9 identifies the dragon as Satan.[264] The 10 horns present symbolically ten kings (Daniel 7:24) who reign simultaneously with the coming world ruler and who are mentioned both in Daniel 7:7 and Revelation 13:1."[265]

v. 4 **"his tail drew the third part of the stars of heaven"** "The interpretation divides into two, first the "stars" connotes a third of the angels which were also cast out of heaven in his rebellion against the Most High during aeon past, or this simply implies satanic power which extends to the heavens and the earth."[266]

v. 4 **"to devour her child"** This is the attempted destruction of Jesus in His infancy phase **(Mathew 2:16)**. "Satanic opposition to Israel and especially to the messianic line is clear in both Testaments."[267]

VERSES 6, 11, 14–17 (Israel's future) Interpreting the Scriptures literally these prophetic days spoken of, 1,260 days, have yet to occur in the past or present history books; it is reserved for a <u>future</u> supernatural deliverance, concerning the especial nation of Israel, when God's face is turned back to His people during the time of Jacob's trouble, Daniel's seventieth week **(Jeremiah 30:7)**.

Again, this woman, "Israel," is given a particular, remarkable deliverance and perseveration for 1,260 days. These days denote the 1,260 latter days of Great Tribulation yet to occur. "This Divine preservation is in a desert hideout, commonly referred as 'Petra.' At the

The City of Petra
"Petra tombs near Kazneh"

proclamation of Christ for the signs of the end, He references the flight of Israel at the beginning of the Great Tribulation to this city hidden in the rocks **(Mark 13:14)**."[268]

The Siq
"The narrow entrance into Petra"

v. 14–17 **"And to the woman were given two wings . . . that she might fly into the wilderness, into her place"** What place is this? The red rock city, Petra. The city Petra is located in the land of Edom. "Petra is also known by the ancient names 'Bozrah' 'Se'lah,' the capital of Edom, situated in the great valley extending from the Dead Sea to the Red Sea."[269]

Daniel 11:41 states the land of Edom will be off limits to the Antichrist, in spite of the fact he will dominate nations, countries, and tongues—"He (Antichrist) shall enter also into the glorious land (Jerusalem), and many countries shall be overthrown: <u>but these shall escape out of his hand</u>, even **Edom**, and Moab,

and the chief of the children of Ammon" (emphasis added). In this fashion the Great Prophet, Jesus, conveys to His Jewish brethren to flee to the mountains when they see the Antichrist enter Jerusalem and stand in the holy place **(Matthew 24:15; Mark 13:14; Daniel 9:27)**.

v. 15 "And the serpent cast out of his mouth water as a flood" Floods in the Bible frequently represent destruction by armies in Jewish perspective—**Jeremiah 46:8**, "Egypt riseth up like a flood" and **Isaiah 59:19**, "When the enemy shall come in like a flood." This denotes the Antichrist will call for an annihilation of the Jewish nation. One familiar with history is aware of the vile hostility toward, or discrimination against, Jews as a religious, ethnic, or racial group in times past.

The Red Rock City
"Another tomb or cave in Petra"

v. 16 "And the earth helped the woman, and the earth opened her mouth, and swallowed up the flood" This is symbolically connoting the earth **(Petra)** will aid the woman (Jews) in their protection during the 1,260 days. Those who flee to the mountains or this red rock city, as directed by the Savior, will not suffer death at the hands of the Antichrist and the various armies to attack Israel in the last days of history.

v. 17 "And the dragon was wroth with the woman, and went to make war with the remnant of her seed" This verse brings clarity to Revelation 13:16–17, exhibiting the Antichrist's wrath with those who pledge faithfulness to the God of the Jewish nation. **It must be noted**: Only those present in the city of Judea, and possibly some in Jerusalem (believing Gentiles also) at the duration of the abomination of desolation of the Temple by the Wicked One will be able to flee to this mountainous region of Petra due to their **locality**; thus, other worshippers of Christ around the globe (the seed of the remnant) will undergo much persecution by the Beast, explaining the draconian law in practice during the Great Tribulation epoch of worshipping the image of the Beast—"And he causeth all, both small and great, rich and poor, free and bond, to receive a mark in their right hand, or in their foreheads: And that no man might buy or sell, save he that had the mark, or the name of the beast, or the number of his name" **(Revelation 13:16–17)**.

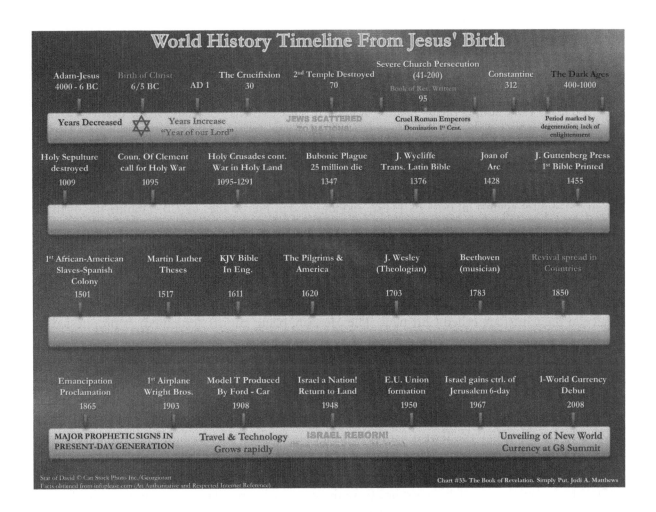

World History Timeline From Jesus' Birth

Adam-Jesus 4000 - 6 BC	Birth of Christ 6/5 BC	AD 1	The Crucifixion 30	2nd Temple Destroyed 70	Severe Church Persecution (41-200) Book of Rev. Written 95	Constantine 312	The Dark Ages 400-1000
Years Decreased ✡	Years Increase "Year of our Lord"		JEWS SCATTERED TO NATIONS		Cruel Roman Emperors Domination 1st Cent.		Period marked by degeneration; lack of enlightenment

Holy Sepulture destroyed 1009	Coun. Of Clement call for Holy War 1095	Holy Crusades cont. War in Holy Land 1095-1291	Bubonic Plague 25 million die 1347	J. Wycliffe Trans. Latin Bible 1376	Joan of Arc 1428	J. Guttenberg Press 1st Bible Printed 1455

1st African-American Slaves-Spanish Colony 1501	Martin Luther Theses 1517	KJV Bible In Eng. 1611	The Pilgrims & America 1620	J. Wesley (Theologian) 1703	Beethoven (musician) 1783	Revival spread in Countries 1850

Emancipation Proclamation 1865	1st Airplane Wright Bros. 1903	Model T Produced By Ford - Car 1908	Israel a Nation! Return to Land 1948	E.U. Union formation 1950	Israel gains ctrl. of Jerusalem 6-day 1967	1-World Currency Debut 2008
MAJOR PROPHETIC SIGNS IN PRESENT-DAY GENERATION	Travel & Technology Grows rapidly		ISRAEL REBORN!			Unveiling of New World Currency at G8 Summit

Star of David © Can Stock Photo Inc./Georgiosart
Facts obtained from infoplease.com (An Authoritative and Respected Internet Reference)

Chart #33- The Book of Revelation. Simply Put. Jodi A. Matthews

WORLD HISTORY TIMELINE FROM
JESUS' BIRTH TO PRESENT

This World History Timeline will highlight key biblical dates and events in history. "Important events, places, and people are detailed together with related historical events and arranged in chronological or date order, providing an actual sequence of the past to present."[270] Timelines help outline the Bible's historical setting and aid greatly in understanding the timing of when events have occurred or shall occur. These fast facts exhibit the especial providential care of the Jewish nation historically. Also dated are interesting facts of the history of the Bible, theologians, technology, and ancestry of the author. The timeline will be expounded with brevity, with special emphasis focused on Israel the nation.

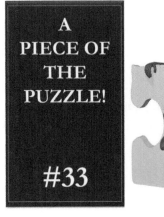

A PIECE OF THE PUZZLE!

#33

6–5 BC—Birth of Christ: "It is interesting to note that the purpose of the BC/AD dating system was to make the birth of Jesus Christ the dividing point of world history. However, when the BC/AD system was being calculated, they actually made a mistake in pinpointing the year of Jesus' birth. Scholars later discovered that Jesus was actually born around 4–6 BC, not AD 1."[271] **BC** stands for "before Christ." **AD** stands for the Latin phrase *anno domini*, which means "in the year of our Lord."

This volume adopts the 6–5 dating system of Christ's birth as a result of the death of Herod the Great (73–4 BC) under whose reign the birth of Christ occurred. "King Herod is best known as the biblical king who ordered a mass slaughter of infants having heard from sages of the birth of another King."[272] The infant Jesus escapes with His family with the aid of an angel appearing to Joseph. This account is recorded in **Matthew 2:13–21**. Herod expired shortly after launching this massive slaughter against all boys two years old and under. Herod dies in 4 BC, dating the birth of Christ two years prior, 6–5 BC.

AD 1—"In the Year of Our Lord": The years in history increase.

AD 30—The Crucifixion: Christ is crucified; a new era called "the Church Age" begins. All who believe in the Christ are called Christians. The Messiah, being cut off (crucified), is prophesied by Daniel the prophet almost six hundred years beforehand **(Daniel 9:26)**.

AD 70—An Important Event in History to the Nation of Israel: "The Temple (worship center of the Jews) is destroyed by the Romans under Titus Flavius Vespasianus."[273] This destruction is prophesied by Daniel the prophet and Jesus Himself almost 530 years prior **(Daniel 9:26; Luke 21:20–24)**. In this light, "the Jewish nation no longer has a place to worship; thus, the Jewish state ceases to exist until its revival in 1948."[274]

This is the "cessation" in the history of the Jewish nation. According to Deuteronomy 32:20–21, God spoke, "I will hide my face from them . . . I will provoke them to anger with a foolish nation (Gentiles)." In this, God paused the seventy weeks, which were progressing prior to Israel's rejection of Christ in the sixty-ninth week, turns His face toward the Gentiles, who accept the Christ, and so world history progresses in the Church Age, where all who call upon the name of the Lord shall be saved.

God's plans and purposes for Israel will commence at the conclusion of the Church Age or end of the sixty-ninth week, therefore inaugurating Daniel's seventieth week upon his people (the Jews) and his city (Jerusalem) **(Daniel 9:24–27)**.

AD 95—The Book of Revelation: Is written by John the apostle in the midst of cruel persecutions to Christians; therefore, this Holy Book offers hope in the midst of dire trials experienced by the first-century Christians.

AD 1455—Johann Guttenberg: Completes first Bible and prints it off the Guttenberg Press.

AD 1611—King James I (KJV Bible): He is best remembered for commissioning the translation into English and publication in 1611 of what is called the Authorized or King James Version of the Bible.

Major Prophetic Signs in the Twentieth Century

AD 1903—First Airplane: Wright brothers, Orville and Wilbur, fly first powered, controlled, heavier-than-air, plane at Kitty Hawk, North Carolina.

AD 1948—Israel a Nation Again!: The nation of Israel is proclaimed and granted entrance back into the land of Israel. Not since AD 70 (1,878 years prior) were the Jews in their land. Note the language and customs retained of this people. It is documented when one has been evicted from his environment, customs, language, and vernaculars are almost always lost, and the surroundings in which he settles are adopted. However, this nation retained its heritage, customs, and language; thus, showing the plans and purposes of God for this people extends into present-day history.

AD 1950—The European Union Formation: Six nations form a union after World War II. The European Union is a group of nations uniting under a common management. This union formation does not cause a problem; except, Daniel reveals there will be a "union" of nations joining together in the **last days** from which the Antichrist will arise. These nations must comprise the precise nations of the ancient Roman Empire to fulfill the prophecy of Daniel 7.

Presently, the EU has grown to over twenty-seven member countries. It is interesting to note the rise of the EU immediately *after* the rebirth of Israel in 1948.

1967—Israel Gains Control of Jerusalem: The war, which ended on June 10, is known as the Six-Day War. Israel declared that it would not give up Jerusalem and that it would hold the other captured territories until significant progress had been made in Arab-Israeli relations. With Israel's capture of Jerusalem, their plans to rebuild a **third Temple** upon its former location of the first and second Temple remains tobe seen.

Major Prophetic Signs in the Twenty-First Century

2008—One World Currency: Russia's president, Dmitry Medvedev, pulled the world's new currency from his pocket at the meeting of G8 leaders in the Italian city of Aquila. Mr. Medvedev, who has been seeking ways to displace the dollar as the world's dominant reserve currency, produced a sample coin of what he described as a united future world currency. The coin, which was minted in Belgium, was presented to all the G8 leaders attending the summit and bears the words "unity in diversity." This minted coin *paves* the way for one-world currency adoption with ease by the Antichrist once in power **(Revelation 13:17)**.

Conclusion

May these "fast facts" assist you in seeing the changing of the times, putting in perspective important dates, events, people, and places in the course of history. It can be clearly seen that some moments in history have evolved before our eyes.

REVELATION CHAPTER 13

Spotlight Chapter

Chapter 13 has been raised to an apex due to its description of the Antichrist and his mark, 666. This chapter causes many to fear and dread reading Revelation, mistakenly distinguishing it as the Revelation of Antichrist instead of the Revelation of Jesus Christ **(Revelation 1:1)**. This manual seeks to debunk the myth of fear and speculation regarding this chapter. I hope you remain ever mindful of a prophecy's purpose: to "prepare" not "scare" the Bible student. Let us move forward with this Spotlight Chapter illuminating details on the man of lawlessness and the false prophet.

Details of the Antichrist

> **Revelation 13:1–2** *¹And I stood upon the sand of the sea, and saw a beast rise up out of the sea, having seven heads and ten horns, and upon his horns ten crowns, and upon his heads the name of blasphemy. ²And the beast which I saw was like unto a leopard, and his feet were as the feet of a bear, and his mouth as the mouth of a lion: and the dragon gave him his power, and his seat, and great authority.*

Depicted Image of the Beast

". . . and the dragon gave him his power, and his seat, and great authority."
(Revelation 13:2)

v. 1 "saw a beast rise up out of the sea" This Beast is symbolic of the man of sin (Antichrist) and the sea and/or waters represents "peoples." He shall arise from the midst of humanity **(Revelation 17:15)**. This connotes the Wicked One will be in man form, not some spiritual or symbolic entity in the earth but human.

v. 1 "ten horns, and upon his horns ten crowns" This parallels with Daniel's vision of the fourth Gentile empire of which the beast shall arise—"After this I saw in the night visions, and behold a fourth beast, dreadful and terrible, and strong exceedingly; and it had great iron teeth: it devoured and brake in pieces, and stamped the residue with the feet of it: and it was diverse from all the beasts that were before it; and it had ten horns" **(Daniel 7:7)**.

v. 2 "and the dragon gave him his power" This dragon is the same dragon in Revelation 12:3 signifying Satan; the Antichrist will be possessed of Satan himself and receive many lying powers from Satan—"Even him, whose coming is <u>after the working of Satan</u> with all power and signs and lying wonders . . ." **(2 Thessalonians 2:9)**.

Revelation 13:3–6 *³And I saw one of his heads as it were wounded to death; and his deadly wound was healed: and all the world wondered after the beast. ⁴And they worshipped the dragon which gave power unto the beast: and they worshipped the beast, saying, Who is like unto the beast? who is able to make war with him? ⁵And there was given unto him a mouth speaking great things and blasphemies; and power was given unto him to continue forty and two months. ⁶And he opened his mouth in blasphemy against God, to blaspheme his name, and his tabernacle, and them that dwell in heaven.*

v. 3 "I saw one of his heads as it were wounded to death" Many speculate the Antichrist will rise from the dead after being assassinated. This is an unfortunate misunderstanding amongst Christians. The Bible says, "as it were wounded to death," denoting it is a fatal wound that should and can cause death, but does not. Miraculous as it will be, the Wicked One will be healed of this wound to full recovery, never resurrected. It must be highlighted that although Satan has great power and will weld it mightily throughout the Great Tribulation, he does not have **"resurrection power."** This power belongs to God alone, thus exhibiting Satan's <u>limited</u> power.

v. 5 "and power was given unto him to continue forty and two months" This is the same forty-two months, equaling only three-and-a-half years or 1,260 days. The Antichrist will not even have authority for the full duration of seven years, only three-and-a-half years, the latter half of the Great Tribulation—"for the devil is come down unto you, having great wrath, because he knoweth that he hath but a short time" **(Revelation 12:12)**. One can affirm three-and-a-half years out of the duration of the history of humanity—from the time of Adam to this future time of wrath of Antichrist—is yet a puny duration in the records of time to have authority given.

Revelation 13:7–8 *⁷And it was given unto him to make war with the saints, and to overcome them: and power was given him over all kindreds, and tongues, and nations. ⁸And all that dwell upon the earth shall worship him, whose names are not written in the book of life of the Lamb slain from the foundation of the world.*

v. 7 "and power was given him" The Antichrist has, yet again, limited power. Those who worship him are those who have not accepted Christ. The saints indicated are Tribulation saints, for many of humanity will accept Christ during the Antichrist's duration of power, thus suffering martyrdom, prison, and captivity **(Revelation 13:10)**. This verse illustrates the Antichrist's difficulty in obtaining complete, total, worldwide worship, for many will reject this proposition and shall be killed **(Revelation 13:15)**.

Revelation 13:9–10 *⁹If any man have an ear, let him hear. ¹⁰He that leadeth into captivity shall go into captivity: he that killeth with the sword must be killed with the sword. Here is the patience and the faith of the saints.*

v. 9 "If any man have an ear" "The conclusion of this speech of the first beast, consisting of two parts, is an exhortation to an attentive audience."[275] "In this verse, these words are evidently introduced to impress the reader with the awfulness of what has just been spoken—all shall worship him whose names are not written in the book of life."[276] This demonstrates that many Tribulation saints will go into captivity and be killed with the sword as a result of not worshipping the Beast, but may the faith of the saints prevail at this juncture.

Details of the False Prophet

Revelation 13:11–12 [11] *And I beheld another beast coming up out of the earth; and he had two horns like a lamb, and he spake as a dragon.* [12] *And he exerciseth all the power of the first beast before him, and causeth the earth and them which dwell therein to worship the first beast, whose deadly wound was healed.*

v. 11 "And I beheld another beast coming up" This beast is the "false prophet"; herein is the **missing link** for those who fruitlessly endeavor to identify the Antichrist with presidential candidates past and present, which leads to infidelity to biblical authority. The beast out of the sea works intensely with the beast out of the earth (false prophet).

The Antichrist is a political leader while the false prophet is a religious leader instituting the worship of the Beast **(vv.13–14)**. Again, many have failed ingloriously in hopes of identifying the present-day man of sin, missing the most **pivotal piece** of another functioning directly beside him: **the false prophet.** Without the accompanying person of the false prophet, one has **not** accurately identified the Antichrist in his lifetime.

Revelation 13:13–15 [13] *And he doeth great wonders, so that he maketh fire come down from heaven on the earth in the sight of men,* [14] *And deceiveth them that dwell on the earth by the means of those miracles which he had power to do in the sight of the beast; saying to them that dwell on the earth, that they should make an image to the beast, which had the wound by a sword, and did live.* [15] *And he had power to give life unto the image of the beast, that the image of the beast should both speak, and cause that as many as would not worship the image of the beast should be killed.*

v. 13 "And he doeth great wonders" The false prophet does many "lying wonders" **(2 Thessalonians 2:9)** causing many to believe in his powers and worship his ally, the Beast (Antichrist).

666—Mark of the Beast

Revelation 13:16–18 [16] *And he causeth all, both small and great, rich and poor, free and bond, to receive a mark in their right hand, or in their foreheads:* [17] *And that no man might buy or sell, save he that had the mark, or the name of the beast, or the number of his name.* [18] *Here is wisdom. Let him that hath understanding count the number of the beast: for it is the number of a man; and his number is Six hundred threescore and six.*

v. 17 "And that no man might buy or sell, save he that had the mark" The number of the Beast, that is the "number of his name" **(Revelation 13:17)**, is the number of a man, and that number is 666. "It is then plain that the number 666 is the number of the name of the beast and this is the man's name."[277] With this mark, the world's economy will be under the control of Antichrist through the powerful infrastructure of technology.

Mark of the Beast
Correct pronunciation of this mark is:
"Six-hundred and sixty-six"

© Can Stock Photo Inc./Kazimala

"The method just described of representing numbers or letters of the alphabet gave rise to a practice among the ancients of representing names also by numbers. Examples of this kind abound in the writings of heathens, Jews, and Christians."[278] During the Great Tribulation, many shall be able to cipher this number identifying who the Antichrist is. This fact is supported in **Daniel 12:4**. Many of the Jews shall "run to and fro," that is, searching the Holy Scriptures; "and knowledge shall be increased," that is, the wise shall understand **(Daniel 12:10; Revelation 13:18)**.

This book seeks to help you in understanding the mark of the Beast, 666. This may be exhibited in the form of a tattoo, which is heavily common and accepted in society. Whatever the form, Christians should not concern themselves with this mark nor be afraid of its numerical value, plummeting one's belief into superstition, of which the Bible forbade the saints—**2 Peter 1:16** "For we have not followed cunningly devised fables, when we made known unto you the power and coming of our Lord Jesus Christ, but were eyewitnesses of his majesty."

REVELATION CHAPTER 14

Spotlight Chapter

As the history of time winds down, the breaking of a New Age is on the horizon. Chapter 14, another Spotlight Chapter, displays images and gives details concerning the 144,000 Jewish witnesses and three angels. It sheds light upon the destruction of Babylon and the battlefield of Armageddon. Chapter 14 will be explained in a flashback.

The 144,000 Jewish Witnesses

> **Revelation 14:1–5** *¹And I looked, and, lo, a Lamb stood on the mount Sion, and with him an hundred forty and four thousand, having his Father's name written in their foreheads. ²And I heard a voice from heaven, as the voice of many waters, and as the voice of a great thunder: and I heard the voice of harpers harping with their harps: ³And they sung as it were a new song before the throne, and before the four beasts, and the elders: and no man could learn that song but the hundred and forty and four thousand, which were redeemed from the earth. ⁴These are they which were not defiled with women; for they are virgins. These are they which follow the Lamb whithersoever he goeth. These were redeemed from among men, being the firstfruits unto God and to the Lamb. ⁵And in their mouth was found no guile: for they are without fault before the throne of God.*

v. 1 "a Lamb stood on the mount Sion, and with him an hundred forty and four thousand" Herein resumes the 144,000 Jewish witnesses from Chapter 7:1–8. These have already been identified as Jews from the twelve tribes of Israel. At this present time, the location of these 144,000 has changed from the earth to heaven.

One is also given great details concerning the sex of the 144,000; they are Jewish virgin men **(v. 4)**, which argues for the integrity against any religion endeavoring to name the 144,000 a group of "anointed" men and women. Not only are they Jewish, but they are virgins as well (never married). It can be positively conjectured the reason for the nonmarriage of these Jewish men is the short time (three-and-a-half years) they have in their commission to save Israel during the first half of the Tribulation.

The 144,000 have been redeemed or raptured from the earth just slightly after the Great Tribulation has begun, for their mandate has been finished successfully, wherein the believing Jews have fled to Petra during the last half of the Tribulation **(Revelation 12:6, 14)** commencing the appearance of the two witnesses **(Revelation 11)**, centered at the heart of Jerusalem where the Antichrist is, who will prophesy the remainder of the Great Tribulation (See Mater Timeline for order of events).

Angels Who Preach?

Revelation 14:6–7 *⁶And I saw another angel fly in the midst of heaven, having the everlasting gospel to preach unto them that dwell on the earth, and to every nation, and kindred, and tongue, and people, ⁷Saying with a loud voice, Fear God, and give glory to him; for the hour of his judgement is come: and worship him that made heaven, and earth, and the sea, and the fountains of waters.*

v. 6 "I saw another angel fly in the midst of heaven, having the everlasting gospel to preach unto them that dwell on the earth" Some commentators speculate whether "angels" will preach the gospel. One can positively adopt this thought since ministers, who are also depicted as "angels of the church," do not possess wings to fly. Hence, interpreting the Scriptures literally, these "angels," during the Great Tribulation epoch (a time in which wonders will be seen in the heavens, Acts 2:19), are flying through the heavens preaching; wherefore **verse 7** declares that which they speak, "Fear God, and give glory to him; for the hour of his judgement is come."

Revelation 14:8 *And there followed another angel, saying, Babylon is fallen, is fallen, that great city, because she made all nations drink of the wine of the wrath of her fornication.*

v. 8 "Babylon is fallen, is fallen, that great city" This has yet to happen, but its pronouncement of coming destruction and utter fall is proclaimed. Chapters 17 and 18 provide the utter damnation and destruction of Babylon; thus, it will be examined later.

The Door of Salvation Shut?

Revelation 14:9–11 *⁹And the third angel followed them, saying with a loud voice, If any man worship the beast and his image, and receive his mark in his forehead, or in his hand, ¹⁰The same shall drink of the wine of the wrath of God, which is poured out without mixture into the cup of his indignation; and he shall be tormented with fire and brimstone in the presence of the holy angels, and in the presence of the Lamb: ¹¹And the smoke of their torment ascendeth up for ever and ever: and they have no rest day nor night, who worship the beast and his image, and whosoever receiveth the mark of his name.*

v. 9 "If any man worship the beast and his image, and receive his mark in his forehead, or in his hand" It has been stated that after the Rapture, no one can be saved; this book cannot support that position. In keeping with numerous Scriptures supporting the saving of men post-rapture, Jesus' superabundance of grace and love is readily seen to the saving of men throughout the Tribulation **(Revelation 7:9–11; Acts 2:21)**.

In contrast to when the "doors of salvation" shall be closed precisely, verses 9–11 indicate the utter sealing of one's fate: **he who worships the beasts and takes the mark of the beast** (v. 9). Then and only then shall one seal his fate with that of Satan. Against this backdrop, God does not "cut off" salvation, so to speak, but man **shreds to pieces** the invitation to receive everlasting life in the face of God when he takes the mark of the Beast. Consequently, "The same shall drink of the wine of the wrath of God . . . whosoever receiveth the mark of his name" **(Revelation 14:10–11)**.

Revelation 14:12–13 *[12]Here is the patience of the saints: here are they that keep the commandments of God, and the faith of Jesus. [13]And I heard a voice from heaven saying unto me, Write, Blessed are the dead which die in the Lord from henceforth: Yea, saith the Spirit, that they may rest from their labours; and their works do follow them.*

v. 12 "Here is the patience of the saints" "The words contain a solemn intimation of the severe trials to which God's faithful servants will be subjected to during the reign of the Beast."[279] Once again, these are Tribulation saints, those who have professed Christ after the Rapture.

An Inner Preview of Armageddon

Revelation 14:14–20 *[14]And I looked, and behold a white cloud, and upon the cloud one sat like unto the Son of man, having on his head a golden crown, and in his hand a sharp sickle. [15]And another angel came out of the temple, crying with a loud voice to him that sat on the cloud, Thrust in thy sickle, and reap: for the time is come for thee to reap; for the harvest of the earth is ripe. [16]And he that sat on the cloud thrust in his sickle on the earth; and the earth was reaped. [17]And another angel came out of the temple which is in heaven, he also having a sharp sickle. [18]And another angel came out from the altar, which had power over fire; and cried with a loud cry to him that had the sharp sickle, saying, Thrust in thy sharp sickle, and gather the clusters of the vine of the earth; for her grapes are fully ripe. [19]And the angel thrust in his sickle into the earth, and gathered the vine of the earth, and cast it into the great winepress of the wrath of God. [20]And the winepress was trodden without the city, and blood came out of the winepress, even unto the horse bridles, by the space of a thousand and six hundred furlongs.*

v. 20 "And the winepress was trodden without the city, and blood came out of the winepress, even unto the horse bridles" These verses convey the preview of the bloodshed of the war of Armageddon. These versus continue from Revelation 6:12–17 and 11:15–18. It will be best to compile the list of casualties in world wars to date. Thus, the casualties lost in WWI[280] and WWII[281] were:

WORLD WAR I:
Total Circa 37 Million

WORLD WAR II:
Total Circa 60 Million

Should these numbers appear staggering, this inner preview of the end of the war of Armageddon enumerates the **"Battle Deaths"**:

WORLD WAR III:
(Battle of Armageddon)
200 Million

Revelation 9:16 addresses this massive army of mounted troops, "two hundred thousand thousand" (two-hundred million), on their way to the battle of Armageddon. "**Armageddon**, as described, is the scene of the final conflict between Christ and Antichrist, which results in the deaths of two-hundred million men; ergo, the bloodshed will be **deep** as blood would be in a field of slaughter where it would come up to the very bridles of the horses."[282] "The idea is that there would be a great slaughter **'by the space of a thousand and six hundred furlongs'** (that is, two hundred miles)—a lake of blood."[283] Set against this backdrop, who is man that he would fight against his Creator?

REVELATION CHAPTER 15

Spotlight Chapter

Chapter 15 is indeed a brief chapter but an informative one. This Spotlight Chapter has a close connection in design with the previous chapter, in that "it pledges and assures that all the enemies of religion would be cut off."[284] It yields details to a marvelous sight of worship to God in heaven, and continues from Revelation 11:19 depicting the seven last plagues to be poured upon the earth, bringing God's wrath to completion. This chapter will also be reviewed in brevity, allowing the Scriptures to speak for themselves.

Worship for Deliverance

Revelation 15:1–4 *¹And I saw another sign in heaven, great and marvellous, seven angels having the seven last plagues; for in them is filled up the wrath of God. ²And I saw as it were a sea of glass mingled with fire: and them that had gotten the victory over the beast, and over his image, and over his mark, and over the number of his name, stand on the sea of glass, having the harps of God. ³And they sing the song of Moses the servant of God, and the song of the Lamb, saying, Great and marvellous are thy works, Lord God Almighty; just and true are thy ways, thou King of saints. ⁴Who shall not fear thee, O Lord, and glorify thy name? for thou only art holy: for all nations shall come and worship before thee; for thy judgements are made manifest.*

v. 1 "seven angels having the seven last plagues" The seven bowls or vials are soon to be poured and God's wrath would be complete.

v. 2 "and them that had gotten victory over the beast" Once again, this group that appears in heaven is not the church saints, but Tribulation saints who have been raptured slightly after the Great Tribulation has begun (the great multitude), for this group no longer appears on earth but in heaven with Christ singing praises to God. "They are now seen in heaven, redeemed and triumphant"[285], before the pouring of the seven vials upon the earth.

Revelation 15:5–6 *⁵And after that I looked, and, behold, the temple of the tabernacle of the testimony in heaven was opened: ⁶And the seven angels came out of the temple, having the seven plagues, clothed in pure and white linen, and having their breasts girded with golden girdles.*

v. 6 "And the seven angels came out of the temple" Notice the employment of angels throughout the book of Revelation. "Here are the administrators or executors coming out of the Temple, they are furnished with instruments of the judgements of God."[286]

Revelation 15:7–8 *⁷And one of the four beasts gave unto the seven angels seven golden vials full of the wrath of God, who liveth for ever and ever. ⁸And the temple was filled with smoke from the glory of God, and from his power; and no man was able to enter into the temple, till the seven plagues of the seven angels were fulfilled.*

Vial
Greek = "phiale"

symbolizes a broad shallow
cup, indicative of bowl
capacity

© Can Stock Photo Inc. / elenaray

v. 7 "And one of the four beasts gave unto the seven angels" Divine creatures working in concert with angels, this manifests the great work taking place in heaven amongst its heavenly creatures. One can be most assured that heaven is a place far beyond the consciousness of rest, but one's activity continues in heaven.

v. 8 "And the temple was filled with smoke" "Smoke, in ancient times, was a usual symbol of the Divine presence in the temple."[287]

v. 8 "From the glory of God" "From the manifestation of the Divine Majesty—that is, the smoke was the proper accompaniment of the Divine Being when appearing in majesty. So on Mount Sinai he is represented as appearing in this manner: 'And Mount Sinai was altogether on a smoke, because the Lord descended on it in fire: and the smoke thereof ascended as the smoke of a furnace, and the whole mount quaked greatly' **(Exodus 19:18)**."[288]

REVELATION CHAPTER 16

Planet Chapter

The previous chapter described the preparation for the seven last plagues that were to come upon that mighty anti-Christian power, to which this series of prophetic visions refer.[289] All is now ready, and this chapter contains the description of those seven last 'plagues' under which this power would reel and fall."[290] Departing from the Spotlight Chapters, Chapter 16 shifts back to earth and is titled a "Planet Chapter," demonstrating what is now taking place upon the earth.

The First Bowl Judgment

> **Revelation 16:1–2** *¹And I heard a great voice out of the temple saying to the seven angels, Go your ways, and pour out the vials of the wrath of God upon the earth. ²And the first went, and poured out his vial upon the earth; and there fell a noisome and grievous sore upon the men which had the mark of the beast, and upon them which worshipped his image.*

v. 2 "and there fell a noisome and grievous sore upon the men" Take note; these sores appear on those who have taken the mark of the Beast; this judgment falls on a particular people, namely those with the mark. "This is also in reference to the sixth Egyptian plague, boils, and blains upon the body **(Exodus 9:8–9)**."[291]

The Second Bowl Judgment

> **Revelation 16:3** *And the second angel poured out his vial upon the sea; and it became as the blood of a dead man: and every living soul died in the sea.*

v. 3 "and it became as the blood of a dead man" "The second angel troubles and molests the sea; it turns into rotten and filthy blood, such as is in dead bodies."[292] This sea turning into blood is different from Revelation 8:8 where a third part of the sea turns to blood. The blood in this area is thick and corrugated liken to mucus or molasses. **"The sea"** may represent the Mediterranean Sea, which boarders Israel and the European area. These bowl judgments seem to be specifically upon the Beast, his kingdom, and his follows as depicted in Revelation 16:2.

The Third Bowl Judgment

> **Revelation 16:4–7** *⁴And the third angel poured out his vial upon the rivers and fountains of waters; and they became blood. ⁵And I heard the angel of the waters say, Thou art righteous, O Lord, which art, and wast, and shalt be, because thou hast judged thus. ⁶For they have shed the blood of saints and prophets, and thou hast given them blood to drink; for they are worthy. ⁷And*

I heard another out of the altar say, Even so, Lord God Almighty, true and righteous are thy judgements.

v. 4 "And the third angel poured out his vial upon the rivers and fountains of waters" Proceeding from this judgment is that all rivers, springs, and fountains of water turn into blood, such that none can drink.

v. 6 "thou hast given them blood to drink" "They thirsted after blood and massacred the saints of God, and now they have got blood to drink!"[293]

<u>**Revelation 16:8–9**</u> *⁸And the fourth angel poured out his vial upon the sun; and power was given unto him to scorch men with fire. ⁹And men were scorched with great heat, and blasphemed the name of God, which hath power over these plagues: and they repented not to give him glory.*

v. 9 "And men were scorched with great heat, and blasphemed . . . and they repented not" Is it a wonder that in the midst of tragedies, men, whose consciences are seared with a hot iron, would not repent **(1 Timothy 4:2)**? The proverbial saying that "troubled times can possibly bring one to seek Christ" demonstrates a weakness in light of this verse. When the heart is in total depravity, it seeks not the Father in good neither bad circumstances, but increases in its hardness toward Christ. This verse also exhibits the survival of man during the Tribulation.

<u>**Revelation 16:12–16**</u> *¹²And the sixth angel poured out his vial upon the great river Euphrates; and the water thereof was dried up, that the way of the kings of the east might be prepared. ¹³And I saw three unclean spirits like frogs come out of the mouth of the dragon, and out of the mouth of the beast, and out of the mouth of the false prophet. ¹⁴For they are the spirits of devils, working miracles, which go forth unto the kings of the earth and of the whole world, to gather them to the battle of that great day of God Almighty. ¹⁵Behold, I come as a thief. Blessed is he that watcheth, and keepeth his garments, lest he walk naked, and they see his shame. 16 And he gathered them together into a place called in the Hebrew tongue Armageddon.*

v. 13 "And I saw three unclean spirits like frogs come out of the mouth of the dragon" These are not literal but spiritual provocation by demon spirits to cause the "kings of the earth" to make war against Christ. Presidents, kings, and prime ministers will unify their armies to make war against the Christ. This passage of Scripture resumes from **Chapter 9:14–16** as it relates to the 200 million-man army. This army is on its way to Armageddon, where the bloodshed will be up to the horses' bridle. Again, this great rebellion is influenced by the dragon himself, Satan, in the person of Antichrist and the false prophet.

v. 15 "Blessed is he that watcheth" This is an admonition for those upon the earth, in light of Armageddon, to be ready for the Second Coming, or Parousia, of Christ. It is sobering to note with all the supernatural events taking place upon the earth, including the pronouncement of Christ coming, an infinite number of humanity will be astonished at His appearing.

Mount of Megiddo

Megiddo remains overlooking the field of Megiddo. A
symbolic name for a place of great slaughter.
(2 Kings 23:29; Judges 5:19; Revelation 16:16)

v. 16 "And he gathered them together into a place called in the Hebrew tongue Armageddon." The mountain of Megiddo is only mentioned in Revelation 16:16. "Megiddo is a city in a great plain at the foot of Mount Carmel, which had been the scene of much slaughter.[294] Under this character, it is referred to in the above text as the place in which God will collect together His enemies for destruction."[295] As one can view, this valley, in which this 200 million-man army will gather, lies full length upon the ground. "This valley also stretches down through Jerusalem into a valley entitled the **Valley of Jehoshaphat**, that is, the 'valley of decision.' The prophet Joel, in a vision, sees the immense array of nations congregating and exclaims '**Multitudes, multitudes,** (Hebraism for immense multitudes) **in the valley of decision'**" (Joel 3:14).[296] Signifying on this day, man wholly **decides** to fight against his Creator and fails ingloriously! **(Revelation 19:11–19)**.

The Seventh Bowl Judgment

> <u>Revelation 16:17</u> *And the seventh angel poured out his vial into the air; and there came a great voice out of the temple of heaven, from the throne, saying, It is done.*

v. 17 "And the seventh angel poured out his vial into the air" "This introduces the final catastrophe in regard to the 'beast'—his complete and utter overthrow accompanied with tremendous judgements."[297]

"saying, It is done" The series of judgments is about to be completed; the dominion of the Beast is about to come to an end forever. "The meaning here is that that destruction was so certain that it might be spoken of as now actually accomplished."[298]

Preview of Babylon the Great Destruction

> <u>Revelation 16:18–21</u> *[18]And there were voices, and thunders, and lightnings; and there was a great earthquake, such as was not since men were upon the earth, so mighty an earthquake, and so great. [19]And the great city was divided into three parts, and the cities of the nations fell: and great Babylon came in remembrance before God, to give unto her the cup of the wine of the fierceness of his wrath. [20]And every island fled away, and the mountains were not found. [21]And there fell upon men a great hail out of heaven, every stone about the weight of a talent: and men blasphemed God because of the plague of the hail; for the plague thereof was exceeding great.*

v. 18 "so mighty an earthquake, and so great." "The seat or standing place of the Antichrist"[299] is leveled to the ground. "This expresses the great and terrible judgements as if the very earth was convulsed and everything was moved out of its place."[300] "What a change this makes in the face of the globe; and yet, the end of the world is not come."[301]

v. 21 "and men blasphemed God because of the plague of the hail" That which the heart is full of, the mouth will speak **(Matthew 12:34)**; thus, men puke their utter hatred toward God.

REVELATION CHAPTER 17

Revelation Chapters 17 and 18 coincide with one another in that Chapter 17 introduces and tells the vision of the great harlot, and chapter 18 proceeds with the great harlot's obituary. These two foci (Chapters 17 and 18) discloses the destruction of Babylon the Great. Hence, it is a Spotlight Chapter, shedding numerous details on this Great Harlot of Ages. The interpretation in this chapter is one of **"spiritual interpretation"** because of the immediate meanings given by an angel after a vision is seen by John. Think spiritually (Revelation 17:3).

Depicted Image of The Great Harlot

". . . having a golden cup in her hand full of abominations and filthiness of her fornication:"
(Revelation 17:4)

An Introduction to the Great Harlot

Revelation 17:1–2 *¹And there came one of the seven angels which had the seven vials, and talked with me, saying unto me, Come hither; I will shew unto thee the judgement of the great whore that sitteth upon many waters: ²With whom the kings of the earth have committed fornication, and the inhabitants of the earth have been made drunk with the wine of her fornication.*

v. 1 "the judgement of the great whore" Voila! Many commentators agree that this woman is not literal, but represents a Satanic system or yet the Church of Satan in the last days. This great harlot, introduced as a woman, represents **all** false religion in the history of time itself. It is the Satanic religious system the Antichrist and false prophet will use in the end times.

"that sitteth upon many waters" Denotes an indefinite number of peoples are involved in the worshipping of false religions **(Revelation 17:15)**; these persons consist of multitudes of nations and tongues that believe in worshipping and following false religions. Take note; "this relation concerning the great whore (city of false worship) and concerning the wife of the Lamb (city of true worship) have the same introduction in token of the exact opposition between them."³⁰² These verses highlight the great whore's influence among humanity, in worshipping false religion, **in contrast** to the City of Jerusalem, the place of true worship to Yahweh. Even so, many false religions today believe there are many paths to God other than through the one door presented—**Christ**.

The Location of the Great Harlot

> **Revelation 17:3** *So he carried me away in the spirit into the wilderness: and I saw a woman sit upon a scarlet coloured beast, full of names of blasphemy, having seven heads and ten horns.*

v. 3 "So he carried me away in the spirit" Again, one must think spiritually. Scripture declares the numerous times a person commits "spiritual adultery"; **James 4:4** says, "Ye adulterers and adulteresses, know ye not that the friendship of the world is enmity with God? whosoever therefore will be a friend of the world is the enemy of God." Israel has been described as committing spiritual adultery (the worshipping of other gods) **(Hosea 2)**. In like manner, this whore is considered the great whore, for in her rests the **root** of every false religion and commercial system.

A Description of the Great Harlot

> **Revelation 17:4** *And the woman was arrayed in purple and scarlet colour, and decked with gold and precious stones and pearls, having a golden cup in her hand full of abominations and filthiness of her fornication:*

v. 4 "full of abominations and filthiness of her fornication" Many in the earth have slept with her (meaning, worshipped other gods) and commit spiritual adultery in refusing to worship the one true God: "Because that, when they knew God, they glorified him not as God, neither were thankful; but became vain in their imaginations, and their foolish heart was darkened" **(Romans 1:21).**

> **Revelation 17:5** *And upon her forehead was a name written, MYSTERY, BABYLON THE GREAT, THE MOTHER OF HARLOTS AND ABOMINATIONS OF THE EARTH.*

v. 5 "MYSTERY, BABYLON THE GREAT" This poses an important question of interpretation: which Babylon is John referring to? Notice that she is called **"MYSTERY, BABYLON."** "Given the description of this place as the center of the Antichrist's government and religion, it is unlikely that it is literally the rebuilt city of ancient Babylon located in modern Iraq."[303] Remember, the seer tells the reader to think spiritually **(Revelation 17:3)**. "More likely is the scenario that the Babylon spoken of here is the **revived Roman Empire**, and by extension the western world."[304] This manual concurs with the latter statement.

Although some want to identify this harlot as ancient Babylon, John the seer identified it as **"MYSTERY, BABYLON"**; it can be positively conjectured that the seer is referring to Rome due to his living during the Roman Empire domination. Thus, he **codes** the name Babylon.

Additionally, in the first century, the name Babylon was used by numerous Christians to signify Rome; hence Peter, in his letter to the saints in Rome during a time of cruel persecution by the Roman Emperors, uses this code name also—"The church that is at **Babylon**, elected together with you, saluteth you; and so doth Marcus my son" **(1 Peter 5:13).**

The Drunkenness of the Great Harlot

Revelation 17:6 *And I saw the woman drunken with the blood of the saints, and with the blood of the martyrs of Jesus: and when I saw her, I wondered with great admiration.*

v. 6 "the woman drunken with the blood of the saints" The phraseology is derived from the barbarous custom, still existent among many pagan nations, of drinking the blood of the enemies slain in way of revenge. "The effect of drinking blood is said to exasperate and to intoxicate with passion and a desire of revenge."[305] This passage also exhibits this great harlot has been around for ages of time, for she is drunk even with the martyrs' blood of Jesus' time.

The Meaning of the Great Harlot

Revelation 17:7–8 [7]*And the angel said unto me, Wherefore didst thou marvel? I will tell thee the mystery of the woman, and of the beast that carrieth her, which hath the seven heads and ten horns.* [8]*The beast that thou sawest was, and is not; and shall ascend out of the bottomless pit, and go into perdition: and they that dwell on the earth shall wonder, whose names were not written in the book of life from the foundation of the world, when they behold the beast that was, and is not, and yet is.*

v. 7 "I will tell thee the mystery of the woman, and of the beast" Take note; the great harlot is not the Beast nor the Beast the great harlot; but both exist together for a certain time during the Tribulation. "This woman rides the beast, not as in a rodeo on a creature, which is trying to buck her off, but sitting relaxed and comfortable holding the reins, obviously a key player in the unfolding drama of the Antichrist's rule over the revived Roman Empire."[306] Again, this harlot is a "Satanic system" and a "city" from which all false religion stems **(v. 9)**.

v. 8 "The beast that thou sawest was, and is not; and shall ascend out of the bottomless pit" "This is a very observable and punctual description of the Beast (Antichrist). His whole duration is here divided into three periods[307]: the Beast **'was'**; his presence has existed for ages such as the great harlot; **'and is not,'** at the time John wrote Revelation his person was not in existence, although his spirit was evident everywhere **(1 John 2:18)**; but in the last days he shall **'ascend out of the bottomless pit'**; he shall arise again with diabolical strength and fury"[308] in personal form, this is yet futurity.

Revelation 17:9–13 [9]*And here is the mind which hath wisdom. The seven heads are seven mountains, on which the woman sitteth.* [10]*And there are seven kings: five are fallen, and one is, and the other is not yet come; and when he cometh, he must continue a short space.* [11]*And the beast that was, and is not, even he is the eighth, and is of the seven, and goeth into perdition.* [12]*And the ten horns which thou sawest are ten kings, which have received no kingdom as yet; but receive power as kings one hour with the beast.* [13]*These have one mind, and shall give their power and strength unto the beast.*

v. 9 "The seven heads are seven mountains, on which the woman sitteth" "The woman must not be separated from the beast that carries her. The beast has seven heads and ten horns. The seven heads symbolize seven mountains (Revelation 17:9) and also seven kings or kingdoms (Revelation 17:10).[309] In keeping with Old Testament imagery, it can be suggested that the seven mountains can be interpreted **geographically** as the seven hills of Rome, but they may also be interpreted **historically** as seven kingdoms."[310]

Let it be stated emphatically; this book does not identify the Roman Catholic Church nor its Papacy as the Antichrist and its system. However, it acknowledges that the City of Rome, of which was the capital of the ancient Roman Empire, will be the capital of the revived Roman Empire, the Euro-Mediterranean providence from which the Antichrist shall arise in the last days per Scripture's literal interpretation concerning the "fourth kingdom" upon the earth **(Daniel 2:40–43; Revelation 17:18)**.

v. 10 "And there are seven kings: five are fallen, and one is, and the other is not yet come" "According to Revelation 17:10, five of these kings (or kingdoms) has passed off the scene, one was present in John's day, and one was yet to come."[311]

If so, then the five past kingdoms would be: **Egypt, Assyria, Babylon, Persia,** and **Greece.** (See chart on following page.) The present kingdom in force at the time of John's writing is **Rome.** "The future kingdom to come is the **revived Roman Empire** (consisting of the exact countries found in the ancient Roman Empire, hence, the European Union presently) and would be that of the beast."[312] Against this backdrop, the prophet Daniel, in his writings, reveals four kingdoms out of the seven: **Babylon, Persia, Greece** and **Rome**—for these four ruled over the nation of Israel and its city Jerusalem distinctly **(Daniel 2:36–44)**.

v. 11 "And the beast . . . even he is the eighth, and is of the seven, and goeth into perdition." The Beast, which Daniel describes as the Antichrist **(Daniel 7:23–24)**, shall build his **own** kingdom that shall become the eighth kingdom. Take note; the eighth kingdom comes out of the seventh kingdom (revived Roman Empire). This comes by way of aid of **ten kings** spoken of by Daniel, noted as **"ten horns"** by the seer, who helps the Antichrist rise into power. But to their dismay, the Antichrist uses them, becomes a tyrant subduing three, with the rest surrendering power and the Antichrist creating his **own kingdom (the eighth)**. The Antichrist is lawless, wicked, and does things according to his own will.

v. 11–13 "the beast that was . . . And the ten horns . . . are ten kings . . . These have one mind" "The beast not only has **seven heads** (kingdoms described by John) but also ten horns, which represent ten kings.[313] One cannot divorce this beast from the ten horns, or "kings," as the seer corroborates with Daniel's exclusive writing concerning the beast and ten kings **(Daniel 7:7–8, 19–20, 23–24)**. In the last days, during the Tribulation epoch, these kings enable the beast to rise to power and are even willing to yield their authority to him" **(v. 13)**.[314] From this power, the Antichrist manifests a new kingdom. (See above image.)

Revelation 17:14 *These shall make war with the Lamb, and the Lamb shall overcome them: for he is Lord of lords, and King of kings: and they that are with him are called, and chosen, and faithful.*

v. 14 "These shall make war with the Lamb" The military power of the nations of these ten kings, along with the Antichrist, shall fight against the Lamb (Christ) in the valley of Megiddo at the war of Armageddon.

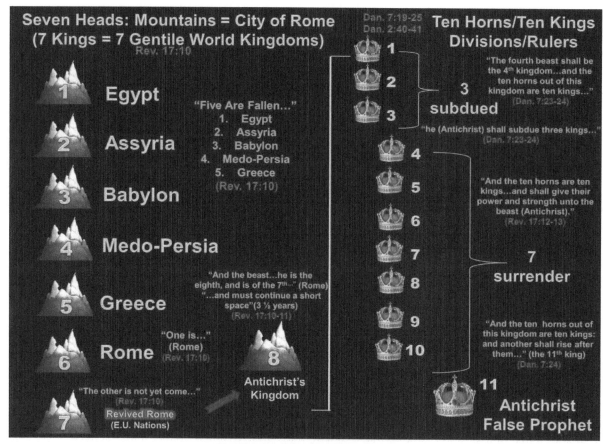

The Scriptures Explained "Visually"
(Revelation 17:10-13 and Daniel 7:19-25)

This image answers how the Antichrist shall arise and gain
power in the end times.

The Great Harlot Vision Explained

> **Revelation 17:15–18** *[15] And he saith unto me, The waters which thou sawest, where the whore sitteth, are peoples, and multitudes, and nations, and tongues. [16] And the ten horns which thou sawest upon the beast, these shall hate the whore, and shall make her desolate and naked, and shall eat her flesh, and burn her with fire. [17] For God hath put in their hearts to fulfill his will, and to agree, and give their kingdom unto the beast, until the words of God shall be fulfilled. [18] And the woman which thou sawest is that great city, which reigneth over the kings of the earth.*

v. 16 "And the ten horns which thou sawest . . . these shall hate the whore" The whore, which represents false religion, proves her reign in the lives of her peoples (v. 15). The fact is readily seen and stated; **people are more devoted to religion than to government.** In this light, the Beast

(Antichrist) and ten kings hate this religious system it carries, for its people are more devoted to her (personal religion) than to them (Antichrist's kingdom).

v. 16 "and shall make her desolate and naked" The betrayal of one of Satan's allies (the whore) should not cause bewilderment, for he uses one for his own gain and volition until such a one is rendered useless; therefore, he destroys that which he uses. Thus, unlike God, the Antichrist's kingdom is divided, ergo, self-destructing itself—**Matthew 12:25** "And Jesus . . . said unto them, Every kingdom divided against itself is brought to desolation; and every city or house divided against itself shall not stand."

REVELATION CHAPTER 18

Spotlight Chapter

Babylon the great has fallen! Here stands the obituary of the harlot, the mother of all false religions; **Birth (eternity past)—Death (future)**. The judgment of **"evil"** in the world has finally come and its fall is great! In one hour, this Satanic system of all ages crumbles off the face of the earth. The prophet Zechariah saw this mystery of wickedness in the earth ("the woman") **(Zechariah 5:5–11)**.

Chapter 18 spotlights the many sins this system bred and the millions of dollars it generated from its worshippers. As this great city falls, the merchants are distraught at its destruction, for with the aid of this city wealth abounds. Let us begin the reading of the fall of Babylon and its wicked kingdom, setting the stage for Christ's millennial kingdom upon the earth **(Revelation Chapter 19)**.

The Violent Fall of Babylon

Revelation 18:1–3 *¹And after these things I saw another angel come down from heaven, having great power; and the earth was lightened with his glory. ²And he cried mightily with a strong voice, saying, Babylon the great is fallen, is fallen, and is become the habitation of devils, and the hold of every foul spirit, and a cage of every unclean and hateful bird. ³For all nations have drunk of the wine of the wrath of her fornication, and the kings of the earth have committed fornication with her, and the merchants of the earth are waxed rich through the abundance of her delicacies.*

v. 2 "And he cried mightily with a strong voice, saying, Babylon the great is fallen, is fallen" "Babylon was not only an ancient city and a powerful empire, but also the symbol of mankind's rebellion against God.[315] In Revelation 18, Babylon represents the world system of the beast, particularly in its economic and political aspects."[316]
"is become the habitation of devils, and the hold of every foul spirit, and a cage of every unclean and hateful bird" Signifying the root of all evil retains its seat in this city, from thence wickedness springs into the rest of the earth.

v. 3 "For all nations have drunk of the wine of the wrath of her fornication" This exhibits the numerous nations in the world that bowed their knee to worship false religions. **"The merchants of the earth"** denotes how many waxed rich by this Satanic system; this can be expressly seen today. The merchandise of the merchants are seen in verses 11–15.

A Second Chance

Revelation 18:4–8 *⁴And I heard another voice from heaven, saying, Come out of her, my people, that ye be not partakers of her sins, and that ye receive not of her plagues. ⁵For her sins have reached unto heaven, and God hath remembered her iniquities. ⁶Reward her even as she rewarded you, and double unto her double according to her works: in the cup which she hath filled fill to her* *double. ⁷How much she hath glorified herself, and lived deliciously, so much torment and sorrow give her: for she saith in her heart, I sit a queen, and am no widow, and shall see no sorrow. 8 Therefore shall her plagues come in one day, death, and mourning, and famine; and she shall be utterly burned with fire: for strong is the Lord God who judgeth her.*

v. 4 "Come out of her, my people" Who are **"my people"**? Some would argue this proves that the church endures the full duration of Tribulation, for many are found partaking of the apostate church when God calls them out; this interpretation is not satisfactory. It is quite clear the Rapture of the church occurs before the Tribulation and even during, for the church is not the object of God's wrath displayed in the Tribulation and Great Tribulation.

It becomes necessary to consider another school of thought, which this guide proposes. This school of thought may answer the questions: **"What becomes of those who are raised or reared in false religions from birth," or "What if one is in a remote place of the globe and has yet to hear of The Christ?"** Although these inquiries are used to garner excuses from those who have heard the invitation of Christ, it begs consideration. Not everyone in false religions are there because of their own stubbornness; some may have been reared from birth. The corpus of this thought reveals this verse possibly speaks of their opportunity to come to Christ at this moment; it also bespeaks the mercy of God that in the final hour mercy still calls one forth to "Come out," lest one share in the fate in which they partake.

v. 7 "for she saith in her heart, I sit a queen, and am no widow, and shall see no sorrow." Oh the pride of this Satanic system, as a result of her wealth, popularity, and worship it is pondered how could she ever fall or come to naught. In fact, in the Old Testament, the kingdom of Nebuchadnezzar fell in one day by the prophetic writing on the wall the day before **(Daniel 5)**; such is this Babylonian system. It shall be brought to nonexistence in one day, in fact, one hour **(v. 8, 17)**.

A Weeping and Lamenting

Revelation 18:9–11 *⁹And the kings of the earth, who have committed fornication and lived deliciously with her, shall bewail her, and lament for her, when they shall see the smoke of her burning, ¹⁰Standing afar off for the fear of her torment, saying, Alas, alas that great city Babylon, that mighty city! for in one hour is thy judgement come. ¹¹And the merchants of the earth shall weep and mourn over her; for no man buyeth their merchandise any more:*

v. 9 "And the kings of the earth, who have committed fornication and lived deliciously with her, shall bewail her" "Merchants who have been accustomed to traffic with her, and who have been enriched by the traffic[317] are impacted. The image is that of a rich and splendid city. Of course such a city depends much on its merchandise, and when it declines and falls, many who had been accustomed to deal with it as merchants or traffickers are affected by it, and have occasion to lament its fall."[318]

Babylon's Wealth and Commodities

Revelation 18:12–14 *¹²The merchandise of gold, and silver, and precious stones, and of pearls, and fine linen, and purple, and silk, and scarlet, and all thyine wood, and all manner vessels of ivory, and all manner vessels of most precious wood, and of brass, and iron, and marble, ¹³And cinnamon, and odours, and ointments, and frankincense, and wine, and oil, and fine flour, and wheat, and beasts, and sheep, and horses, and chariots, and slaves, and souls of men. ¹⁴And the fruits that thy soul lusted after are departed from thee, and all things which were dainty and goodly are departed from thee, and thou shalt find them no more at all.*

v. 12 "The merchandise of gold, and silver, and precious stones" Here are the commodities of goods that made men rich, even so today: "gold, and silver, and the precious stones" speak to European marble, which costs greatly to furnish one's house with. **"Purple, and silk"** bespeaks the fine linen or high-brand fashions shipped from overseas. **"Odours, and ointments"** were the authentic perfumes produced in the land. This list of commodities creates great wealth for those who have investments in its sales.

v. 13 "and slaves, and souls of men" "Nowadays this is termed 'sweatshops.' A sweatshop employs workers at low wages, for long hours, and under poor conditions."[319] There is even the illegal selling and trafficking of **(souls of men)** occupying sweatshops and other vile conditions, which aids the merchants who commit fornication with this Babylonian system of Satanic wealth.

Revelation 18:15–19 *¹⁵The merchants of these things, which were made rich by her, shall stand afar off for the fear of her torment, weeping and wailing, ¹⁶And saying, Alas, alas that great city, that was clothed in fine linen, and purple, and scarlet, and decked with gold, and precious stones, and pearls! ¹⁷For in one hour so great riches is come to nought. And every shipmaster, and all the company in ships, and sailors, and as many as trade by sea, stood afar off, ¹⁸And cried when they saw the smoke of her burning, saying, What city is like unto this great city! ¹⁹And they cast dust on their heads, and cried, weeping and wailing, saying, Alas, alas that great city, wherein were made rich all that had ships in the sea by reason of her costliness! for in one hour is she made desolate.*

v. 18 "And cried when they saw the smoke of her burning" "As they had a deep interest in it, they will on their own account, as well as hers, lift up the voice of lamentation."[320]

A Command to Rejoice!

Revelation 18:20–24 *²⁰Rejoice over her, thou heaven, and ye holy apostles and prophets; for God hath avenged you on her. ²¹And a mighty angel took up a stone like a great millstone, and cast it into the sea, saying, Thus with violence shall that great city Babylon be thrown down, and shall be found no more at all. ²²And the voice of harpers, and musicians, and of pipers, and trumpeters, shall be heard no more at all in thee; and no craftsman, of whatsoever craft he be, shall be found any more in thee; and the sound of a millstone shall be heard no more at all in thee; ²³And the light of a candle shall shine no more at all in thee; and the voice of the bridegroom and of the bride shall be* *heard no more at all in thee: for thy merchants were the great men of the earth; for by thy sorceries were all nations deceived. ²⁴And in her was found the blood of prophets, and of saints, and of all that were slain upon the earth.*

v. 20 "Rejoice over her, thou heaven, and ye holy apostles and prophets" A command to praise at the fall of Babylon! Heaven rejoices because evil has finally been given her just reward, for the nations have been deceived by this Satanic system.

REVELATION CHAPTER 19

Planet Chapter

Chapter 19 resumes the praise of Chapter 18, indeed it is a transitional chapter. This chapter commences in heaven and ends on earth with the coming of Christ and His saints. At this opening episode, Revelation pauses once again to render "praise" to the King for His righteous judgment of Babylon. Now that Babylon has been judged, her husband, the Antichrist and false prophet, assumes position of judgment. Chapter 19 unveils a special time for the believers.

Praise for the Fall of Babylon!

Revelation 19:1–4 *¹And after these things I heard a great voice of much people in heaven, saying, Alleluia; Salvation, and glory, and honour, and power, unto the Lord our God: ²For true and righteous are his judgements: for he hath judged the great whore, which did corrupt the earth with her fornication, and hath avenged the blood of his servants at her hand. ³And again they said, Alleluia And her smoke rose up for ever and ever. ⁴And the four and twenty elders and the four beasts fell down and worshipped God that sat on the throne, saying, Amen; Alleluia.*

v. 1 "I heard a great voice of much people in heaven, saying, Alleluia" Here is the adoring exclamation to Yahweh, found only in this blessed book: **"Alleluia"**! The once-silent heaven at the opening of the seventh seal, God's judgment **(Revelation 8:1)**, has burst forth in a boisterous exclamation at the finishing of God's judgment of evil in the fall of Babylon **(v. 2)**.

Praise for the Marriage Supper of the Lamb

Revelation 19:5–10 *⁵And a voice came out of the throne, saying, Praise our God, all ye his servants, and ye that fear him, both small and great. ⁶And I heard as it were the voice of a great multitude, and as the voice of many waters, and as the voice of mighty thunderings, saying, Alleluia: for the Lord God omnipotent reigneth. ⁷Let us be glad and rejoice, and give honour to him: for the marriage of the Lamb is come, and his wife hath made herself ready. ⁸And to her was granted that she should be arrayed in fine linen, clean and white: for the fine linen is the righteousness of saints. ⁹And he saith unto me, Write, Blessed are they which are called unto the marriage supper of the Lamb. And he saith unto me, These are the true sayings of God. ¹⁰And I fell at his feet to worship him. And he said unto me, See thou do it not: I am thy fellowservant, and of thy brethren that have the testimony of Jesus: worship God: for the testimony of Jesus is the spirit of prophecy.*

v. 7 "Let us be glad and rejoice, and give honour to him: for the marriage of the Lamb is come" This is a special time for believers. "The relation of God, and especially of the Messiah, to the church is often in the Scriptures represented under the image of marriage."[321] There have been minor arguments on "the Body of Christ" and "the Bride of Christ"; how can the church be both? The answer divides into two: just as the first Adam's wife, Eve, was of his body—yet his wife **(Genesis 2:21)**, so it is with the Second Adam, Christ; the church is of His body and yet, is His wife **(1 Corinthians 15:45; Ephesians 5:21–32)**.

The True Christ!

> <u>**Revelation 19:11–16**</u> *[11]And I saw heaven opened, and behold a white horse; and he that sat upon him was called Faithful and True, and in righteousness he doth judge and make war. [12]His eyes were as a flame of fire, and on his head were many crowns; and he had a name written, that no man knew, but he himself. [13]And he was clothed with a vesture dipped in blood: and his name is called The Word of God. [14]And the armies which were in heaven followed him upon white horses, clothed in fine linen, white and clean. [15]And out of his mouth goeth a sharp sword, that with it he should smite the nations: and he shall rule them with a rod of iron: and he treadeth the winepress of the fierceness and wrath of Almighty God. [16]And he hath on his vesture and on his thigh a name written, KING OF KINGS, AND LORD OF LORDS.*

v. 11 "and behold a white horse; and he that sat upon him was called Faithful and True" This passage reveals the **"True Christ"** in sharp contrast to the "Antichrist" **(Revelation 6:2)**, whose weaponry is deceptive in that he has a bow with no arrows **(Revelation 6:2)**.

Notice the eight significant contrasts of this One riding a white horse, this Rider:

> **1)** is Faithful and True **(v. 11)**
> **2)** has many crowns **(v.12)**
> **3)** possesses the unutterable name of God, (YHVH) **(v.12)**
> **4)** has clothes dipped in blood, (sacrificed Lamb) **(v. 13)**
> **5)** name is called, "The Word of God" **(v. 13; John 1:1)**
> **6)** is followed by the armies of heaven **(v. 14)**
> **7)** out of His mouth goes a sharp sword **(v. 15)**
> **8)** has written upon His clothes and His flesh, "KING OF KINGS" and "LORD OF LORDS" **(v.16)**

This is undeniably the Christ! The interpretation betwixt the rider in Revelation 6:1 **(Antichrist)** and the Rider here in 19:11 **(the Christ)** should be attended with no particular difficulty in distinguishing. To repeat Swete's most persuasive statement: "It is tempting to identify the Antichrist with the Rider on the white horse in 19:11, whose name is 'the Word of God'; tempting. But the two riders have nothing in common beyond the white horse."[5] The Antichrist would not exist as the Christ, less some similarities; except, upon close examination he is reckoned a "pseudo-Christ."

---

[5] Henry Barclay Swete, *Robertson, A. T. Word Pictures in the New Testament* (Nashville, TN: Broadman Press, 1933).

"The Riders on the White Horse"
Significant Differences

The Christ!
(Revelation 19:11-16)

1. Is Faithful & True!
2. Has "many" crowns
3. Know the secret name of God (YHVH)
4. Clothes are dipped in blood
5. Called, "The Word of God"
6. Followed by armies of heaven
7. Has a sharp sword
8. Embossed with "KING OF KINGS" and LORD OF LORDS"

The Antichrist!
(Revelation 6:1-2)

1. Is unfaithful & a liar!
2. Has a "crown" given to him
3. Does not "know" God
4. Causes "bloodshed"
5. Called a "Deceiver" (bow and no arrows)
6. Has to gather armies for war
7. Has no sword
8. Desires to be "KING OF KINGS and LORD OF LORDS"

v. 14 "And the armies which were in heaven followed him upon white horses" This army is not angels, but the church who has been raptured to heaven at the onset of the Tribulation. Notice the church's clothes: **"fine linen, white and clean."** Throughout Scripture, the church is conveyed not only as sheep, the Body of Christ, and the Bride of Christ, but it declares the church is identified also as "Army men" **(Ephesians 6:11–18; Romans 13:12; 1 Thessalonians 5:8)**. The Scriptures repeatedly liken the church to one on the battlefield, hence, the old spiritual hymn chorus sung, "I am on the battlefield for my Lord." This army who follows Christ back to earth are the saints of the Living God.

The Great Supper of God

Revelation 19:17–19 *¹⁷And I saw an angel standing in the sun; and he cried with a loud voice, saying to all the fowls that fly in the midst of heaven, Come and gather yourselves together unto the supper of the great God; ¹⁸That ye may eat the flesh of kings, and the flesh of captains, and the flesh of mighty men, and the flesh of horses, and of them that sit on them, and the flesh of all men, both free and bond, both small and great. ¹⁹And I saw the beast, and the kings of the earth, and their armies, gathered together to make war against him that sat on the horse, and against his army.*

v. 17 "Come and gather yourselves together unto the supper of the great God" This verse resumes from the massive earthquake that takes place at the Second Coming of Christ. The earlier chapters (Revelation 6:12–17, 11:13–18, 14:14–20) are preparatory to this verse.

This verse is not to be confused with the "marriage supper of the Lamb," which is for believers. This great supper of God is a preannouncement to all the fowls of the air, for after the battle of Armageddon **(in which there will be massive bloodshed and bodies)** God will use these fowls of the air to cleanse the land of the flesh and dead bodies of the kings of the earth who fought in Armageddon. These fowls will be used as the coroner's vehicle disposing of the dead.

v. 19 "And I saw the beast, and the kings of the earth, and their armies, gathered together to make war against him that sat on the horse, and against his army." The vivid details of the outcome of Armageddon is depicted in **Zechariah Chapter 14**, in which the Scriptures explain the reason for the "massive" earthquake at the Second Coming of Christ as a result of when Christ returns to Mount Olivet, as He foretold **(Acts 1:9–12)**. When His feet touch this mountain (Mount Olivet), instantaneously, topographical changes occur. Mount Olivet, which has remained on the earth for centuries, shall "split apart," making a wide valley, for half the mountain will move toward the north and half toward the south **(Zechariah 14:4)**.

The Beast and False Prophet Destroyed

Revelation 19:20–21 *²⁰And the beast was taken, and with him the false prophet that wrought miracles before him, with which he deceived them that had received the mark of the beast, and them that worshipped his image. These both were cast alive into a lake of fire burning with brimstone. ²¹And the remnant were slain with the sword of him that sat upon the horse, which sword proceeded out of his mouth: and all the fowls were filled with their flesh.*

v. 20 "These both were cast alive into a lake of fire burning with brimstone" The myth of the Antichrist being assassinated during the Tribulation indicates infidelity to biblical authority, as he bears the judgment of his punishment in **full strength**, being cast into the lake of fire "alive."

This event follows, in succession, to have the Antichrist and false prophet bowing on their knees to the Christ declaring, **JESUS IS LORD!** "For it is written, As I live, saith the Lord, <u>every knee</u> shall bow to me, and <u>every tongue</u> shall confess to God" **(Romans 14:11)**.

Planet Chapter

REVELATION CHAPTER 20

This chapter is not the end of the world but the *beginning* of a new dispensation called **kingdom** (see image below). When Christ returns, the dispensation of grace ceases, and the next epoch in operation opens—the Millennial Reign of Christ! Wherefore, "the government shall be upon his shoulder" as prophesied by Isaiah the prophet **(Isaiah 9:6)**.

At this juncture, various **"pieces of the puzzle"** should be reviewed for the fitting of the pieces and comparison to see the full picture **(Chart #4, "Three Millennium Views," Chart #13, "Dispensations,"** as well as the **Master Revelation Timeline)**.

As you may have observed, the pieces of the puzzle have lessened as you progresses through Revelation, for each piece further completes the **whole** of the prophetic puzzle; thus, there are not many pieces left to place. The re-examination of pieces aids greatly as you are introduced to the magnificent millennial kingdom of Christ in this chapter!

THE DISPENSATIONS "GOD'S PLAN FOR THE AGES"

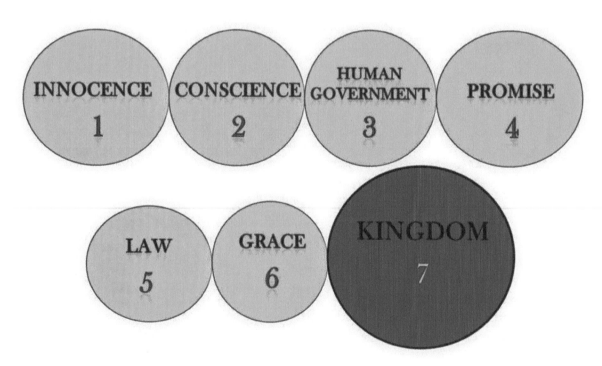

Based upon the works of C.I. Scofield and Charles C. Ryire
Image-The Book of Revelation. Simply Put. Jodi A. Matthews

The 1,000 Years

> **Revelation 20:1–3** *¹And I saw an angel come down from heaven, having the key of the bottomless pit and a great chain in his hand. ²And he laid hold on the dragon, that old serpent, which is the Devil, and Satan, and bound him a thousand years, ³And cast him into the bottomless pit, and shut him up, and set a seal upon him, that he should deceive the nations no more, till the thousand years should be fulfilled: and after that he must be loosed a little season.*

FIT THE MISSING PIECES!

See **Piece #34** for further explanation on the 1,000-Year Millennium Dispensation

v. 2 "And he laid hold on the dragon . . . and bound him a thousand years" The word *millennium*, denoting one thousand, appears six times in Revelation 20 defining the duration of Christ's kingdom. The Millennium refers to one thousand years of Christ's future reign on earth. This manual supports the futurist view that during the Millennium, Christ will reign in time, space, and human form, and Satan, our adversary, will be bound for one thousand years.

Those who hold to a millennialism view believe Satan was bound at Christ's first appearance on earth two thousand years ago; this interpretation is proper, in a sense, for Satan was bound *spiritually.* However, the interpretation should be followed by Satan's literal, *physical binding* **(v. 3)** where he shall be under **"house arrest,"** unable to wreak havoc in the earth for one thousand years.

Take note; the numeral six often refers to "man" in the Scriptures. Using deduction, with the reference of a one thousand-year reign mentioned six times in Revelation 20, as it relates to Christ's reign on earth, one can conclude and harmonize from numerous Scriptures that Christ will be in **man form** during this duration of the thousand years. This isn't a promise to the church, but God's promise to the Jewish nation of an earthly King from the house of David who will reign King of the Jews and universal King of the world **(Luke 1:32, Zechariah 14:9).**

The Judging of the Nations

> **Revelation 20:4** *And I saw thrones, and they sat upon them, and judgement was given unto them: and I saw the souls of them that were beheaded for the witness of Jesus, and for the word of God, and which had not worshipped the beast, neither his image, neither had received his mark upon their foreheads, or in their hands; and they lived and reigned with Christ a thousand years.*

FIT THE MISSING PIECES!

See **Chart #35** for further explanation of the 75-Day Intermission

v. 4 "And I saw thrones, and they sat upon them, and judgement was given unto them:" This epoch, kingdom dispensation, will be unlike any other. It can be rightfully stated there will reside a number of "groups" of people upon the earth; hence, there will be: **1) the Jewish Messiah** (Christ in man form); **2) the church** (clothed in new bodies reigning with Christ); **3) the nation of Israel** (in man form—fulfilling her national calling); **4) the Tribulation populace** (in man form—nations of people who survived the duration of the Tribulation).

Now, what does this have to do with the people sitting upon thrones judging (v. 4)? Herein stands one of the final pieces to the prophetic puzzle. At the return of Christ, after the war of Armageddon, there remains the inauguration of the kingdom of God; in fact, there is a cessation or interval time lapse of seventy-five days, spoken of by the prophet Daniel **(Daniel 12:11–12)**.

The First and Second Resurrections

> **Revelation 20:5–6** *⁵But the rest of the dead lived not again until the thousand years were finished. This is the first resurrection. ⁶Blessed and holy is he that hath part in the first resurrection: on such the second death hath no power, but they shall be priests of God and of Christ, and shall reign with him a thousand years.*

v. 6 "Blessed and holy is he that hath part in the first resurrection" Scripture declares there are two resurrections: the "first resurrection" and the "second resurrection." Although there are two resurrections, there will be **five distinct judgements**: first judgment **(believers)**; second judgment **(Israel)**; third judgment **(nations)**; fourth judgment **(angels)**; fifth judgment **(wicked)**.

Satan's Final Revolt

> **Revelation 20:7–10** *⁷And when the thousand years are expired, Satan shall be loosed out of his prison, ⁸And shall go out to deceive the nations which are in the four quarters of the earth, Gog, and Magog, to gather them together to battle: the number of whom is as the sand of the sea. ⁹And they went up on the breadth of the earth, and compassed the camp of the saints about, and the beloved city: and fire came down from God out of heaven, and devoured them. ¹⁰And the devil that deceived them was cast into the lake of fire and brimstone, where the beast and the false prophet are, and shall be tormented day and night for ever and ever.*

FIT THE MISSING PIECES!

See **Chart #36** for further explanation of Five Distinct Judgements

v. 7 "And when the thousand years are expired, Satan shall be loosed" "The earth shall have its golden age but it shall not last forever. Satan shall, when many ages have rolled away, be loosed for a little season."[322] It must be noted the many births of humans during this golden age, for those left of the nations and considered blessed have entered the Millennium in human capacity; therefore, many shall bear children and repopulate the earth. The vast difference in the children born during this dispensation is that none has experienced Satan nor temptation, for this group of persons has matured under the kingdom dispensation.

v. 8 "And shall go out to deceive the nations which are in the four quarters of the earth, Gog, and Magog" At this juncture, Satan does not use "human" means to accomplish his evil rampage on humanity; he employs himself. **"Gog and Magog":** Magog a general name for the northern nations, and according to Ezekiel, Gog is their prince. However interpreted, Satan shall gain a vast following in rebellion against the King of the earth, Christ, upon his release from the abyss of one thousand years.

v. 9–10 And they went up on the breadth of the earth, and compassed the camp of the saints about, and the beloved city [Jerusalem] . . . And the devil that deceived them was cast into the lake of fire" Satan compels one final revolt against Christ but to no avail. The enemy has not taken heed to the Scriptures: saints win, he loses (v. 10)! Satan is cast into the lake of fire prepared for him where he cannot implement evil in heaven, earth, or hell. Satan does not reign as "king" of hades; therefore, he has **no** kingdom. Hell causes him great torment; hence, it was prepared for him **(Matthew 25:41; Revelation 20:10)**.

The Final Judgment

> **Revelation 20:11–15** *[11]And I saw a great white throne, and him that sat on it, from whose face the earth and the heaven fled away; and there was found no place for them. [12]And I saw the dead, small and great, stand before God; and the books were opened: and another book was opened, which is the book of life: and the dead were judged out of those things which were written in the books, according to their works. [13]And the sea gave up the dead which were in it; and death and hell delivered up the dead which were in them: and they were judged every man according to their works. [14]And death and hell were cast into the lake of fire. This is the second death. [15]And whosoever was not found written in the book of life was cast into the lake of fire.*

v. 11–12 "And I saw a great white throne . . . And I saw the dead, small and great, stand before God" This Great White Throne is the judgment seat of the Holy God, the Father. **"The dead, small and great"** are the wicked dead exclusively.

v. 12 "and the books were opened: and another book . . . which is the book of life" None who appear at the great White Throne Judgment shall enter heaven; this judgment is reserved for condemnation to the lake of fire. Those who appear at the great White Throne Judgment shall be judged according to **"their works" (v.12)**.

Herein is the significance of the great work of Christ wrought upon the cross, which graces those who trust in **this work** (the cross); wherein the church is judged according to His work and not their own works. The wicked dead who has chosen to reject **His work (the cross)**, must bear the penalties of sin themselves before the just, holy, and righteous God; brutally stated, none of their works qualifies them as being righteous before God, for there lies only one door **(Jesus)**, which constitutes righteousness before the eyes and judgment of God.

v. 14 "And death and hell were cast into the lake of fire" "The order there of closing events is the resurrection, the judgement, and the casting of death and hell (hades—the grave) into the lake of fire."[323] **1 Corinthians 15:26** states, "The last enemy that shall be destroyed is death."

v. 14 "This is the second death" (see **Chart #36** for explanation of first and second resurrections.)

THE MILLENNIUM: WHAT HAPPENS?

"The Millennium, what is it?—a thousand years, the name given to the era mentioned in Revelation 20:1–7."[324] The Bible discusses a period of time upon the earth in which there will be **perfect peace**. This utopia (a place of ideal perfection especially in laws, government, and social conditions) upon the earth fulfills the writings of the Old Testament prophets concerning their Jewish King and the state of affairs in the world. The advanced writings of these specific prophets **(Zechariah, Isaiah, Ezekiel, and Daniel)** puzzle scholars even today, for these prophets wrote beyond their reality, stretching beyond the present reality (twenty-first century), peering into the **kingdom age** where Christ will rule and reign on the earth. **(see Dispensation Image Below)**

A PIECE OF THE PUZZLE!

#34

Nowadays, one cannot fathom the thought of a world in utopia; it is considered illusory. But the prophets of old debunk this thought of imaginary thinking, expounding truth in a utopian state of the world to come. When one examines their writings in this light, the comprehension of these prophetic pieces is readily visible.

This manual will discuss the Millennium in imagery form, for the interpretation is attended with no particular difficulty. In laying the foundation to comprehend this "age of utopia," you must understand the term *government*.

What Is a Government?

"A government is a system of social control under which the right to make laws, and the right to enforce them, is vested in a particular group in society.[325] There are many classifications of government. According to the classical formula, governments are distinguished by whether power is held by one man, a few men, or a majority.[326] Set against this background and in light of one's locale upon the earth, one's governmental powers may be identified as: **a president** (a presiding officer of a governmental body); **prime minister** (a chief minister, ruler of a state; chief executive of a government); or a **king** (a male monarch of a major territorial unit; especially one who rules for life)."

Christ the King: One Lord!

When Christ returns to the earth, He returns as King! This fulfills the Davidic Covenant, of whose linage kings descend and under whose dynasty continues forever **(2 Samuel 7:16)**. When Christ walked the earth in the first century, He did not overthrow the Roman Empire and sit upon the throne of His father David, but He was crucified **("cut off"; Daniel 9:26)**. Even so, after His resurrection and before His ascension, His Jewish disciples inquired once again regarding the kingdom, saying, "Lord, wilt thou at this time restore again the kingdom to Israel?" **(Acts 1:6)**. Simply put, "Are you now going to overthrow this Roman Empire and restore the Jews as head of the nations and You as ruling Monarch over all, as the Scriptures declare of You?" Yet, Christ did not take the throne but ascended into heaven; however, Christ did not leave His disciples hopeless, but stated He will return.

This introduces into the narration the Millennial Reign of Christ as spoken of in Revelation 20:1–7. During this time, the government shall be upon His shoulders **(Isaiah 9:6)**. This simply means, Christ will take the government of law, economy, security, and justice upon His shoulders, executing what former presidents, prime ministers, and kings could *not* accomplish—**one world order and peace!**—under which men study war no more.

In the manner of imagery, let's discover this age of utopia (**note:** this glimpse into the Millennium is not to be confused with the "eternal heaven," whereas this epoch lasts for a duration of one thousand years precisely).

THE MILLENNIUM WHAT WILL HAPPEN?

The Millennial Kingdom is the title given to the 1000-year reign of Jesus Christ on the earth; defining the duration of Christ's literal, visible Kingdom with the physical eyes of man!
(Revelation 20:1-7)

THE GOVERNMENT:
"For unto us a child is born, unto us a son is given: and **the government** shall be upon his shoulder:"
(Isaiah 9:6)

THE GOVERNMENT

 RELIGION

✡ ENERGY & ENVIRONMENT

✡ HOMELAND SECURITY

✡ ECONOMY

✡ HEALTH CARE

"And the LORD shall be king over all the earth: in that day shall there be one LORD, and His name one."

(meaning, his name alone will be worshipped)

(Zechariah 14:9)

Millennium Scripture References

Acts 1:6-11

Zechariah 14

Zechariah 6:12-13

Daniel 12:11-13

Revelation 20:1-7

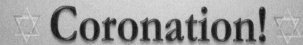 ✡ **Coronation!** ✡

Other Millennium Scriptures:

Isaiah 2:1-5, 9:6-7, 11:6-9, 35, 65:17-25

Ezekiel Chapters 40-48

THE RELIGION:

- 1-World Religion: Christendom!
- Earth full of the knowledge of God!

KING JESUS,

Ruler of the World!
physically located in Israel
on Mount Moriah, in the Temple
upon the Throne of David,
ruling with an iron rod!

One World Government!
(Zechariah 14)

Momentous Topographical Changes!
(Isaiah 35:8-10)

ENERGY & ENVIRONMENT

Tremendous Environmental Transformation!

- No desserts
- No earthquakes or Tsunamis
- No day or night: (1 day)
- No air pollution, smoke, oil spills
- A Highway Called:
  "Highway of Holiness"
- The Dead Sea becomes a Living Sea

HOMELAND SECURITY

• No Satan
(Bound 1,000 years!)
•No Wars!
•No Violence!
•No Crime!
•No Evil!
•No Prisons!
•No Temptations!
•No wild animals!
•No child left behind!

The Accuser Bound!
("Spiritually" & "Literally")
(Revelation 20:1-3)

The Fountain Of Youth Established!
(Ezekiel 47:8-9)

HEALTHCARE

• No Healthcare!
(The Adamic curse reversed!)
•Man will live up to age 1,000!
•Man considered a child at age 100!

LANGUAGE
•Main Language upon the earth: Hebrew!

ECONOMY:
•No poor, middle class
•Work will be easy
•Easy to make a living

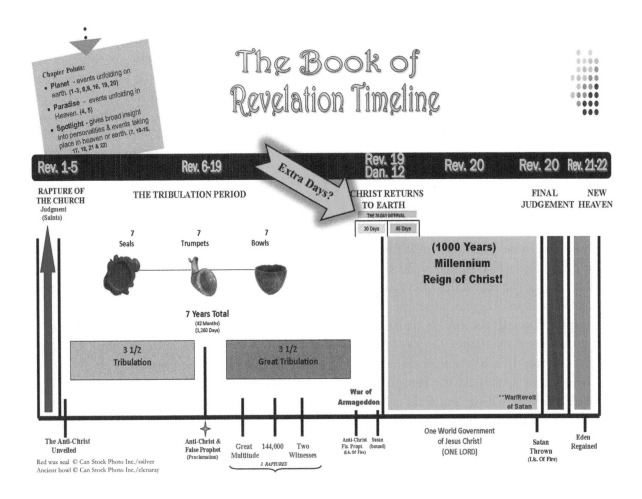

The Book of Revelation Timeline

Chapter Points:
• Planet - events unfolding on earth. (1-3, 8,9, 16, 19, 20)
• Paradise - events unfolding in Heaven. (4, 5)
• Spotlight - gives broad insight into personalities & events taking place in heaven or earth. (7, 10-15, 17, 18, 21 & 22)

| Rev. 1-5 | Rev. 6-19 | Extra Days? | Rev. 19 Dan. 12 | Rev. 20 | Rev. 20 | Rev. 21-22 |

RAPTURE OF THE CHURCH
Judgment (Saints)

THE TRIBULATION PERIOD

CHRIST RETURNS TO EARTH
THE 75-DAY INTERVAL
30 Days | 45 Days

FINAL JUDGEMENT

NEW HEAVEN

7 Seals   7 Trumpets   7 Bowls

(1000 Years) Millennium Reign of Christ!

7 Years Total
(42 Months)
(1,260 Days)

3 1/2 Tribulation

3 1/2 Great Tribulation

War of Armageddon

**War/Revolt of Satan

The Anti-Christ Unveiled

Anti-Christ & False Prophet (Proclamation)

Great Multitude   144,000   Two Witnesses
3 RAPTURES

Anti-Christ Fls. Prcpt. (Lk. Of Fire)   Satan (bound)

One World Government of Jesus Christ! (ONE LORD)

Satan Thrown (Lk. Of Fire)

Eden Regained

Red wax seal © Can Stock Photo Inc./ssilver
Ancient bowl © Can Stock Photo Inc./elenaray

THE SEVENTY-FIVE DAY INTERMISSION

On the Revelation timeline, slightly before the millennial kingdom begins, one will see a **seventy-five-day interval color coded in orange**. What does this reference and mean? We will undertake this study with the aid of *Willimington's Bible Handbook* by H. L. Willimington. One must first look to the prophet Daniel who gives a great quantity and quality of information on the end times and can be viewed as a commentary to Revelation. Daniel's writings underscore the end times such that Jesus instructs the Jews to read his writings in the last days.

A PIECE OF THE PUZZLE!

#35

Key Verse

Daniel 12:11–13 *"And from the time that the daily sacrifice shall be taken away, and the abomination that maketh desolate set up, there shall be a thousand two hundred and ninety days [1,290]. 12 Blessed is he that waiteth, and cometh to the thousand three hundred and five* *and thirty days [1,335]. 13 But go thou thy way till the end be: for thou shalt rest, and stand in thy lot at the end of the days" (emphasis added).*

In this instance of Chapter 12, Willimington points out interesting facts; Daniel continues with many inquiries as relates to the end times. "In his final writing, Daniel asks the angel to explain the visions further **(Daniel 12:8)**. The angel reassured Daniel that these things would not happen until 'the time of the end'" **(Daniel 12:9)**[327], as relates to the 1,260 days of Tribulation and Great Tribulation. Yet, he also left Daniel two more cryptic references of **time** to ponder:

The 1,290 Days:

- "From the time when the Antichrist turns against Israel and desecrates its worship there will be 1,290 days **(12:11)**—this is <u>30 days longer</u> than the 1,260 days. These extra 30 days may allow"[328] for the rebuilding of a fourth temple, as prophesied, for the third temple would have been desecrated by the Antichrist. In this light, Christ, **the Branch, shall build the fourth temple Himself** wherein He shall be situated in the midst of His people, the Jews, sitting upon the throne of His father David—"And speak unto him, saying, Thus speaketh the LORD of hosts, saying, Behold the man whose name is **The BRANCH**; and he shall grow up out of his place, and he shall build the Temple of the LORD" **(Zechariah 6:12)**. Scripture declares **"The BRANCH"** is Christ, and Him only—"And there shall come forth a rod out of the stem of Jesse, and **a Branch** [Jesus] shall grow out of his roots" **(Isaiah 11:1)**.

The 1,335 Days:

- "The angel then suggested that the final half of the Tribulation will last 1,335 days—another <u>forty-five days longer</u> than the 1,290 days of 12:11! Since those who 'wait' for the full 1,335 days will be blessed, this may represent the time at which Christ's Millennial Reign begins"[329] and whether one may enter into His kingdom; thus, we have the separation of the "sheeps" and the "goats" (judgment of the nations) **(Matthew 25:31–46)**. **(This will be expounded further in Chart #36, "Five Distinct Judgments.")**

This is not the ultimate answer; however, it moves beyond guess and speculation proving a plausible theory based upon the facts of Scriptures in relation to one another.

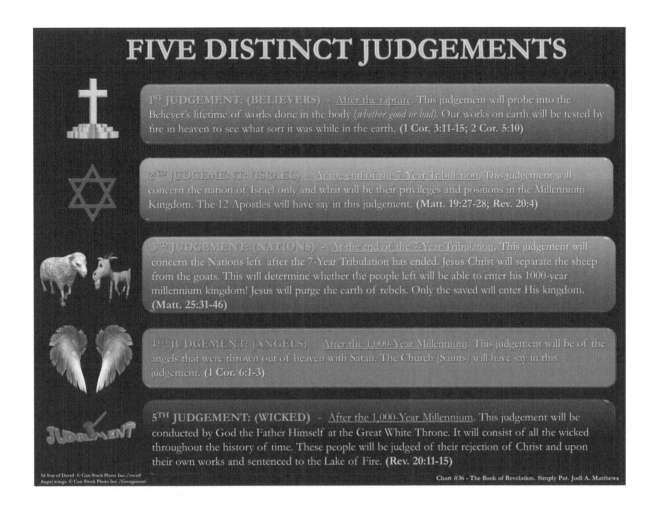

FIVE DISTINCT JUDGEMENTS

1ˢᵀ JUDGEMENT: (BELIEVERS) - <u>After the rapture</u>. This judgement will probe into the Believer's lifetime of works done in the body (*whether good or bad*). Our works on earth will be tested by fire in heaven to see what sort it was while in the earth. **(1 Cor. 3:11-15; 2 Cor. 5:10)**

2ᴺᴰ JUDGEMENT: (ISRAEL) - <u>At the end of the 7-Year Tribulation</u>. This judgement will concern the nation of Israel only and what will be their privileges and positions in the Millennium Kingdom. The 12 Apostles will have say in this judgement. **(Matt. 19:27-28; Rev. 20:4)**

3ᴿᴰ JUDGEMENT: (NATIONS) - <u>At the end of the 7-Year Tribulation</u>. This judgement will concern the Nations left after the 7-Year Tribulation has ended. Jesus Christ will separate the sheep from the goats. This will determine whether the people left will be able to enter his 1000-year millennium kingdom! Jesus will purge the earth of rebels. Only the saved will enter His kingdom. **(Matt. 25:31-46)**

4ᵀᴴ JUDGEMENT: (ANGELS) - <u>After the 1,000-Year Millennium</u>. This judgement will be of the angels that were thrown out of heaven with Satan. The Church (Saints) will have say in this judgement. **(1 Cor. 6:1-3)**

5ᵀᴴ JUDGEMENT: (WICKED) - <u>After the 1,000-Year Millennium</u>. This judgement will be conducted by God the Father Himself at the Great White Throne. It will consist of all the wicked throughout the history of time. These people will be judged of their rejection of Christ and upon their own works and sentenced to the Lake of Fire. **(Rev. 20:11-15)**

3d Star of David © Can Stock Photo Inc./rven0
Angel wings © Can Stock Photo Inc./Georgiosart

Chart #36 - The Book of Revelation. Simply Put. Jodi A. Matthews

FIVE DISTINCT JUDGMENTS
(The First and Second Resurrections)

Although there are two resurrections, there will be five distinct judgments. **Chart #36** lists the different judgments that Scripture declares will take place. The first three (believers, Israel, and nations) encompasses the first resurrection. Although taking place at different intervals, these are all inclusive of the **First Resurrection**.

"Physical death does not end human existence."[330] "It is the peculiar glory of the New Testament that it makes a full revelation of this great doctrine[331], the resurrection." "Without a doubt, one of the most comforting and reassuring parts of God's Word is the doctrine of the resurrection. Scripture describes a series of resurrections, and in each case one must ask who is being resurrected and when."[332]

A PIECE OF THE PUZZLE!

#36

The First Resurrection

"The first resurrection occurs at various times throughout history and the future. In light of the ones first mentioned, this also includes: the Savior **(Romans 6:9)**; selected Old Testament saints **(Matthew 27:50–53)**; the saved who have died **(1 Thessalonians 4:13–18)**; the Two Witnesses **(Revelation 11:9–12)**; Tribulation martyrs **(Revelation 20:4–6)**; Old Testament saints **(Daniel 12:1–2)**. Each of these named has taken part in the first resurrection at different intervals."[6] **Hebrews 9:27** says, "it is appointed unto men once to die, but after this the judgement." As you may read, all humanity will be **judged**, even the saints at the bema seat of Christ **(Romans 14:10)**. Each one of these resurrections has happened or will happen at different intervals.

The judgment of the nations is two-fold, for **Daniel 12:12** states, "Blessed is he that waiteth, and cometh to the thousand three hundred and five and thirty days." This is after the judgment of the nations has taken place, during the extra "forty-five days" **(which encompasses the seventy-five-day intermission)** before the inauguration of the millennial kingdom. Those who make it to the end of the 1,335 days, after judgment (the sheep), will enter His glorious Millennial Reign; hence, they are blessed to enter in. The wicked (goats) have been judged and will not enter this glorious kingdom **(Matthew 25:31–41)**.

The Second Resurrection

The final resurrection, the resuscitation of the **unsaved**, occurs at the end of history after the Millennium. "The lost of all ages will be collected from the place of the dead (hades) and brought before the great white throne **(Revelation 20:11–15)**, where they will be condemned to spend eternity in the lake of fire.[333] This is a universal resurrection of the unredeemed"[334] of all ages. This truth ought to render hope in the redeemed for the simple reason no evil shall escape judgment and punishment. In the wake of **unsolved crimes**, at the Great White Throne Judgment, no criminal shall escape through the laws of "technicalities" for the Righteous Judge judgeth.

Let's look at a distinction of the Great White Throne Judgment. This judgment is reserved for the wicked exclusively, not the saints. This misconception may come from the assumption of a white throne, which can confuse many. The saints are judged at "the judgement seat of Christ" **(Romans 14:10)**, while the wicked are judged at "the great white throne" **(Revelation 20:12)**. Please retain this distinction.

The Judgment of the Nation of Israel

With regard to the resurrection of Israelites, it encompasses the first and second resurrections mentioned above. Those righteous in the Lord are included in the first; those who rejected Christ (wicked) will be resurrected with the rest of the wicked dead and judged then **(Revelation 20:12)**.

However, in the Millennial Reign of Christ upon the throne of His father David, of which earthly kingdom the Jews eagerly await to arrive (Acts 1:6), there will be certain rights, ranks, and privileges assigned to the nation of Israel during the Millennial Reign. Christ will allow the **twelve**

---

[6] Tim LaHaye and Ed Hinson, *The Popular Encyclopedia of Bible Prophecy* (Eugene, OR: Harvest House Publishers, 2004, p. 331).

Jewish apostles (Israel's brethren) to assign the rights, ranks, and privileges of each individual Jew during the kingdom epoch. This is described in **Matthew 19:28**: "And Jesus said unto them, Verily I say unto you, That ye which have followed me, in the regeneration when the Son of man shall sit in the throne of his glory, ye also shall sit upon twelve thrones, <u>judging</u> the twelve tribes of Israel."

"This judgement is not in light of heaven or hell, for the final sentence belongs to Christ alone, but in honor, rights, rank, and privileges in the 1000-year kingdom decisions."[335]

REVELATION CHAPTER 21

Spotlight Chapter

The God of history completes "His story" in the culmination of the history of creation and it is very good **(Genesis 1:31)**. Revelation Chapters 21 and 22 describe the eternal state of the new heavens and new earth. These "twin" chapters give vast information of the glorious state of the new earth and heaven. There is a beauty in reading the Scriptures for the *pure joy* of it. As such, these final chapters will speak for themselves, treating explanation of passages with brevity.

All Things New!

> <u>Revelation 21:1–2</u> *¹And I saw a new heaven and a new earth: for the first heaven and the first earth were passed away; and there was no more sea. ²And I John saw the holy city, new Jerusalem, coming down from God out of heaven, prepared as a bride adorned for her husband.*

v. 1 "And I saw a new heaven and a new earth" "This is not the creation of an additional earth and heaven, but this word new denotes 'freshness.' The old creation must make way for the new creation if God is to be glorified.[336] Jesus calls this event 'the regeneration' of the earth **(Matthew 19:28),** and Peter explained it as a cleansing and renewing by fire **(2 Peter 3:10–13)**."[337] This action can be best described as "renovating." Merriam-Webster's dictionary defines *renovate* as "to restore to a former better state as by cleaning, repairing, or rebuilding." In this shall God restore the earth by melting its former elements by fire, as if to gut out the earth's interior while maintaining its exterior shell.

v. 2 "And I John saw the holy city, new Jerusalem, coming down" This city has never before been inhabited, for this is the prepared place Christ speaks of in John 14:1–3. One can conclude the new Jerusalem shall come down from heaven and rest upon the new earth at the sight of the old Jerusalem. This city, once more, is distinct, for none has inhabited this place to date; all the saints rest in the destination of paradise **(Luke 23:43)**.

God Abides Among Men

> <u>Revelation 21:3–5</u> *³And I heard a great voice out of heaven saying, Behold, the tabernacle of God is with men, and he will dwell with them, and they shall be his people, and God himself shall be with them, and be their God. ⁴And God shall wipe away all tears from their eyes; and there shall be no more death, neither sorrow, nor crying, neither shall there be any more pain: for the former things are passed away. ⁵And he that sat upon the throne said, Behold, I make all things new. And he said unto me, Write: for these words are true and faithful.*

v. 3 "the tabernacle of God is with men, and he will dwell with them" Amazingly stated is the abode of God Himself, in this new earth and heaven, He shall walk among men in the cool of the day once again **(Genesis 3:8)**; for He shall be in the tabernacle or "at home" with man **(Leviticus 26:11–12; Ezekiel 43:7)**.

v. 4 "And God shall wipe away all tears from their eyes" The proximity of God is such that He uses His fingers to wipe away tears of those who are crying. Unlike today, where tears are numerous from the babe to the senior, in the eternal state no tears shall be found; in addition, this new earth shall not possess any cemeteries.

Amen and Amen!

Revelation 21:5 *And he that sat upon the throne said, Behold, I make all things new. And he said unto me, Write: for these words are true and faithful.*

v. 5 "And he that sat upon the throne said" God Himself speaks unto John to write that the weight of these words found in this blessed book are not sensationalized words but are **true** and shall come to pass, for God is faithful to bring it to pass.

A Proclamation of Praise!

Revelation 21:6–8 *⁶And he said unto me, It is done. I am Alpha and Omega, the beginning and the end. I will give unto him that is athirst of the fountain of the water of life freely. ⁷He that overcometh shall inherit all things; and I will be his God, and he shall be my son. ⁸But the fearful, and unbelieving, and the abominable, and murderers, and whoremongers, and sorcerers, and idolaters, and all liars, shall have their part in the lake which burneth with fire and brimstone: which is the second death.*

v. 6 "I will give unto him that is athirst of the fountain of the water of life freely" The invitation to Christ costs one nothing but **trust** in the work that Christ wrought upon the cross; this is less any secret society, special group of persons, monetary gift, or elite mass of persons. God gives unto **ALL** the gift of freely drinking of the water of life found in Christ.

v. 8 "But the fearful, and unbelieving, and the abominable, . . . shall have their part in the lake which burneth with fire and brimstone" This unrepentant group of persons, having been judged **(Revelation 20:11–15)**, are not found in this new earth.

Details of the New City

Revelation 21:9–10 *⁹And there came unto me one of the seven angels which had the seven vials full of the seven last plagues, and talked with me, saying, Come hither, I will shew thee the bride, the Lamb's wife. ¹⁰And he carried me away in the spirit to a great and high mountain, and shewed me that great city, the holy Jerusalem, descending out of heaven from God,*

Depicted image of the New Cubic Jerusalem
coming down out of heaven.
(Revelation 21:9-10)

vv. 9–10 "Come hither, I will shew thee the bride, the Lamb's wife And he carried me away in the spirit" "In sharp contrast to the great whore; that city who sat on many waters **(Revelation 17:1)**"[338], the abode of every kind of wickedness and the bride of Satan—here is described this great city, Jerusalem. This is the abode of the saints and righteousness of God, the Lamb's wife in the spirit.

<u>Revelation 21:11–21</u> *[11]Having the glory of God: and her light was like unto a stone most precious, even like a jasper stone, clear as crystal; [12]And had a wall great and high, and had twelve gates, and at the gates twelve angels, and names written thereon, which are the names of the twelve tribes of the children of Israel: [13]On the east three gates; on the north three gates; on the south three gates; and on the west three gates. [14]And the wall of the city had twelve foundations, and in them the names of the twelve apostles of the Lamb. [15]And he that talked with me had a golden reed to measure the city, and the gates thereof, and the wall thereof. [16]And the city lieth foursquare, and the length is as large as the breadth: and he measured the city with the reed, twelve thousand furlongs. The length and the breadth and the height of it are equal. [17]And he measured the wall thereof, an hundred and forty and four cubits, according to the measure of a man, that is, of the angel. [18]And the building of the wall of it was of jasper: and the city was pure gold, like unto clear glass. [19]And the foundations of the wall of the city were garnished with all manner of precious stones. The first foundation was jasper; the second, sapphire; the third, a chalcedony; the fourth, an emerald; [20]The fifth, sardonyx; the sixth, sardius; the seventh, chrysolite; the eighth, beryl; the ninth, a topaz; the tenth, a chrysoprasus; the eleventh, a jacinth; the twelfth, an amethyst. [21]And the twelve gates were twelve pearls; every several gate was of one pearl: and the street of the city was pure gold, as it were transparent glass.*

v. 11–21 "and her light was like unto a stone most precious, even like . . . like unto . . . as it were" Notice how the seer uses terms *even like, like unto,* and *as it were,* denoting the lack of the human mind to understand the quality of the elements in this metropolis. In the comprehension of the new Jerusalem, this great city, the mind cannot fathom its beauty; it exceeds the capacity of the intellect to be understood. There are stones mentioned in the list that are familiar, as well as unfamiliar, to man.

v. 16 "and he measured the city with the reed, twelve thousand furlongs" "The description seems to be that of a vast cube, which may suggest the Holy of Holies of the tabernacle, which was of that shape, but opinions vary.[339] The twelve thousand furlongs would be 1378.97 (1,300) miles.[340] The New Living Translation marks it 1,400 miles in length, width, and height, measuring the walls to be 216 feet thick."

No Churches, No Sun, No Moon

> **Revelation 21:22–27** *²²And I saw no temple therein: for the Lord God Almighty and the Lamb are the temple of it. ²³And the city had no need of the sun, neither of the moon, to shine in it: for the glory of God did lighten it, and the Lamb is the light thereof. ²⁴And the nations of them which are saved shall walk in the light of it: and the kings of the earth do bring their glory and honour into it. ²⁵And the gates of it shall not be shut at all by day: for there shall be no night there. ²⁶And they shall bring the glory and honour of the nations into it. ²⁷And there shall in no wise enter into it any thing that defileth, neither whatsoever worketh abomination, or maketh a lie: but they which are written in the Lamb's book of life.*

v. 22 "And I saw no temple therein" This eternal state is drastically different from the millennial state in that the eternal state has no Temple, for the Lord God Almighty and the Lamb is now the tabernacle among men: "And I will set my tabernacle among you: and my soul shall not abhor you. And I will walk among you, and will be your God, and ye shall be my people" **(Leviticus 26:11–12)**.

v. 23 "And the city had no need of the sun, neither of the moon, to shine in it" "The City's illumination shall be by the visible splendor of His glory that supplies light in place of the sun and the moon."[341]

v. 25 "And the gates of it shall not be shut at all by day" "This implies that the city has no fear of any foes; these have all been conquered and subdued."[342] The saved shall approach and depart freely.

"All Manner of Precious Stones & Gems"
(Rev. 21:19-20)

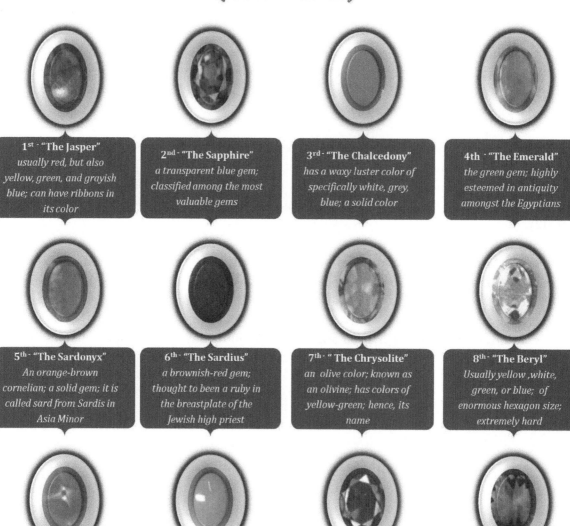

1st - "The Jasper"
usually red, but also yellow, green, and grayish blue; can have ribbons in its color

2nd - "The Sapphire"
a transparent blue gem; classified among the most valuable gems

3rd - "The Chalcedony"
has a waxy luster color of specifically white, grey, blue; a solid color

4th - "The Emerald"
the green gem; highly esteemed in antiquity amongst the Egyptians

5th - "The Sardonyx"
An orange-brown cornelian; a solid gem; it is called sard from Sardis in Asia Minor

6th - "The Sardius"
a brownish-red gem; thought to been a ruby in the breastplate of the Jewish high priest

7th - " The Chrysolite"
an olive color; known as an olivine; has colors of yellow-green; hence, its name

8th - "The Beryl"
Usually yellow ,white, green, or blue; of enormous hexagon size; extremely hard

9th - "The Topaz"
a transparent stone, whose color shades are blue, green yellow, with a glass appearance

10th - "The Chrysoprasus"
normally apple-green; a solid gem; a cryptocrystalline, meaning, composed of crystals

11th - "The Jacinth"
properly a flower, reddish blue or deep purple (hyacinth) or zircon stone of that color

12th - "The Amethyst"
violet to purple in color, a rare stone gem; in the Gk. its meaning connote "non drunkenness

Gem & Stone bases obtained from www.gemselect.com
With the exception of: Jasper, Sardonyx, Sardius, Chrisolite, obtained from Wikipedia.com
Definitions obtained from Infoplease.com

Image – The Book of Revelation. Simply Put. Jodi A. Matthews

REVELATION CHAPTER 22

Spotlight Chapter

Here we have the concluding chapter that rounds out the seer's literary work. This chapter is a continuation of Chapter 21; hence the term, "twin chapters," for they mirror each other in description and devotion. Chapter 22, a Spotlight Chapter, highlights the quickness of Jesus' Second Coming, encouraging the book's reading and teaching in the churches, in light of saluting its veracity.

The Flow of It All

Depicted image of the Tree of Life

"And the leaves of the tree were for the healing of the nations . . ."
(Revelation 22:2)

Revelation 22:1–5 *¹And he shewed me a pure river of water of life, clear as crystal, proceeding out of the throne of God and of the Lamb. ²In the midst of the street of it, and on either side of the river, was there the tree of life, which bare twelve manner of fruits, and yielded her fruit every month: and the leaves of the tree were for the healing of the nations. ³And there shall be no more curse: but the throne of God and of the Lamb shall be in it; and his servants shall serve him: ⁴And they shall see his face; and his name shall be in their foreheads. ⁵And there shall be no night there; and they need no candle, neither light of the sun; for the Lord God giveth them light: and they shall reign for ever and ever.*

v. 1 "And he shewed me a pure river of water of life" "The ever fresh and fruitful effluence of the Holy Ghost, where also the trees are mentioned which 'yielded her fruit every month,' that is, perpetually."[343]

vv. 2–3 "and the leaves of the tree were for the healing of the nations And there shall be no more curse" The sickness of the disease-stricken soul, and/or physical body, no longer remains sick or even falters to its original state of sickness. Alongside the river of life are preventable measures ("the leaves") maintaining the health, vigor, and strength of the nations, wherefore the trees habitually harvests its leaves every month year round.

Revelation 22:6 *And he said unto me, These sayings are faithful and true: and the Lord God of the holy prophets sent his angel to shew unto his servants the things which must shortly be done.*

v. 6 "And he said unto me, These sayings are faithful and true" Once again, a salutation to the truthfulness of every word expressed of the Father, seen and written of John the seer

(Revelation Chapters 1–22). **"To shew unto his servants"** denotes to whom this message (book) ought to be testified (preached) to, in the churches **(Revelation 22:16)**; **"the things which must shortly be done"** (see Revelation 1:1 for an explanation of the word, **"shortly."**)

Jesus Is Coming Quickly

> **Revelation 22:7–9** *⁷Behold, I come quickly: blessed is he that keepeth the sayings of the prophecy of this book. ⁸And I John saw these things, and heard them. And when I had heard and seen, I fell down to worship before the feet of the angel which shewed me these things. ⁹Then saith he unto me, See thou do it not: for I am thy fellowservant, and of thy brethren the prophets, and of them which keep the sayings of this book: worship God.*

v. 7 "Behold, I come quickly" Today, the proverbial phrase "Jesus is coming soon" is often spoken, except Jesus' statement of His return is **"quickly,"** that is, the action shall be swift when He appears.

Unlike "NASA space shuttles as they prepare to reenter earth's atmosphere where prepping time can take up to four hours, then perhaps the next day perform the deorbit burn at the behest of Mission Controls, touching down on earth within an hour,"[344] Christ's reentry into earth's atmospheric heavens is quite different; it shall be without delay, *swift*.

v. 8 "when I had heard and seen, I fell down to worship before the feet of the angel which shewed me these things" The awesomeness of the angel speaking with John and hearing those things spoken of by him cause John to fall and worship the angel; in sharp contrast to Lucifer (the adversary) who desires worship, this angel directed John to whom worship wholly belongs— **God! (v.9)**

Do Not Seal This Prophecy

> **Revelation 22:10** *And he saith unto me, Seal not the sayings of the prophecy of this book: for the time is at hand.*

v. 10 "And he saith unto me, Seal not the sayings of the prophecy of this book" Again, this is in sharp contrast to Daniel in his days **(dispensation of law)**, who was told to "seal up those things" representing the far distant future **(Daniel 9:24; 12:4)**. In John's days, the last days **(dispensation of grace)**, the seer is told to keep this book open for all to see and its testimonies to be read.

Affirmation of His Coming

> **Revelation 22:11–15** *¹¹He that is unjust, let him be unjust still: and he which is filthy, let him be filthy still: and he that is righteous, let him be righteous still: and he that is holy, let him be holy still. ¹²And, behold, I come quickly; and my reward is with me, to give every man according*

as his work shall be. ¹³I am Alpha and Omega, the beginning and the end, the first and the last.
¹⁴Blessed are they that do his commandments, that they may have right to the tree of life, and may
enter in through the gates into the city. ¹⁵For without are dogs, and sorcerers, and whoremongers, and
murderers, and idolaters, and whosoever loveth and maketh a lie.

      v. 11 "He that is unjust, let him be unjust still" An admonishment to those insisting and/
or refusing to believe, retaining their filthiness, for these shall remain without **(v.15)**. The Gospel
comes not by force, none shall be saved who desires not, none shall be forgotten who desires to, and
the Water of Life is available to all such who hunger and thirst after righteousness **(Matthew 5:6)**.

Read, Preach, Teach This Book

      <u>**Revelation 22:16**</u> *I Jesus have sent mine angel to testify unto you these things in the churches. I*
am the root and the offspring of David, and the bright and morning star.

      v. 16 "I Jesus have sent mine angel to testify unto you these things in the churches."
If any should hear, if any must read, if any shall preach, let it arise in the churches. Christ gives
direct and especial designation for those whom this book is purposed, to share this information
with **the churches**.

How to Handle This Book

      <u>**Revelation 22:17–19**</u> *¹⁷And the Spirit and the bride say, Come. And let him that heareth say,*
Come. And let him that is athirst come. And whosoever will, let him take the water of life freely.
¹⁸For I testify unto every man that heareth the words of the prophecy of this book, If any man
shall add unto these things, God shall add unto him the plagues that are written in this book:
¹⁹And if any man shall take away from the words of the book of this prophecy, God shall take
away his part out of the book of life, and out of the holy city, and from the things which are
written in this book.

      v. 17 "And the Spirit and the bride say, Come. And let him that heareth say,
Come." Wherefore, the Holy Spirit instructs and proclaims an invitation to <u>**ALL**</u> that hear the
words of this prophecy: **Come.** Come to the Savior and take the water of life freely, for this
is the hour of salvation.

      v. 18 "If any man shall add unto these things" "This means any who may furnish a
more full and complete revelation, or has a profession that new truth has been communicated
by inspiration as relates to this Book, the reference here is to the Book of Revelation only, for
at that time the books that now constitute what we call the Bible were not collected into a single
volume"³⁴⁵—he, she, or they shall suffer from the plagues described within Revelation. **"God shall**
add unto him the plagues that are written in this book:"

A Final Reminder and Farewell

Revelation 22:20–21 *²⁰He which testifieth these things saith, Surely I come quickly. Amen. Even so, come, Lord Jesus. ²¹The grace of our Lord Jesus Christ be with you all. Amen.*

v. 20 "Surely I come quickly. Amen." This is a strong reminder that Christ's return shall befall "quickly," not in the sense of time but *speed*.

v. 21 "The grace of our Lord Jesus Christ be with you all. Amen." "May the favor and powerful influence of Jesus Christ be with all: the seven churches, the whole Church of Christ in every part of the earth, and through all periods of time."[346]

v. 21 "Amen" This word means "firm, trustworthy." "In Judaism, the use of *Amen* is widespread and firmly established. An extraordinary value is attached to its utterance,"[347] "rendered also as 'truth.' This word, often at the end of a sentence relates, 'truly,' 'surely,' 'certainly.'[348] It thus confirms the preceding words and invokes their fulfillment: 'so be it.'"[349]

EPILOGUE

The reading of these lively, sharp, and intense details causes some to say that the Scriptures are sensationalized, but that is not the design of this literary work. However, you can stand on the words of Christ that **"These sayings are faithful and true" (Revelation 22:6)**. There is a devotion to the truthfulness of every word expressed in Revelation.

After this study, I pray you see that God did not "scribble script" Revelation, making it dauntingly confusing, scary, and mysterious. This visual commentary was written to inform, educate, and excite God's people and others who **"have an ear"** (Revelation 2:7) to understand its writing with clarity, confidence, and surety.

This literary work was aided by many sound Holy Ghost-filled Bible scholars, experts, and articles. Although I take the position of "futurist," an absolute respect remains toward my fellow brethren who also exhort the teaching of this blessed book. In light of their positional view, their labor in ministry is held in highest respect, such that many **"pieces"** were clearly understood through the aid of studying the other views of interpretation, which are well written and argued.

Let me reiterate, the pinnacle design, purpose, and calling of this piece is to fulfill **Acts 8:27–35**, as it relates to understanding difficult passages or books of Scripture.

"Until the coming of our LORD, do not forsake the assembling of yourselves, but exhort one another so much the more as you see the day of His arrival coming" (Hebrews 10:25).

May His *shalom* be with you!

ACTS 8:27-35

"Behold, a man of Ethiopia, a eunuch of great authority had come to Jerusalem to worship. And sitting in his chariot he read Isaiah the prophet…And Philip ran there to him and heard him read the prophet Isaiah, and said:

Do you indeed understand what you are reading?

And he said, How can I unless some man should guide me?

And he asked Philip to come up and sit with him. Then Philip opened his mouth and began at the same Scripture and preached the gospel of Jesus to him."

(Modern King James Version)

Shalom
A Jewish greeting and farewell signifying "Peace"

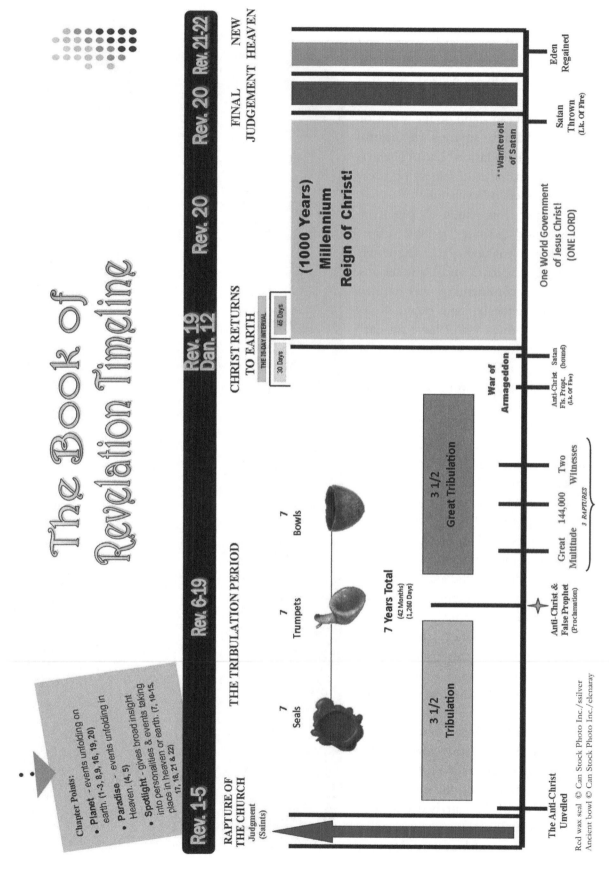

The Book of Revelation Timeline

| Rev. 1-5 | Rev. 6-19 | Rev. 19 Dan. 12 | Rev. 20 | Rev. 20 | Rev. 21-22 |

Chapter Points:
- **Planet** - events unfolding on earth. (1-3, 8,9, 16, 19,20)
- **Paradise** - events unfolding in Heaven. (4, 5)
- **Spotlight** - gives broad insight into personalities & events taking place in heaven or earth. (7, 10-15, 17, 18, 21 & 22)

RAPTURE OF THE CHURCH
Judgment (Saints)

THE TRIBULATION PERIOD

CHRIST RETURNS TO EARTH

FINAL JUDGEMENT

NEW HEAVEN

7 Seals

7 Trumpets

7 Bowls

7 Years Total
(42 Months)
(1,260 Days)

THE 75-DAY INTERVAL

30 Days

45 Days

(1000 Years)
Millennium Reign of Christ!

**War/Revolt of Satan

3 1/2 Tribulation

3 1/2 Great Tribulation

War of Armageddon

One World Government of Jesus Christ! (ONE LORD)

Eden Regained

Satan Thrown (Lk. Of Fire)

The Anti-Christ Unveiled

Anti-Christ & False Prophet (Proclamation)

Great Multitude

Great 144,000

Two Witnesses

3 RAPTURES

Anti-Christ Fls. Prophet. (Lk. Of Fire)

Satan (bound)

Red wax seal © Can Stock Photo Inc./ssilver
Ancient bowl © Can Stock Photo Inc./elenaray

CHART INDEX

WANT REVELATION TAUGHT IN YOUR CHURCH?

"I, Jesus, have sent My angel to testify to you these things in the churches" – REVELATION 22:16 (NKJV).

By Email:
Website: jodimatthews.org
Jodi@jodimatthews.org

By Mail:
Jodi A. Matthews
P.O. Box 173
Farmington, MI 48332

Want to know what's on Jodi's mind? Let's be friends! (FACEBOOK)
Want to start your day on a positive note? Follow me. Daily inspirations! (TWITTER)

OTHER BOOKS BY JODI A. MATTHEWS

Grasping for Sweet Things & Finding Nothing Inside:
A Spiritual Empowerment Book for Women

BIBLIOGRAPHY

Primary Sources:

Gentry, Kenneth L., Sam Hamstra, Jr., Marvin C. Pate, and Robert L. Thomas, *The Four Views on the Book of Revelation*. Grand Rapids: Zondervan, 2010.

Hill, Andrew & John Walton. *A Survey of the Old Testament*. Grand Rapids: Zondervan, 2009.

Kirsch, Jonathan. *A History of the End of the World: How the Most Controversial Book in the Bible Changed the Course of Western Civilization*. New York, NY: Harper Collins, 2007.

LaHaye, Tim & Thomas Ice. *Charting The End Times: A Visual Guide to Understanding Bible Prophecy*. Eugene: Harvest House Publishers, 2001.

LaHaye, Tim and Ed Hindson. *The Popular Encyclopedia of Bible Prophecy*. Eugene: Harvest House Publishers, 2004.

Secondary Sources:

Barnes, Albert. *Albert Barne's New Testament Commentary*. Public domain. Reproduced in Power Bible CD {CD-ROM}. Bronson: Online Publishing, Inc., 2000.

Boyd, Robert T. *World's Bible Handbook*. Eugene: Harvest House Publishers, 1991.

Burkitts, William. *William Burkitt's Notes on the New Testament,* 40th edition, 1807. Public domain. Reproduced in Power Bible CD {CD-ROM}. Bronson: Online Publishing, Inc., 2000.

Carson, D.A. *New Bible Commentary: 21st Century Edition*. Reproduced in Logos Bible Software {CD-ROM}. Downers Grove: Inter-Varsity Press, 1994.

Clarke, Adam. *Adam Clarke's Commentary*. Reproduced in Power Bible CD {CD-ROM}. Concord, NC: 1995-97.

Duck, Daymond R., and Larry, Richards, ed. *The Book of Revelation: The Smart Guide to the Bible Series*. Nashville, TN, 2006.

Easton, M.G. *Easton's 1897 Bible Dictionary*. Public domain. Reproduced in Power Bible CD {CD-ROM}. Bronson: Online Publishing, Inc., 2000.

Family Bible Notes. Public domain. Reproduced in PowerBible CD {CD-ROM}. Bronson: Online Publishing, Inc., 2000.

Fausset, Jamieson R, Fausset, A.R., Brown, A.R. D. & Brown, D. *A Commentary, Critical and Explanatory, on the Old and New Testaments.* Reproduced in Logos Bible Software {CD-ROM}. Oak Harbor: Logos Research Systems, Inc., 1997.

Geneva Bible Notes. Published 1599. Public domain. Reproduced in Power Bible CD {CD-ROM}. Bronson: Online Publishing, Inc., 2000.

Henry, Matthew. *Matthew Henry's Commentary on the Whole Bible.* Public domain. Reproduced in Power Bible CD {CD-ROM}. Bronson: Online Publishing, Inc., 2000.

Hughes, R.B., and Laney, J.C. *Tyndale Concise Bible Commentary.* Reproduced in Logos Bible Software {CD-ROM}.Wheaton: Tyndale House, 2001.

Jeremiah, David. *What In the World Is Going On? 10 Prophetic Clues You Cannot Afford to Ignore."* Nashville: Thomas Nelson, 2008.

Johnson, B.W. *People's New Testament Commentary.* Public domain. Reproduced in Power Bible CD {CD- ROM}. Bronson: Online Publishing, Inc., 2000.

Rand, William W. and Robinson, Edward. *American Tract Society Bible Dictionary.* Published 1859, public domain. Reproduced in Power Bible CD {CD-ROM}. Bronson: Online Publishing, Inc., 2000.

Richards, L.O. *The Bible Reader's Companion.* Reproduced in Logos Bible Software {CD-ROM}. Wheaton: Victor Books, 1996.

Smith, William. *Smith's Bible Dictionary.* Public domain. Reproduced in Power Bible CD {CD-ROM}. Bronson: Online Publishing, Inc., 2000.

Spence-Jones H.D.M., Ed., *The Pulpit Commentary: Zechariah.* Reproduced in Logos Bible Software {CD-ROM}. Bellingham: Logos Research Systems, Inc., 2004.

Walvoord, J. F., Zuck, R. B. and Dallas Theological Seminary. *The Bible Knowledge Commentary.* Reproduced in Logos Bible Software {CD-ROM}.Wheaton: Victor Books, 1983-1985.

Wesley, John. *John Wesley's Notes on the Old and New Testaments.* Reproduced in Power Bible CD {CD-ROM}. Concord, NC: 1995-97.

Woodson, Carter G. *The Mis-Education of the Negro.* Seven Treasures Publications, 2010.

ENDNOTES

PREFACE

[1] Rogers, James. "The Dictionary of Clichés". New York, NY: Ballantine Books, 1985.

[2] The Jargon File, Version 4.4.7. http://catb.org/jargon/html/K/KISS-Principle.html (January 10, 2012).

[3] Kirsch, Jonathan "A History of the End of the World: How the Most Controversial Book in the Bible Changed the Course of Western Civilization." New York, NY: Harper Collins, 2007, p.7. Quoted in Paul Boyer, "The Growth of Fundamentalist Apocalyptic in the United States," in Stein, Apocalypticism 164-65 (adapted).

[4] "World-Country Profiles, US Department of State Background: Israel." Infoplease.com. http://www.infoplease.com/country/profiles/israel.html (November 9, 2011).

[5] Brubaker, Don. "Introduction to Learning Styles Handout." Adapted from: Catherine Jester, Learning Disability Specialist, Copyright 2000 for educational uses only. The Kings College and Seminary, Van Nuys, CA.

[6] Kirsch, Jonathan "A History of the End of the World: How the Most Controversial Book in the Bible Changed the Course of Western Civilization." New York: Harper Collins, 2007, p.3, 4.

ABOUT THE AUTHOR

[7] Duck, Daymond R., and Richards, Larry, ed. "The Book of Revelation: The Smart Guide to the Bible Series." Nashville, TN: Nelson Reference, a Division of Thomas Nelson, Inc., 2006, Introduction, iii.

A PERSONAL WORD FROM THE AUTHOR

[8] Adapted from Kirsch, Jonathan "A History of the End of the World: How the Most Controversial Book in the Bible Changed the Course of Western Civilization." New York: Harper Collins, 2007, p.2.

[9] Jeremiah, David. "What In the World Is Going On? 10 Prophetic Clues You Cannot Afford to Ignore." Nashville: Thomas Nelson, 2008, p.214.

[10] Ibid., 214

[11] "World-Country Profiles, US Department of State Background: Israel." Infoplease.com. http://www.infoplease.com/country/profiles/israel.html (November 9, 2011).

[12] Adapted from: Chuck Missler, Former International Executive, Eternal-Productions.org, "Countdown to Eternity: The Classic 1997 Bible Prophecy Documentary." Division Chapter 4. United States: Eternal Productions, 2006. DVD.

[13] "Timeline: Social Media, Key Dates in the Evolution of Social Media." Infoplease.com. http://www.infoplease.com/science/computers/social-media-timeline.html (November 9, 2011).

[14] Ibid., (November 9, 2011)

[15] Woodson, Carter G. "The Mis-Education of the Negro." Printed in U.S.A.: Seven Treasures Publications, 2010. Amazon Digital Services, Kindle Edition, ePub, Location 465.

BEFORE YOU BEGIN! THE BLUEPRINT: IMPORTANT STUDY HELPS TO KEEPING IT SIMPLE

[16] Dialogue Queen, "How to Build a House Foundation." eHow.com.1999-2012. http://www.ehow.com/how_2311562_build-foundation-house.html#ixzz1jpgUNqbL (January 18, 2012).

[17] Daniels, Stephanie, "Types of House Foundations." eHow.com http://www.ehow.com/about_5410145_types-house-foundations.html#ixzz1jpkwTLr6 (January 18, 2012)

[18] Boyd, Robert T. World's Bible Handbook. Eugene: Harvest House Publishers, 1991.

[19] Gentry, Kenneth L., Hamstra, Sam Jr., Pate, Marvin C., and Thomas, Robert L. "The Four Views on the Book of Revelation." Grand Rapids: Zondervan, ePub Edition, Location 63 of 4407, 2010.

[20] Ibid, location 63 of 4407

[21] Ice, Thomas, "Why I Believe The Bible Teaches Rapture Before Tribulation." Pre-trib.org. http://www.pre-trib.org/articles/view/why-i-believe-bible-teaches-rapture-before-tribulation. (January 2, 2012).

[22] Zukeran, Patrick, "Four Views of Revelation." Probe Ministries. 2009. http://www.probe.org/site/c.fdKEIMNsEoG/b.5110361/k.5D09/Four_Views_of_Revelation.htm (January 23, 2012)

[23] Ibid

[24] Ibid

[25] Ibid

[26] Zukeran, Patrick, "Four Views of Revelation." Probe Ministries. 2009. http://www.probe.org/site/c.fdKEIMNsEoG/b.5110361/k.5D09/Four_Views_of_Revelation.htm (January 23, 2012)

[27] Ibid

[28] Ibid

[29] Ibid

[30] Ibid

[31] LaHaye, Tim & Ice, Thomas, "Charting The End Times: A Visual Guide to Understanding Bible Prophecy." Eugene, OR: Harvest House Publishers, 2001, p 106.

[32] LaHaye, Tim and Hindson, Ed, "The Popular Encyclopedia of Bible Prophecy." Eugene, OR: Harvest House Publishers, 2004, p.311.

[33] Ibid., p. 309, 311

[34] Ibid., p. 385.

[35] Ibid., p.234, 235.

[36] Ibid., p.235.

[37] Ibid., p.280.

[38] LaHaye, Tim, Hindson, Edward, Ice, Thomas, Combs, James, Baker, Warren, eds. "Tim LaHaye Prophecy Study Bible, NKJV: Article by Mal Couch, "The Millennial Views" Chattanooga: AMG Publishers, 2001, p. 1530.

[39] LaHaye, Tim and Hindson, Ed, "The Popular Encyclopedia of Bible Prophecy." Eugene: Harvest House Publishers, 2004, p.282.

[40] Ibid., p.234.

[41] Ibid., 282

[42] Ibid., 283

[43] Robertson, A.T. "Robert's NT Word Pictures," reproduced in Power Bible CD{CD-ROM}. Bronson: Online Publishing, Inc., 2000.

[44] Ibid

[45] Burkitts, William. "William Burkitt's Notes on the New Testament," 40th edition, 1807, Public Domain, reproduced in Power Bible CD {CD-ROM}. Bronson: Online Publishing, Inc., 2000.

[46] LaHaye, Tim & Ice, Thomas, "Charting The End Times: A Visual Guide to Understanding Bible Prophecy." Eugene: Harvest House Publishers, 2001, p 12.

[47] Ibid., p. 7

[48] LaHaye, Tim and Hindson, Ed, "The Popular Encyclopedia of Bible Prophecy." Eugene: Harvest House Publishers, 2004, p.1.

[49] Hill, Andrew E. and Walton, John H. "A Survey of the Old Testament." Grand Rapids: Zondervan, 2009, p. 507.

[50] LaHaye, Tim & Ice, Thomas, "Charting The End Times: A Visual Guide to Understanding Bible Prophecy." Eugene: Harvest House Publishers, 2001, p 11.

[51] Rand, William W. and Robinson, Edward. "American Tract Society Bible Dictionary," published 1859, public domain, reproduced in Power Bible CD{CD-ROM}. Bronson: Online Publishing, Inc., 2000.

[52] Ibid

[53] Hill, Andrew E. and Walton, John H. "A Survey of the Old Testament." Grand Rapids: Zondervan, 2009, p. 554.

[54] Galvin, James, "Life Application Study Bible Vital Statistics." Wheaton: Tyndale House Publishers, Inc., 1996, p. 2034.

[55] Boyd, Robert T. "World's Bible Handbook." Eugene: Harvest House Publishers, 1991, p. 674.

REVELATION CHAPTER 1

[56] Adapted from: Duck, Daymond R., and Richards, Larry, ed. "The Book of Revelation: The Smart Guide to the Bible Series." Nashville: Nelson Reference, a Division of Thomas Nelson, Inc., 2006, p. 3.

[57] Burkitts, William. "William Burkitt's Notes on the New Testament," 40th edition, 1807, Public Domain, reproduced in Power Bible CD {CD-ROM}. Bronson: Online Publishing, Inc., 2000.

[58] CBN TV, cbn.com, Chris Mitchell, Reporter. "Building The Third Temple."http://www.cbn.com/media/index.aspx?s=/vod/EZ3_WPatsComments_040308

59 Fausset, Jamieson R, Fausset, A.R., Brown, A.R. D. & Brown, D. "A Commentary, Critical and Explanatory, on the Old and New Testaments," reproduced in Logos Bible Software {CD-ROM}. Oak Harbor: Logos Research Systems, Inc., 1997.

60 Ibid

61 "Geneva Bible Notes," Published 1599, public domain, reproduced in Power Bible CD {CD-ROM}. Bronson: Online Publishing, Inc., 2000.

62 Richards, L.O. "The Bible Reader's Companion," reproduced in Logos Bible Software {CD-ROM}. Wheaton: Victor Books, 1996.

63 Hughes, R.B., and Laney, J.C. "Tyndale Concise Bible Commentary," reproduced in Logos Bible Software {CD-ROM}. Wheaton: Tyndale House, 2001.

64 Walvoord, J. F., Zuck, R. B. and Dallas Theological Seminary. "The Bible Knowledge Commentary: An exposition of the Scriptures," reproduced in Logos Bible Software {CD-ROM}. Wheaton: Victor Books, 1983-1985.

65 Ibid

66 Ibid

67 Gentry, Kenneth L., Hamstra, Sam Jr., Pate, Marvin C., and Thomas, Robert L., "The Four Views on the Book of Revelation." Grand Rapids: Zondervan, ePub Edition, Location 203 of 4407, 2010.

68 LaHaye, Tim and Hindson, Ed, "The Popular Encyclopedia of Bible Prophecy." Eugene: Harvest House Publishers, 2004, p.390.

69 Ibid., p. 390

70 Fruchtenbaum, Arnold, "Premillennialism in the Old Testament (Part I)" Ariel Ministries.2012. http://ldolphin.org/otpremill.html (February 20, 2012).

71 LaHaye, Tim and Hindson, Ed, "The Popular Encyclopedia of Bible Prophecy." Eugene: Harvest House Publishers, 2004, p.390.

72 Gentry, Kenneth L., Hamstra, Sam Jr., Pate, Marvin C., and Thomas, Robert L. "The Four Views on the Book of Revelation." Grand Rapids: Zondervan, ePub Edition, Location 161 of 4407, 2010.

73 LaHaye, Tim and Hindson, Ed, "The Popular Encyclopedia of Bible Prophecy." Eugene: Harvest House Publishers, 2004, p.390.

74 Ibid., p. 82

[75] Ibid., p. 84

[76] Johnson, B.W. "People's New Testament Commentary," public domain, reproduced in Power Bible CD {CD-ROM}. Bronson: Online Publishing, Inc., 2000.

[77] Smith, William. "Smith's Bible Dictionary," public domain, reproduced in Power Bible CD {CD-ROM}. Bronson: Online Publishing, Inc., 2000.

[78] LaHaye, Tim and Hindson, Ed, "The Popular Encyclopedia of Bible Prophecy." Eugene: Harvest House Publishers, 2004, p.83.

[79] "What is replacement theology /supersessionism?" Got Questions.org. 2002-2012. http://www.gotquestions.org/replacement-theology.html

[80] Ibid

REVELATION CHAPTER 2

[81] Richards, L.O. "The Bible Reader's Companion," reproduced in Logos Bible Software {CD-ROM}. Wheaton: Victor Books, 1996.

[82] Fausset, Jamieson R, Fausset, A.R., Brown, A.R. D. & Brown, D. "A Commentary, Critical and Explanatory, on the Old and New Testaments," reproduced in Logos Bible Software {CD-ROM}. Oak Harbor: Logos Research Systems, Inc., 1997.

[83] Ibid

[84] Overstreet, Larry R. "The Temple of God in the Book of Revelation." Bibliotheca Sacra 166 (October-December 2009): 446-62.

[85] Ibid

[86] Fausset, Jamieson R, Fausset, A.R., Brown, A.R. D. & Brown, D. "A Commentary, Critical and Explanatory, on the Old and New Testaments," reproduced in Logos Bible Software {CD-ROM}. Oak Harbor: Logos Research Systems, Inc., 1997.

[87] Richards, L.O. "The Bible Reader's Companion," reproduced in Logos Bible Software {CD-ROM}. Wheaton: Victor Books, 1996.

[88] Fausset, Jamieson R, Fausset, A.R., Brown, A.R. D. & Brown, D. "A Commentary, Critical and Explanatory, on the Old and New Testaments," reproduced in Logos Bible Software {CD-ROM}. Oak Harbor: Logos Research Systems, Inc., 1997.

[89] Ibid

⁹⁰ Overstreet, Larry R. "The Temple of God in the Book of Revelation." Bibliotheca Sacra 166 (October-December 2009): 446-62.

⁹¹ Ibid

⁹² Ibid

⁹³ Hindson, Ed. "The Revelation Study Guide, Part 1: Keys to Unlocking the Future," Study Guide from World Prophetic Ministry, Inc., Colton, CA: (November 11, 2011)

⁹⁴ Fausset, Jamieson R, Fausset, A.R., Brown, A.R. D. & Brown, D. "A Commentary, Critical and Explanatory, on the Old and New Testaments," reproduced in Logos Bible Software {CD-ROM}. Oak Harbor: Logos Research Systems, Inc., 1997.

⁹⁵ Jamieson, Robert, Fausset A.R., and Brown, David, "Jamieson-Fausset-Brown Commentary" 1871, public domain, reproduced in Power Bible CD {CD-ROM}. Bronson: Online Publishing, Inc., 2000

⁹⁶ Clarke, Adam, "Adam Clarke's Commentary," reproduced in Power Bible CD {CD-ROM}. Concord, NC: 1995-97.

⁹⁷ Fausset, Jamieson R, Fausset, A.R., Brown, A.R. D. & Brown, D. "A Commentary, Critical and Explanatory, on the Old and New Testaments," reproduced in Logos Bible Software {CD-ROM}. Oak Harbor: Logos Research Systems, Inc., 1997.

⁹⁸ Overstreet, Larry R. "The Temple of God in the Book of Revelation." Bibliotheca Sacra 166 (October-December 2009): 446-62.

⁹⁹ Ibid

¹⁰⁰ Ibid

¹⁰¹ Fausset, Jamieson R, Fausset, A.R., Brown, A.R. D. & Brown, D. "A Commentary, Critical and Explanatory, on the Old and New Testaments," reproduced in Logos Bible Software {CD-ROM}. Oak Harbor: Logos Research Systems, Inc., 1997.

¹⁰² Smith, William. "Smith's Bible Dictionary", public domain, reproduced in Power Bible CD {CD-ROM}. Bronson: Online Publishing, Inc., 2000.

¹⁰³ Fausset, Jamieson R, Fausset, A.R., Brown, A.R. D. & Brown, D. "A Commentary, Critical and Explanatory, on the Old and New Testaments," reproduced in Logos Bible Software {CD-ROM}. Oak Harbor: Logos Research Systems, Inc., 1997.

¹⁰⁴ Ibid

[105] Overstreet, Larry R. "The Temple of God in the Book of Revelation." Bibliotheca Sacra 166 (October-December 2009): 446-62.

[106] Ibid

[107] Fausset, Jamieson R, Fausset, A.R., Brown, A.R. D. & Brown, D. "A Commentary, Critical and Explanatory, on the Old and New Testaments," reproduced in Logos Bible Software {CD-ROM}. Oak Harbor: Logos Research Systems, Inc., 1997.

[108] Ibid

[109] Overstreet, Larry R. "The Temple of God in the Book of Revelation." Bibliotheca Sacra 166 (October-December 2009): 446-62.

[110] Richards, L.O. "The Bible Reader's Companion", reproduced in Logos Bible Software {CD-ROM}. Wheaton: Victor Books, 1996.

[111] Ibid

[112] Ibid

REVELATION CHAPTER 3

[113] Overstreet, Larry R. "The Temple of God in the Book of Revelation." Bibliotheca Sacra 166 (October-December 2009): 446-62.

[114] Ibid

[115] Ibid

[116] Smith, William. "Smith's Bible Dictionary", public domain, reproduced in Power Bible CD {CD-ROM}. Bronson: Online Publishing, Inc., 2000.

[117] Ibid

[118] Richards, L.O. "The Bible Reader's Companion", reproduced in Logos Bible Software {CD-ROM}. Wheaton: Victor Books, 1996.

[119] Clarke, Adam, "Adam Clarke's Commentary", reproduced in Power Bible CD {CD-ROM}. Concord, NC: 1995-97.

[120] Fausset, Jamieson R, Fausset, A.R., Brown, A.R. D. & Brown, D. "A Commentary, Critical and Explanatory, on the Old and New Testaments", reproduced in Logos Bible Software {CD-ROM}. Oak Harbor: Logos Research Systems, Inc., 1997.

[121] Ibid

[122] Ibid

[123] Overstreet, Larry R. "The Temple of God in the Book of Revelation." Bibliotheca Sacra 166 (October-December 2009): 446-62.

[124] Ibid

[125] Carson, D.A. "New Bible Commentary: 21st Century Edition" reproduced in Logos Bible Software {CD-ROM}. Downers Grove:Inter-Varsity Press, 1994.

[126] Richards, L.O. "The Bible Reader's Companion", reproduced in Logos Bible Software {CD-ROM}. Wheaton: Victor Books, 1996.

[127] Overstreet, Larry R. "The Temple of God in the Book of Revelation." Bibliotheca Sacra 166 (October-December 2009): 446-62.

[128] Richards, L.O. "The Bible Reader's Companion", reproduced in Logos Bible Software {CD-ROM}. Wheaton: Victor Books, 1996.

[129] Ibid

[130] Ibid

[131] Fausset, Jamieson R, Fausset, A.R., Brown, A.R. D. & Brown, D. "A Commentary, Critical and Explanatory, on the Old and New Testaments", reproduced in Logos Bible Software {CD-ROM}. Oak Harbor: Logos Research Systems, Inc., 1997.

[132] Ibid

[133] Carson, D.A. "New Bible Commentary: 21st Century Edition" reproduced in Logos Bible Software {CD-ROM}. Downers Grove: Inter-Varsity Press, 1994, Rev 3:14-22

[134] Ibid, Rev 3:14-22

[135] Clarke, Adam, "Adam Clarke's Commentary", reproduced in Power Bible CD{CD-ROM}. Concord, NC: 1995-97.

[136] Barnes, Albert, "Albert Barne's New Testament Commentary", public domain, reproduced in Power Bible CD{CD-ROM}. Bronson: Online Publishing, Inc., 2000.

REVELATION CHAPTER 4

[137] Fausset, Jamieson R, Fausset, A.R., Brown, A.R. D. & Brown, D. "A Commentary, Critical and Explanatory, on the Old and New Testaments", reproduced in Logos Bible Software {CD-ROM}. Oak Harbor: Logos Research Systems, Inc., 1997.

[138] Ibid

[139] Edwards, Justin, "Family Bible Notes", public domain, reproduced in Power Bible CD {CD-ROM}. Bronson: Online Publishing, Inc., 2000.

REVELATION CHAPTER 5

[140] Fausset, Jamieson R, Fausset, A.R., Brown, A.R. D. & Brown, D. "A Commentary, Critical and Explanatory, on the Old and New Testaments", reproduced in Logos Bible Software{CD-ROM}. Oak Harbor: Logos Research Systems, Inc., 1997.

[141] Ibid

[142] Rand, William W. and Robinson, Edward. "American Tract Society Bible Dictionary", published 1859, public domain, reproduced in Power Bible CD {CD-ROM}. Bronson: Online Publishing, Inc., 2000.

[143] "The Population of the World Reached 7 Billion on October 31, 2011" Infoplease.com. http://www.infoplease.com/world/statistics/world-population-seven-billion.html#ixzz1nEU3B4 cM (February 23, 2012).

[144] "Leading Causes of Mortality Throughout the World, 2002" Infoplease.com, http://www.infoplease.com/ipa/A0933893.html, (February 23, 2012).

[145] M.G. Easton, "Easton's 1897 Bible Dictionary", public domain, reproduced in Power Bible CD{CD-ROM}. Bronson: Online Publishing, Inc., 2000.

[146] Ibid

[147] Rand, William W. and Robinson, Edward, "American Tract Society Dictionary of the Holy Bible", Published in 1859, public domain, reproduced in Power Bible CD v2.8 {CD-ROM}. Bronson: Online Publishing, Inc., 2000.

[148] M.G. Easton, "Easton's 1897 Bible Dictionary", public domain, reproduced in Power Bible CD{CD-ROM}. Bronson: Online Publishing, Inc., 2000.

[149] Carson, D.A. "New Bible Commentary: 21st Century Edition", reproduced in Logos Bible Software {CD-ROM}. Downers Grove: Inter-Varsity Press, 1994.

[150] Fausset, Jamieson R, Fausset, A.R., Brown, A.R. D. & Brown, D. "A Commentary, Critical and Explanatory, on the Old and New Testaments", reproduced in Logos Bible Software {CD-ROM}. Oak Harbor: Logos Research Systems, Inc., 1997.

[151] Carson, D.A. "New Bible Commentary: 21st Century Edition", reproduced in Logos Bible Software {CD-ROM}. Downers Grove: Inter-Varsity Press, 1994.

[152] Ibid

[153] Campbell, Henry, Nolan, Joseph and Nolan-Haley Jacqueline and others "Black's Law Dictionary", St. Paul: West Publishing, 1990.

[154] Ibid

[155] Spence-Jones H.D.M., Ed., "The Pulpit Commentary: Zechariah", reproduced in Logos Bible Software {CD-ROM}. Bellingham: Logos Research Systems, Inc., 2004.

[156] Hughes, R.B & Laney, J.C. "Tyndale Concise Bible Commentary" reproduced in Logos Bible Software {CD-ROM}. Wheaton: Tyndale House Publishers, 2001.

[157] Slick, Matthew J. "What Is Biblical Numerology?" Christian Apologetics and Research Ministry.1995-2011. http://carm.org/what-biblical-numerology (February 22, 2012).

[158] Rand, William W. and Robinson, Edward. "American Tract Society Bible Dictionary", published 1859, public domain, reproduced in Power Bible CD {CD-ROM}. Bronson: Online Publishing, Inc., 2000.

[159] M.G. Easton, "Easton's 1897 Bible Dictionary", public domain, reproduced in Power Bible CD {CD-ROM}. Bronson: Online Publishing, Inc., 2000.

REVELATION CHAPTER 6

[160] Easton, M.G. "Easton's Bible Dictionary". Oak Harbor, WA: Logos Research Systems, Inc., 1996.

[161] Ewell, Walter A. and Philip Wesley Comfort. "Tyndale Bible Dictionary". Tyndale reference library. Wheaton, IL: Tyndale House Publisher, 2001.

[162] Ibid

[163] Ibid

[164] Ibid

[165] Jamieson, Robert, A.R. Fausset and David Brown." Commentary Critical and Explanatory on the Whole Bible." Oak Harbor, WA: Logos Research Systems, Inc., 1997.

[166] Johnson, B.W. "People's New Testament Commentary", public domain, reproduced in Power Bible CD {CD-ROM}. Bronson: Online Publishing, Inc., 2000.

[167] Ibid

[168] Johnson, B.W. "People's New Testament Commentary", public domain, reproduced in Power Bible CD {CD-ROM}. Bronson: Online Publishing, Inc., 2000.

[169] Fausset, Jamieson R, Fausset, A.R., Brown, A.R. D. & Brown, D. "A Commentary, Critical and Explanatory, on the Old and New Testaments", reproduced in Logos Bible Software {CD-ROM}. Oak Harbor: Logos Research Systems, Inc., 1997.

[170] Hindson, Ed. "The Revelation Study Guide: Keys to unlocking the Future, Part I." World Prophetic Ministry. Colton, CA. www.thekingiscoming.com.

[171] Fausset, Jamieson R, Fausset, A.R., Brown, A.R. D. & Brown, D. "A Commentary, Critical and Explanatory, on the Old and New Testaments", reproduced in Logos Bible Software {CD-ROM}. Oak Harbor: Logos Research Systems, Inc., 1997.

[172] Ibid

[173] Hindson, Ed. "The Revelation Study Guide: Keys to unlocking the Future, Part I." World Prophetic Ministry. Colton, CA. www.thekingiscoming.com.

[174] Ibid, p. 11

[175] Fausset, Jamieson R, Fausset, A.R., Brown, A.R. D. & Brown, D. "A Commentary, Critical and Explanatory, on the Old and New Testaments", reproduced in Logos Bible Software {CD-ROM}. Oak Harbor: Logos Research Systems, Inc., 1997.

[176] Rand, William W. and Robinson, Edward. "American Tract Society Bible Dictionary", published 1859, public domain, reproduced in Power Bible CD {CD-ROM}. Bronson: Online Publishing, Inc., 2000.

[177] Ibid

[178] Jamieson, Robert, Fausset A.R., and Brown, David, "Jamieson-Fausset-Brown Commentary" 1871, public domain, reproduced in Power Bible CD {CD-ROM}. Bronson: Online Publishing, Inc., 2000

[179] Miller, Stephen R. Vol. 18, Daniel. The New American Commentary, (Leupold, Daniel, 406). Nashville: Broadman & Holman Publisher, 1994.

[180] M.G. Easton, "Easton's 1897 Bible Dictionary", public domain, reproduced in Power Bible CD {CD-ROM}. Bronson: Online Publishing, Inc., 2000.

[181] Ibid

[182] Ibid

[183] Ibid

[184] Miller, Stephen R. Vol. 18, Daniel. The New American Commentary, (Leupold, Daniel, 406). Nashville: Broadman & Holman Publisher, 1994.

[185] Ibid

[186] Ibid

[187] Ibid

[188] Clarke, Adam, "Adam Clarke's Commentary", reproduced in Power Bible CD{CD-ROM}. Concord, NC: 1995-97.

[189] Jamieson, Robert, Fausset A.R., and Brown, David, "Jamieson-Fausset-Brown Commentary" 1871, public domain, reproduced in Power Bible CD {CD-ROM}. Bronson: Online Publishing, Inc., 2000

[190] Ibid

[191] Clarke, Adam, "Adam Clarke's Commentary", reproduced in Power Bible CD{CD-ROM}. Concord, NC: 1995-97.

[192] Jamieson, Robert, Fausset A.R., and Brown, David, "Jamieson-Fausset-Brown Commentary" 1871, public domain, reproduced in Power Bible CD {CD-ROM}. Bronson: Online Publishing, Inc., 2000

[193] Clarke, Adam, "Adam Clarke's Commentary", reproduced in Power Bible CD {CD-ROM}. Concord, NC: 1995-97.

[194] Miller, Stephen R. Vol. 18, Daniel. The New American Commentary. Nashville: Broadman & Holman Publisher, 1994.

[195] Miller, Stephen R. Vol. 18, Daniel. The New American Commentary. Nashville: Broadman& Holman Publisher, 1994.

[196] Ibid, (with adaptations)

[197] Ibid, (with adaptations)

[198] Ibid

[199] Ibid

[200] Ibid

[201] Ibid

[202] The Columbia Electronic Encyclopedia, 6th ed "Rome, city, Italy." Infoplease.com. 2000-2012. http://www.infoplease.com/ce6/world/A0842326.html#ixzz1qKvzVlzj (March 27, 2012).

[203] Ibid

[204] Hindson, Ed. "The Prophecies of Daniel: Triumph Over Terror, Part I Study Guide." World Prophetic Ministry. Colton, CA. www.thekingiscoming.com.

[205] Ibid

[206] Ibid

[207] Hindson, Ed. "The Prophecies of Daniel: Triumph Over Terror, Part II Study Guide." World Prophetic Ministry. Colton, CA. www.thekingiscoming.com.

[208] Ibid

[209] Ibid

[210] "EU Symbols." Europa.eu. 2012.http://europa.eu/about-eu/basic-information/symbols/index_en.htm (March 27, 2012).

[211] "The History of the European Union." Europa.eu. 2012.http://europa.eu/about-eu/eu-history/index_en.htm (March 27, 2012).

[212] Ibid

[213] "A Growing Union." Europa.eu. 2012.http://europa.eu/about-eu/growing-eu/index_en.htm (March 27, 2012).

[214] "EU Symbols." Europa.eu. 2012.http://europa.eu/about-eu/basic-information/symbols/index_en.htm (March 27, 2012).

[215] "Leading Causes of Mortality Throughout the World" Infoplease.com http://www.infoplease.com/ipa/A0933893.html (March 28, 2012).

[216] "The Population of the World Reached 7 Billion on October 31, 2011" Infoplease.com http://www.infoplease.com/world/statistics/world-population-seven-billion.html#ixzz1nEU 3B4cM (February 23, 2012).

[217] Ibid

[218] Clarke, Adam, "Adam Clarke's Commentary", reproduced in Power Bible CD {CD-ROM}. Concord, NC: 1995-97.

REVELATION CHAPTER 7

[219] Walvoord, J. F., Zuck, R. B. and Dallas Theological Seminary. "The Bible Knowledge Commentary", reproduced in Logos Bible Software {CD-ROM}. Wheaton: Victor Books, 1983-1985.

[220] Ibid

[221] Ibid

[222] "Are Jews Saved because they are God's Chosen People? Do Jews Have To Believe In Jesus Christ to Be Saved?" Got Questions. 2002-2012. http://www.gotquestions.org/Jews-saved.html (March 29, 2012).

[223] Ibid

[224] Walvoord, J. F., Zuck, R. B. and Dallas Theological Seminary. "The Bible Knowledge Commentary", reproduced in Logos Bible Software {CD-ROM}. Wheaton: Victor Books, 1983-1985.

[225] Ibid

[226] Ryrie, Charles Caldwell. "A Survey of Bible Doctrine." reproduced in Logos Bible Software {CD-ROM}, Chicago: Moody Press, 1972.

REVELATION CHAPTER 8

[227] Slick, Matthew J. "What Is Biblical Numerology?" Christian Apologetics and Research Ministry.1995-2011. http://carm.org/what-biblical-numerology (February 22, 2012).

[228] "What Causes A Falling Star?" Nasa. 2012. http://starchild.gsfc.nasa.gov/docs/ StarChild/questions/question12.html (March 30, 2012).

[229] "Asteroids, Comets, Meteorites." JPL Nasa. 2012. http://www.jpl.nasa.gov/asteroidwatch/ asteroids-comets.cfm (March 30, 2012).

[230] "Geneva Bible Notes", Published 1599, public domain, reproduced in Power Bible CD {CD-ROM}. Bronson: Online Publishing, Inc., 2000.

REVELATION CHAPTER 9

[231] Clarke, Adam, "Adam Clarke's Commentary", reproduced in Power Bible CD {CD-ROM}. Concord, NC: 1995-97.

[232] Ibid

[233] Ryrie, Charles Caldwell. "A Survey of Bible Doctrine." reproduced in Logos Bible Software {CD-ROM}, Chicago: Moody Press, 1972.

[234] Elwell, Walter A. and Philip Wesley Comfort. Tyndale Bible Dictionary. Reproduced in Logos Bible Software {CD-ROM}, Tyndale reference library. Wheaton, IL: Tyndale House Publishers, 2001.

[235] Barnes, Albert, "Albert Barne's New Testament Commentary", public domain, reproduced in Power Bible CD {CD-ROM}. Bronson: Online Publishing, Inc., 2000.

[236] Jamieson, Robert, A. R. Fausset and David Brown. Commentary Critical and Explanatory on the Whole Bible. Reproduced in Logos Bible Software {CD-ROM}, Oak Harbor, WA: Logos Research Systems, Inc., 1997.

[237] Ibid

[238] "World Population Milestones." Infoplease. 2000-2012. http://www.infoplease.com/ipa/ A0883352.html (March 31, 2012)

[239] "World's 50 Most Populas Countries: 2011." Infoplease. 2000-2012. http://www. infoplease.com/world/statistics/most-populous-countries.html (March 31, 2012)

REVELATION CHAPTER 10

[240] Robertson, A.T. "Word Pictures in the New Testament." Reproduced in Logos Bible Software {CD-ROM}, Oak Harbor: Logos Research Systems, 1997.

[241] Barnes, Albert, "Albert Barne's New Testament Commentary", public domain, reproduced in Power Bible CD {CD-ROM}. Bronson: Online Publishing, Inc., 2000.

[242] Wesley, John, "John Wesley's Notes on the Old and New Testaments", reproduced in PowerBible CD {CD-ROM}. Concord, NC: 1995-97.

[243] Jamieson, Robert, Fausset A.R., and Brown, David, "Jamieson-Fausset-Brown Commentary", 1871, public domain, reproduced in Power Bible CD {CD-ROM}. Bronson: Online Publishing, Inc., 2000

[244] "Family Bible Notes", public domain, reproduced in PowerBible CD {CD-ROM}. Bronson: Online Publishing, Inc., 2000.

[245] Clarke, Adam, "Adam Clarke's Commentary", reproduced in Power Bible CD {CD-ROM}. Concord, NC: 1995-97.

[246] Ibid

[247] Ibid

REVELATION CHAPTER 11

[248] Henry, Matthew. "Matthew Henry's Commentary on the Whole Bible", public domain, reproduced in Power Bible CD {CD-ROM}. Bronson: Online Publishing, Inc., 2000.

[249] "Dome of the Rock." Infoplease.com. 2000-2012. http://dictionary.infoplease.com/dome-of-the-rock (April 3, 2012).

[250] CBN TV, cbn.com, Chris Mitchell, Reporter. "Building The Third Temple." http://www.cbn.com/media/index.aspx?s=/vod/EZ3_WPatsComments_040308

[251] Ibid

[252] Ibid

[253] Jamieson, Robert, Fausset A.R., and Brown, David, "Jamieson-Fausset-Brown Commentary", 1871, public domain, reproduced in Power Bible CD {CD-ROM}. Bronson: Online Publishing, Inc., 2000

[254] Wesley, John, "John Wesley's Notes on the Old and New Testaments", reproduced in PowerBible CD {CD-ROM}. Concord, NC: 1995-97.

[255] Barnes, Albert, "Albert Barne's New Testament Commentary", public domain, reproduced in Power Bible CD {CD-ROM}. Bronson: Online Publishing, Inc., 2000.

[256] Ibid

[257] Ibid

[258] Barnes, Albert, "Albert Barne's New Testament Commentary", public domain, reproduced in Power Bible CD {CD-ROM}. Bronson: Online Publishing, Inc., 2000.

<u>REVELATION CHAPTER 12</u>

[259] Walvoord, J. F., Zuck, R. B. and Dallas Theological Seminary. "The Bible Knowledge Commentary", reproduced in Logos Bible Software {CD-ROM}. Wheaton: Victor Books, 1983-1985.

[260] Ibid

[261] Ibid

[262] Ibid

[263] Ibid

[264] Ibid

[265] Ibid

[266] Ibid

[267] Ibid

[268] Ibid

[269] M.G. Easton, "Easton's 1897 Bible Dictionary", public domain, reproduced in Power Bible CD{CD-ROM}. Bronson: Online Publishing, Inc., 2000.

[270] "History Timelines," History-timelines.org.2011. http://www.history-timelines.org.uk/, (April 3, 2012).

[271] "What is the meaning of BC and AD?" Got Questions.org. 2002-2012. http://www. gotquestions.org/Printer/BC-AD-PF.html

[272] "Herod Biography (Biblical Figure)" Infoplease.com.2007. http://www.infoplease.com/ biography/var/herod.html#ixzz1rYUzWtb1, (April 9, 2012).

[273] "Titus Flavius Vespasianus," Infoplease.com. 2007. http://www.infoplease.com/ biography/var/titus.html

[274] Gundry, Robert H. "A Survey of the New Testament." Grand Rapids, MI: Zondervan, 2003, p.15-16.

REVELATION CHAPTER 13

[275] "Geneva Bible Notes", Published 1599, public domain, reproduced in Power Bible CD {CD-ROM}. Bronson: Online Publishing, Inc., 2000.

[276] Clarke, Adam, "Adam Clarke's Commentary", reproduced in Power Bible CD {CD-ROM}. Concord, NC: 1995-97.

[277] Johnson, B.W. "People's New Testament Commentary", public domain, reproduced in Power Bible CD {CD-ROM}. Bronson: Online Publishing, Inc., 2000.

[278] Clarke, Adam, "Adam Clarke's Commentary", reproduced in Power Bible CD {CD-ROM}. Concord, NC: 1995-97.

REVELATION CHAPTER 14

[279] "Family Bible Notes", public domain, reproduced in PowerBible CD {CD-ROM}. Bronson: Online Publishing, Inc., 2000.

[280] "Casualties in World War I," Infoplease.com. 2007. http://www.infoplease.com/ipa/A0004617.html (April 9, 2012)

[281] "Casualties in World War II," Infoplease.com. 2007.http://www.infoplease.com/ipa/A0004619.html (April 9, 2012)

[282] Barnes, Albert, "Albert Barne's New Testament Commentary", public domain, reproduced in Power Bible CD {CD-ROM}. Bronson: Online Publishing, Inc., 2000.

[283] Ibid

REVELATION CHAPTER 15

[284] Barnes, Albert, "Albert Barne's New Testament Commentary", public domain, reproduced in Power Bible CD {CD-ROM}. Bronson: Online Publishing, Inc., 2000.

[285] Barnes, Albert, "Albert Barne's New Testament Commentary", public domain, reproduced in Power Bible CD {CD-ROM}. Bronson: Online Publishing, Inc., 2000.

[286] "Geneva Bible Notes", Published 1599, public domain, reproduced in Power Bible CD {CD-ROM}. Bronson: Online Publishing, Inc., 2000.

[287] Barnes, Albert, "Albert Barne's New Testament Commentary", public domain, reproduced in Power Bible CD {CD-ROM}. Bronson: Online Publishing, Inc., 2000.

[288] Ibid

REVELATION CHAPTER 16

[289] Barnes, Albert, "Albert Barne's New Testament Commentary", public domain, reproduced in Power Bible CD{CD-ROM}. Bronson: Online Publishing, Inc., 2000.

[290] Ibid

[291] Clarke, Adam, "Adam Clarke's Commentary", reproduced in Power Bible CD {CD-ROM}. Concord, NC: 1995-97.

[292] "Geneva Bible Notes", Published 1599, public domain, reproduced in Power Bible CD{CD-ROM}. Bronson: Online Publishing, Inc., 2000, (with adaptations).

[293] Clarke, Adam, "Adam Clarke's Commentary", reproduced in Power Bible CD{CD-ROM}. Concord, NC: 1995-97.

[294] Rand, William W. and Robinson, Edward. "American Tract Society Bible Dictionary", published 1859, public domain, reproduced in Power Bible CD {CD-ROM}. Bronson: Online Publishing, Inc., 2000.

[295] Ibid

[296] Jamieson, Robert, Fausset A.R., and Brown, David, "Jamieson-Fausset-Brown Commentary", 1871, public domain, reproduced in Power Bible CD {CD-ROM}. Bronson: Online Publishing, Inc., 2000

[297] Barnes, Albert, "Albert Barne's New Testament Commentary", public domain, reproduced in Power Bible CD{CD-ROM}. Bronson: Online Publishing, Inc., 2000.

[298] Ibid

[299] "Geneva Bible Notes", Published 1599, public domain, reproduced in Power Bible CD{CD-ROM}. Bronson: Online Publishing, Inc., 2000.

[300] Barnes, Albert, "Albert Barne's New Testament Commentary", public domain, reproduced in Power Bible CD{CD-ROM}. Bronson: Online Publishing, Inc., 2000.

[301] Wesley, John, "John Wesley's Notes on the Old and New Testaments", reproduced in PowerBible CD{CD-ROM}. Concord, NC: 1995-97.

REVELATION CHAPTER 17

[302] Wesley, John, "John Wesley's Notes on the Old and New Testaments", reproduced in PowerBible CD {CD-ROM}. Concord, NC: 1995-97.

[303] Hindson, Ed. "The Revelation Study Guide, Part 3: The Fall of Babylon", Study Guide from World Prophetic Ministry, Inc., Colton, CA: (April 10, 2012)

[304] Ibid, p. 2

[305] Barnes, Albert, "Albert Barne's New Testament Commentary", public domain, reproduced in Power Bible CD {CD-ROM}. Bronson: Online Publishing, Inc., 2000.

[306] Hunt, Dave, "Mystery Babylon Identified" Pre-trib.org.http://www.pre-trib.org/articles/view/mystery-babylon-identified, (April 9, 2012).

[307] Barnes, Albert, "Albert Barne's New Testament Commentary", public domain, reproduced in Power Bible CD {CD-ROM}. Bronson: Online Publishing, Inc., 2000.

[308] Ibid

[309] Wiersbe, Warren W., "The Bible Exposition Commentary", reproduced in Logos Bible Software {CD-ROM}. Wheaton, IL: Victor Books, 1996.

[310] Ibid

[311] Ibid

[312] Ibid

[313] Ibid

[314] Ibid

REVELATION CHAPTER 18

[315] Wiersbe, Warren W., "The Bible Exposition Commentary", reproduced in Logos Bible Software {CD-ROM}. Wheaton, IL: Victor Books, 1996.

[316] Ibid

[317] Barnes, Albert, "Albert Barne's New Testament Commentary", public domain, reproduced in Power Bible CD {CD-ROM}. Bronson: Online Publishing, Inc., 2000.

[318] Ibid

[319] "Sweatshop", Infoplease.com. 1997. http://dictionary.infoplease.com/sweatshop#ixzz1rlMmczST

[320] Barnes, Albert, "Albert Barne's New Testament Commentary", public domain, reproduced in Power Bible CD{CD-ROM}. Bronson: Online Publishing, Inc., 2000.

REVELATION CHAPTER 19

[321] Barnes, Albert, "Albert Barne's New Testament Commentary", public domain, reproduced in Power Bible CD{CD-ROM}. Bronson: Online Publishing, Inc., 2000.

REVELATION CHAPTER 20

[322] Johnson, B.W. "People's New Testament Commentary", public domain, reproduced in Power Bible CD{CD-ROM}. Bronson: Online Publishing, Inc., 2000.

[323] Ibid

[324] M.G. Easton, "Easton's 1897 Bible Dictionary", public domain, reproduced in Power Bible CD{CD-ROM}. Bronson: Online Publishing, Inc., 2000.

[325] "Government." Infoplease.com. 2000-2012. http://www.infoplease.com/ce6/history/A0821419.html#ixzz1sDLfFzFV (April 16, 2012).

[326] Ibid

[327] Willimington, H. L. "Willimington's Bible Handbook", reproduced in Logos Bible Software {CD-ROM}. Wheaton, Ill: Tyndale House Publisher, 1997, p. 439. (with adaptations)

[328] Ibid, p. 439-40 (with adaptations)

[329] Ibid, p. 440 (with adaptations)

[330] LaHaye, Tim and Hindson, Ed, "The Popular Encyclopedia of Bible Prophecy." Eugene, OR: Harvest House Publishers, 2004, p.331.

[331] Rand, William W. and Robinson, Edward. "American Tract Society Bible Dictionary", published 1859, public domain, reproduced in Power Bible CD{CD-ROM}. Bronson: Online Publishing, Inc., 2000.

[332] LaHaye, Tim and Hindson, Ed, "The Popular Encyclopedia of Bible Prophecy." Eugene, OR: Harvest House Publishers, 2004, p.331.

[333] Ibid., p. 332

[334] Ibid, p. 332

[335] "Family Bible Notes", public domain, reproduced in PowerBible CD {CD-ROM}. Bronson: Online Publishing, Inc., 2000.

REVELATION CHAPTER 21

336 Wiersbe, Warren W. "The Bible Exposition Commentary", reproduced in Logos Bible Software 3.0 {CD-ROM}. Wheaton: Tyndale House Publishers, 2001.

337 Ibid

338 Jamieson, Robert, Fausset A.R., and Brown, David, "Jamieson-Fausset-Brown Commentary", 1871, public domain, reproduced in Power Bible CD {CD-ROM}. Bronson: Online Publishing, Inc., 2000

339 Vincent, Marvin Richard. "Word Studies in the New Testament", reproduced in Logos Bible Software, public domain, {CD-ROM} New York: Charles Scribner's Sons, 1887.

340 Ibid

341 Barnes, Albert, "Albert Barne's New Testament Commentary", public domain, reproduced in Power Bible CD{CD-ROM}. Bronson: Online Publishing, Inc., 2000.

342 Johnson, B.W. "People's New Testament Commentary", public domain, reproduced in Power Bible CD{CD-ROM}. Bronson: Online Publishing, Inc., 2000.

REVELATION CHAPTER 22

343 Wesley, John, "John Wesley's Notes on the Old and New Testaments", reproduced in PowerBible CD {CD-ROM}. Concord, NC: 1995-97.

344 Ryba, Jeneene " Landing 101", NASA. 2007. http://www.nasa.gov/mission_pages/shuttle/launch/landing101.html (April 17, 2012).

345 Barnes, Albert, "Albert Barne's New Testament Commentary", public domain, reproduced in Power Bible CD{CD-ROM}. Bronson: Online Publishing, Inc., 2000.

346 Clarke, Adam, "Adam Clarke's Commentary", reproduced in Power Bible CD{CD-ROM}. Concord, NC: 1995-97.

347 Kittel, Gerhard, Bromiley W. Geoffrey and Gerhard, Friedrich, "Theological Dictionary of the New Testament", reproduced in Logos Bible Software {CD-ROM}. Grand Rapids, MI: Eerdmans, 1964.

348 Zodhiates, Spiros. "The Complete Word Study Dictionary: New Testament.", reproduced in Logos Bible Software{CD-ROM} Chattanooga, TN: AMG Publishers, 2000.

349 Ibid

CPSIA information can be obtained at www.ICGtesting.com
Printed in the USA
BVOW100017290113

311809BV00001B/1/P